D0148331

Florissant Valley Library
St. Louis Community College
3400 Pershall Road
Ferguson, MO 63135-1499
314-513-4514

UN PEACEKEEPING

Praeger Security International Advisory Board

Board Cochairs

Loch K. Johnson, Regents Professor of Public and International Affairs, School of Public and International Affairs, University of Georgia (U.S.A.)

Paul Wilkinson, Professor of International Relations and Chairman of the Advisory Board, Centre for the Study of Terrorism and Political Violence, University of St. Andrews (U.K.)

Members

Eliot A. Cohen, Robert E. Osgood Professor of Strategic Studies and Director, Philip Merrill Center for Strategic Studies, Paul H. Nitze School of Advanced International Studies, The Johns Hopkins University (U.S.A.)

Anthony H. Cordesman, Arleigh A. Burke Chair in Strategy, Center for Strategic and International Studies (U.S.A.)

Thérèse Delpech, Senior Research Fellow, CERI (Atomic Energy Commission), Paris (France)

Sir Michael Howard, former Professor of History of War, Oxford University, and Professor of Military and Naval History, Yale University (U.K.)

Lieutenant General Claudia J. Kennedy, USA (Ret.), former Deputy Chief of Staff for Intelligence, Headquarters, Department of the Army (U.S.A.)

Paul M. Kennedy, J. Richardson Dilworth Professor of History and Director, International Security Studies, Yale University (U.S.A.)

Robert J. O'Neill, former Chichele Professor of the History of War, All Souls College, Oxford University (Australia)

Shibley Telhami, Anwar Sadat Chair for Peace and Development, Department of Government and Politics, University of Maryland (U.S.A.)

Jusuf Wanandi, co-founder and member, Board of Trustees, Centre for Strategic and International Studies (Indonesia)

Fareed Zakaria, Editor, Newsweek International (U.S.A.)

UN PEACEKEEPING

Myth and Reality

ANDRZEJ SITKOWSKI

Foreword by Tadeusz Mazowiecki

PRAEGER SECURITY INTERNATIONAL
Westport, Connecticut • London

Library of Congress Cataloging-in-Publication Data

Sitkowski, Andrzej, 1928–

UN peacekeeping : myth and reality / Andrzej Sitkowski; foreword by Tadeusz Mazowiecki.

p.   cm.

Includes bibliographical references and index.

ISBN 0–275–99214–4 (alk. paper)

1. United Nations—Peacekeeping forces.   2. Peacekeeping forces.   I. Title.   II. Title: United Nations peacekeeping.

JZ6374.S58   2006

341.5′84–dc22   2006026027

British Library Cataloguing in Publication Data is available.

Copyright © 2006 by Andrzej Sitkowski

All rights reserved. No portion of this book may be reproduced, by any process or technique, without the express written consent of the publisher.

Library of Congress Catalog Card Number: 2006026027

ISBN: 0–275–99214–4

First published in 2006

Praeger Security International, 88 Post Road West, Westport, CT 06881

An imprint of Greenwood Publishing Group, Inc.

www.praeger.com

Printed in the United States of America

The paper used in this book complies with the Permanent Paper Standard issued by the National Information Standards Organization (Z39.48–1984).

10 9 8 7 6 5 4 3 2 1

The author's biographical information printed in this book and on its jacket is incorrect. The publisher regrets the error. The correct information is as follows:

About the Author

Andrzej Sitkowski is an independent researcher who has worked with the UN as a consultant, advisor, and staff member for 18 years. He also served in the UN peacekeeping mission in Namibia (UNTAG).

In memory of Barbara

"We do not think United Nations failed, we think it has never been tried."

U.S. Senator William Fulbright

"Excellencies, you are the United Nations."

United Nations Secretary General Kofi Annan to the heads of states
and other representatives at the General Assembly Session in
New York on September 23, 2003.

Contents

Foreword[*]

THE HISTORY OF MANKIND is branded with armed conflicts of greater or lesser cruelty. In the twentieth century, which was no exception, violent conflagrations reached, in fact, a tragic peak in the number of mainly civilian victims and in the scale of abhorrent crimes committed. The drama of the Second World War and the suffering of victims of the totalitarian Nazi and Stalinist regimes gave rise to a search for effective international countermeasures. The United Nations Charter and the Universal Human Rights Declaration were supposed to provide the foundations of a new order in international relations which would make it possible, not only to react effectively to brutal violations of basic human rights, but also to prevent such violations; a strong desire prevailed among the communities affected by war atrocities as well as their elite: no more Auschwitz, Katyn, Hiroshima, or mass deportations. The cold war put an early end to such hopes. The genocide perpetrated on the people of Cambodia, though without doubt the largest in scale, was only one example of the atrocities committed in defiance of basic human values. The United Nations, an international organization that came into existence to prevent such crimes, proved to be helpless.[1]

The objective of Solidarnosc, the popular Polish movement of the 1980s, was to reclaim personal freedom and dignity through recognition and respect of basic human rights. The struggle against the totalitarian regime on the domestic front was also a struggle for a reshaping of international relations. Both the democratic transformations in Poland and the coming down of the Berlin Wall in 1989, along with its symbolism, gave rise to expectations that international organizations would change their ways as well. Such hopes looked closest to fulfillment in Europe.

---

* Translated from Polish by Ireneusz Adach.

The early 1990s seemed to provide a solid basis for optimism. Peaceful development in international relations was solemnly heralded in Paris. NATO invited new members to join the alliance, the European Union announced its intention of enlargement, the Organization for Security and Cooperation in Europe became more active, and democratic transformations were being felt throughout the continent. In this context the war in Yugoslavia came as a complete shock. Initially Europe hoped to be able to deal with the conflict by itself. It soon turned out, however, that the European structures were incapable of coping with armed conflicts of this kind, and the involvement of the United Nations became indispensable. Significantly enough, it was not until August 1992 that the UN Human Rights Commission started considering the subject: and only after the drama of Vukovar's fall, after the beginning of the siege of Sarajevo, and many other tragic manifestations of that war.

In the August of 1992, I accepted nomination as the Special Rapporteur of the UN Commission on Human Rights in the former Yugoslavia, not without serious doubts. Still, while being aware of the large scale of war crimes committed there, I was overwhelmed with what the reality represented. I noticed at the same time that the attitude to the conflict of the international community was equivocal and full of contradictions. On the one hand, there were calls for peace, mediation, numerous appeals for a cease-fire, a wide stream of humanitarian aid, and, on the other, an evident lack of political will to engage forcefully in stopping the conflict. The performance of the UN peacekeeping forces in the Balkans provided a dramatic illustration of this attitude.

The author of this work presents the mechanisms of the functioning of peacekeeping operations very convincingly. Time and again, I was witness to the disheartening effects of the overall confusion concerning the role of the United Nations troops in Bosnia. But, reflecting on the impact of the particular military commanders, or on the contribution of these or other national contingents of the Blue Helmets to the outcome of the mission, is of rather limited usefulness. There are far more important issues to be discussed. Is the present system of reacting to such conflicts adequate to the challenge? In his book, Andrzej Sitkowski attempts to give answers to all these questions. I am not going to make an assessment of the solutions suggested by the author, but I fully share his diagnosis of the present state of affairs. My assignment in the former Yugoslavia made me once again acutely aware of the old truth: in order to avoid war one has to be equipped with tools of effective action, armed operations included, and be prepared to make use of them.

Is it ever possible to devise a universal tool kit that will be applicable wherever armed conflicts cause a breakdown of law and order and massive victimization of whole nations, a system equally applicable to Bosnia, Rwanda, East Timor, or Chechnya? Experience prompts a negative reply, but we should not give up trying to work out a better system of international relations. We must not indulge in repeating the words "never again" without supporting them with changes in the way we respond to threats to international peace. Without the wholehearted support of the international community, however, the efforts of individuals or particular governments will not suffice. We all need to realize that the responsibility for the drama of Srebrenica does not only rest with a handful of Dutch peacekeeping soldiers and their commanders.

As members of the United Nations, we all bear the responsibility, because it was in our name that a safe area was established there, only to become an area of death. If the horror of Srebrenica is not to remain just an item on a long list of mass atrocities committed in the world, it has to generate a buildup toward finding more articulate and effective ways of dealing with similar risks. I hope that this book will contribute toward an in-depth analysis of the subject discussed.

Tadeusz Mazowiecki (PM of Poland 1989–1991)

Acknowledgments

I WISH TO ACKNOWLEDGE the generosity of Tadeusz Mazowiecki for writing the foreword. He was the first democratically elected Prime Minister of Poland after the dissolution of the Soviet Bloc in 1989. Nominated later the United Nations Special Rapporteur for Human Rights in ex-Yugoslavia, Tadeusz Mazowiecki resigned from this assignment after the fall of the safe area in Srebrenica in 1995 in protest over the futility of the UN peacekeeping involvement in that country.

I am most appreciative to the former UNPROFOR Commander in Bosnia and Herzegovina, General Francis Briquemont for sharing with me his experience and for helpfully leading me to important sources of information for my research. General Briquemont also left his assignment in disagreement with the unrealistic and futile course imposed on the mission.

In writing this book I have drawn heavily on the superb historical narratives relating to the UN and peacekeeping by one of its main architects, Sir Brian Urquhart. Anyone who wants to learn about the origins and evolution of that unique concept of controlling international conflicts cannot omit his *Hammarskjold* and *A Life in Peace and War.* I was also inspired by an unusually direct account of the experience of a UN military leader as presented in the book *Fighting For Peace* by General Michael Rose who succeeded General Briquemont in Bosnia. I also greatly benefited from works of the late Marianne Heiberg on Middle East and Lebanon.

I am grateful to Marion Kozak for her enthusiastic and unwavering support for this book since its initial concept, for reading the manuscript at different stages, and for giving me the benefit of her informed judgment. I am also deeply appreciative of the encouragement of Robert E. Shepard and Richard R. Valcourt, without whose support I might have given up this project altogether.

Giulio Dente and John Arild Jenssen read the draft manuscript and gave me substantive comments that helped me to put it in shape for submission to the publisher. James J. Sadkovich read the revised draft and was a tremendous critical help and encouragement. Leonce Bloch and Jane M.O. Sharp read parts of the text and offered friendly advice and critical insight. Dick Schoonoord offered helpful suggestions on the text concerning the fall of Srebrenica in Bosnia and Herzegovina. To all of them I am grateful for the friendship and assistance. Needless to say, the responsibility for any errors in this book is mine alone.

Hadassa Kosak used her skill, patience, and acumen in helping me trough the maze of contemporary data research and I am most indebted for her effectiveness in dealing with my inquiries. I would like also to thank Rani Dogra, Jeanine van Erk, JoAnne Beck, Tom Kennedy, Czeslaw Marcinkowski, and Jan Woroniecki for helping me to obtain information that contributed to improvement of this book.

But it would never reach the reader without the support of the publisher. I greatly appreciate the interest and advice obtained from Alexander Andrusyszyn, Elizabeth Demers, and Heather Staines. I also do appreciate contribution of all the other persons involved in the production of this book.

Finally, I wish to thank my immediate family. To my daughter Joanna Sitkowska-Bayle for many discussions and for scanning of the francophone sources for me and to my wife, Uschi Ostermeier-Sitkowski, for her unstinting support, patience in living with a writer, and for help whenever it was needed.

Abbreviations

AG	Administrator General
AMIS	African Mission in Sudan
ANC	Congolese National Army
AU	African Union
CIVPOL	Civilian Police
CPA	Comprehensive Peace Agreement
DPKO	Department of Peacekeeping Operations
DTA	Democratic Turnhalle Alliance
EU	European Union
FUNCINPEC	United Front for an Independent, Neutral, Peaceful, and Cooperative Cambodia
GA	United Nations General Assembly
ICJ	International Court of Justice
ICRC	International Committee of the Red Cross
ICTR	International Criminal Tribunal for Rwanda
IDF	Israeli Defense Force
ISAF	International Security Assistance Force
JMMC	Joint Military Monitoring Commission
JNA	Yugoslav People's Army
KPFNLF	Khmer People's Liberation Front
MAC	Mixed Armistice Commission
MONUC	United Nations Mission in the Democratic Republic of Congo
MP	Member of Parliament
MPLA	Angola People's Liberation Movement

NATO	North Atlantic Treaty Organization
NIOD	Netherland's Institute of War Documentation
NUPI	Norwegian Institute of Foreign Affairs
ONUC	United Nations Mission in Congo
OP	Observation Post
PDK	Party of Democratic Kampuchea
PLO	Palestine Liberation Organization
PM	Prime Minister
PRT	Provincial Reconstruction Team
RGF	Rwandese Government Forces
ROE	RULES OF ENGAGEMENT
RPF	Rwandese Patriotic Front
SA	South Africa
SADF	South African Defense Force
SC	United Nations Security Council
SG	United Nations Secretary General
SHIRBERG	United Nations Standby Forces High Readiness Brigade
SFOR	Stabilization Force
SLA	South Lebanese Army
SNC	Supreme National Council
SRSG	Special Representative of the United Nations Secretary General
SWA	South West Africa
SWAPO	South West Africa People's Organization
SWAPOL	South West African Police
UAR	United Arab Republic
UK	United Kingdom of Great Britain and Northern Ireland
UN	United Nations
UNAMIC	United Nations Advance Mission in Cambodia
UNAMIR	United Nations Assistance Mission for Rwanda
UNASOG	United Nations Aouzou Strip Observer Group
UNCRO	United Nations Confidence Restoration Operation in Croatia
UNDOF	United Nations Disengagement Observer Force
UNEF I	First United Nations Emergency Force
UNEF II	Second United Nations Emergency Force
UNFICYP	United Nations Peacekeeping Force in Cyprus
UNHCR	Office of the United Nations High Commissioner for Refugees
UNIFIL	United Nations Interim Force in Lebanon
UNITA	National Union for Total Independence of Angola
UNITAF	Unified Task Force
UNMEE	United Nations Mission in Ethiopia and Eritrea
UNMIS	United Nations Mission in Sudan
UNMOGIP	United Nations Military Observer Group in India and Pakistan
UNOGIL	United Nations Observation Group in Lebanon
UNOMUR	United Nations Observer Mission Uganda–Rwanda

UNOSOM I	United Nations Operation in Somalia I
UNOSOM II	United Nations Operation in Somalia II
UNPA	United Nations Protected Area
UNPF	United Nations Peace Forces
UNPREDEP	United Nations Preventive Deployment Force
UNPROFOR	United Nations Protection Force
UNSAS	United Nations Standby Arrangements System
UNSCOP	United Nations Special Commission for Palestine
UNTAC	United Nations Transitional Authority in Cambodia
UNTAES	United Nations Transitional Administration for Eastern Slavonia, Baranja and Western Sirmium
UNTAG	United Nations Transition Assistance Group
UNTEA	United Nations Temporary Executive Authority
UNTSO	United Nations Truce Supervision Organization
WPK	Wider Peacekeeping

Introduction

SOLDIERS from all corners of the world congregate under the Blue Flag in god-forsaken places they have difficulty of finding on a map. What brings together young men from Zimbabwe and France, from Russia and Fiji, from Poland and Bangladesh, from Argentina and UK, and, rarely, even from the United States of America? Their common cause is United Nations peacekeeping, which in words of the UN Secretary General, Boutros Boutros-Ghali, ". . . stands out, as one of the Organization's most original and ambitious undertakings in its efforts to control conflict and promote peace."[1] But Fred Cuny, an American from Texas, the legendary international relief leader, liked to say that, if the United Nations had been around in 1939, we would all be speaking German.[2] He was not alone in thinking that the contribution of the colorful contingents fell miserably short of the grand expectations people had of them.

I shared these expectations. The experience of the Second World War in Warsaw (Poland) made me to believe in the need for a world in which peace and freedom for people is internationally protected. The United Nations Charter contained such a promise. A few decades later, I was lucky enough to participate in a UN operation that delivered on that promise by ushering Namibia (South West Africa or SWA) into its independence in 1989. But that success was an exception rather then a rule and what followed was not a New World Order, promised also by the U.S. President in the wake of the first Gulf War, but a string of UN failures and humiliations in Somalia, Rwanda, and the former Yugoslavia. Not convinced by confusing, contradictory, and simplistic explanations of these debacles offered by the media and by the politicians, I begun to search for more plausible answers on what went wrong and why. There were no simple answers in sight and I embarked on a closer examination of the subject the results of which I am sharing with the reader of this book.

Ultimately, I have come to believe that the UN doctrine and practice informed by the alleged contradiction between peacekeeping and peace enforcement is divorced from the reality of most contemporary armed conflicts. It is wasteful and cripples all levels of a UN peacekeeping mission. Abdication in advance of peace enforcement by UN peacekeeping contingents has severely limited their effectiveness and allowed aggressors and warlords to carry on their trade of war, atrocities, and ethnic cleansing with impunity.[3] As Edward N. Luttwak rightly observed, the very presence of UN FORCES unable to effectively protect civilians inhibits the normal remedy of escape from war. Deluded into thinking that they would be protected, the endangered people stay in place, until it is too late to flee.[4]

FROM SUEZ CANAL TO RWANDA AND SREBRENICA

The first UN peacekeeping operation, United Nations Emergency Force (UNEF), was deployed in 1956 to separate belligerents in the Suez Canal War. It acted under three guiding principles: consent of the parties to the conflict, impartiality, and use of force only in self-defense.[5] Until its premature and forced withdrawal, it was a success. Peacekeeping was never formally defined by any UN organ or by its Secretariat. But this was not necessarily a problem, because the lack of an official definition could have been an advantage, allowing the UN to tailor its missions in keeping with the nature of the conflicts. Yet, although Brian Urquhart, one of the major architects of peacekeeping, considered the UN mission in Egypt to have been a face-saving operation of a unique kind,[6] the UN choose to codify the UNEF's guidelines as a doctrine which it has subsequently applied indiscriminately for some 50 years. As a result, international military contingents have deployed with the same face-saving guidelines as those formulated for UNEF, even when one of the faces to be saved was that of a genocidal killer, as it happened in the Rwanda of 1994. The ill-conceived and abusive deployment of lightly armed international contingents in areas of armed conflagrations has gradually made peacekeeping a travesty of the initially brilliant concept.

In 1995 the "safe area" of Srebrenica in Bosnia was overrun by Serbs despite the presence of a UN battalion which did not put any resistance to the attackers who massacred thousands of Bosnians afterward. The Security Council (SC) in resolution 836, which established the safe areas, explicitly authorized use of force to deter attacks on them. But the UN Secretariat argued that such an authorization should be read in the context of self-defense, which does not imply defense of a territory. It also pointed out that "deterrence" is different from "defense" or "protection." As a high UN official in charge of the ex-Yugoslavia desk in the New York headquarters explained before the fall of Srebrenica ". . . we were deployed to help extinguish the flames of war, not to fan them." After the enclave's fall, he maintained that peacekeepers were being blamed for failing to do things that they were not mandated to do.[7] It was not just UN officials who promoted this view. In Yugoslavia the media shaped the perceptions and influenced the actions of their audiences by disseminating an image of peacekeepers made impotent by some undefined "international laws." Parroting their sources and trotting out stereotypes, journalists bore considerable responsibility for the failure of the American and the international public to understand the conflict and to grasp the UN role in it.[8] Indeed, the media has shaped our perceptions of other troubled UN missions to other tortured nations as well.

But the United Nations is too noble a project to debase itself by turning a blind eye to areas of its military deployment becoming killing fields, as it did in Rwanda and Srebrenica.[9]

DOCTRINAL CONFUSION AND CONCEPTUAL VOID

The real nature of the UN military interventions is obscured by the existing confusion about "peacekeeping" and "peace enforcement," neither of which appears in the UN Charter. Both are open to differing interpretations, but in the UN view, first and foremost, are incompatible. According to Ghali: "The logic of peacekeeping flows from premises that are quite distinct from those of enforcement. . . . To blur the distinction between the two can undermine the viability of a peacekeeping operation and endanger its personnel."[10] But the guidelines for UNEF II, established in the aftermath of the Yom Kippur Arab–Israeli War in 1973, provided that the UN troops can use force in self-defense, "which would include resistance to attempts by forceful means to prevent it from discharging its duties under the Security Council's mandate . . ."[11] In less diplomatic language it means that force can be used in defense of the mandate, and such an action is nothing else than enforcement. These guidelines become standard for the future operations but that fact did not disturb the UN in repeating its mantra of a strict contradiction between peacekeeping and peace enforcement.

Members of UN Forces from the Commander to the privates face, therefore, hard choices. Is a forcible removal of an illegal roadblock on the way of a UN convoy an act of peacekeeping or an act of peace enforcement? The UN mission to Cambodia illustrated mutually exclusive but seemingly correct interpretations of the UN policy. The Force's Commander, General John M. Sanderson, and his Deputy, General Michel Loridon, differed on the appropriate strategy toward the Khmer Rouge who, contrary to previous agreements, prevented UN peacekeepers from entering their zone. The Deputy rightly insisted that it was within the mission's mandate to use force, if need be, to compel rebels to honor their own pledges and to maintain the UN troops' freedom of movement. The Commander believed that such an action would amount to an offensive, which was outside the mission's mandate. Both generals could have claimed to be following UN principles but the Deputy was sent packing.[12] It was a telling illustration of a conceptual confusion that reigned at all levels of the UN peacekeeping operations. The results of that confusion and of the conceptual void proved to be tragic for everyone concerned.

The incompatibility of the original concept of peacekeeping with the nature of the prevailing intrastate conflicts has not gone unnoticed. But the UN Secretary General Kofi Annan's bold admission of failures and errors in Srebrenica fell short of calling into question the peacekeeping doctrine itself. "It became apparent that the old rules of the game no longer held," declared Annan in his report on the fall of the enclave. Yet, he again insisted that peacekeeping and peace enforcement were distinct activities that should not be confused. A report produced in 2000 by a panel of experts contained a fitting analysis of the existing shortcomings, but confirmed the validity of the consensual peacekeeping principles, unchanged from the time of the Suez Canal crisis.[13]

Outside of the UN system, military strategists and academia produced in the last decade a vast body of theoretical contributions on peacekeeping's doctrinal adjustment to the new challenges. To describe better the complex realities new ideas and semantic innovations have been introduced, such as "robust," "wider," "expanded peacekeeping," "peace support," "peace restoration," or "inducement" and also "humanitarian" operations—to name a few. As for peace enforcement a consensus seems emerging in considering it a subdivision of UN operations, falling into a "gray area" between peacekeeping and war fighting.[14] But the existing debates have not affected policies and practices of peacekeeping, yet. Whatever turn these debates may take in the future, their participants cannot afford neglecting stark realities of peacekeeping on the ground, because what can be easily differentiated on paper may defy such a distinction in the field. Neither theoreticians nor practitioners should overlook the experience of the former commander of the United Nations Protection Force (UNPROFOR) in Bosnia, General Michael Rose. According to the general, "... it is impossible to draw a clear line between the permissible use of force in a peacekeeping operation and an act of war."[15] Until the theoretical questions are resolved, a common sense principle could be perhaps agreed upon: before deploying peacekeeping operations the UN should make sure that its military contingents are ready to defend themselves and their mandate and that they have means to do so. Otherwise it is better for the organization and for the soldiers that they stay home.

CONSTRAINTS OF CHANGE

An effective UN peacekeeping faces serious constraints on the part of the Secretariat of the organization and of the troop contributing governments. The leaders of the organization never came to terms with the idea that war sometime must be fought to keep up or create peace. The governments shy from commitments to operation exposing their troops to casualties. Thus, changing the UN peacekeeping doctrine or introducing more robust rules of engagement cannot by itself radically alter how the organization confronts challenges to international peace. The roots of the malaise reach deep, growing out of a soil fertilized by ubiquitous contradictions and an illusion. The first contradiction is a declared desire for peace but an unwillingness to pay its price. Equally contradictory is the nature of the United Nations composition. The very offenders of peace and human rights are among its members and exercise a corroding influence on the organization's capability in challenging these violations. The illusion is the belief, widely spread in the West before September 11, 2001, that conflicts in distant, exotic places do not affect our own safety.

The reluctance of states to undertake risky interventions in foreign conflicts in the interest of an abstract concept of international peace found an institutional expression in a profound, if undeclared, shift in role of the United Nations. The world body whose Charter enabled it to restrain aggressors and prevent wars became in 1948 in Palestine an organization offering good offices for mediating, monitoring, and reporting from areas of conflict. The member governments either welcomed that shift or did not mind. That shift articulated during the cold war into the replacement of the collective security sought by the UN founding members by a less ambitious strategy called "peacekeeping," which William Durch defined as "carving out a more narrow security role."[16]

But the Great Powers, which exercise the veto over the Security Council's resolutions, did not have a common agenda even after the cold war was over. Initial hopes for a more assertive role by the organization quickly floundered, thus. By 1996, a clear confirmation of the old stance came from Ghali, who pronounced the UN "a neutral intervening force and honest broker."[17] He did so in spite of the Charter of the organization, which in Chapter VII provides for a collective response to threats to international peace, including, as the last resort, military actions against the aggressors (see Appendix).[18] Ghali's confirmed retreat from the original aims of the UN was an expression of the institutional culture of neutrality that took a firm hold in the organization and Annan's pronunciations to the contrary proved insufficient to break up that lock.

The ambiguity of the current official language on use of force by the UN remains an obstacle to any meaningful reform. It is best exposed by the contradictory interpretation of the mandates of the SC formulated in resolutions 678 and 836. Both resolutions authorized the intervening international contingents to employ "all necessary means" to discharge their mandates. The former was interpreted as an authorization for a flat-out war with Iraq or Desert Storm by a U.S.-led coalition of the willing. The latter was deemed insufficient for inducing a UN battalion to use force either in deterrence of attacks on the safe area of Srebrenica or in defense of itself.[19]

WHAT THE FUTURE HOLDS

Short of a radical rewriting of the present peacekeeping rules, the Secretary General has no reason for wearing the sheriff's star. The UN Secretariat should then follow its own logic of neutrality and disarm by restricting its peacekeeping missions to the dispatch of military observers. The organization can only gain from abandoning the false promises of peacekeeping by noncombatant troops, maintained at tremendous costs and to no avail. Building up its negotiating and mediating capabilities has a greater potential for the support of peace than feeble sable rattling. The money wasted on failed interventions could be released for a better use.[20] Moreover, with UN pretences abandoned, neither islanders from Fiji, paratroopers from Belgium, nor young men from any other country would need to die in places like Bosnia, Lebanon, or Rwanda in actions that are no more than exercises in international hypocrisy, provided that the North Atlantic Treaty Organization (NATO) and coalitions of the willing who already replace Blue Helmets in UN authorized peacekeeping operations will learn from the organization's failures.

But as the organization proved capable of absorbing the results of worst failures without a visible damage or change of its course, it may well be that peacekeeping will just continue in its present frame. The symbolic presence of international troops provides a smokescreen, a substitute for an effective intervention, and there is a constant demand for such a commodity on the international political market. It was recently confirmed in Afghanistan. After the American defeat of the Taliban regime in 2001, a multinational International Security Assistance Force (ISAF) authorized by the UN Security Council has been restricted to patrolling the relatively calm capital city of Kabul, while the provinces were left to their fate—armed clashes between competing factions, common banditry, and flourishing narco-business. NATO, which took over the command of the operation in August 2003, went outside of Kabul (after the U.S. administration dropped its opposition to that move).[21] But it restricted the initial deployment to a symbolic force in the one and only, relatively calm region of Kunduz with the task of protecting a Provincial Reconstruction Team (PRT). NATOS' minimalist response to the risk of Afghanistan sliding into anarchy again shows that it is not immune to the UN peacekeeping syndrome of expecting to alter the behavior of warring parties by a symbolic presence of international noncombat troops. Some of the alliance's members even believe that their peacekeepers need to obtain assurances of security before being deployed.[22]

When even NATO, the most powerful military alliance in the world, wavers in deployment of its might, may the UN play any significant role in what is called peacekeeping? It is an open question, but even in face of failures and shortcomings only too obvious, the organization cannot be dismissed easily. On the second anniversary of the terrorist attack of September 9, 2001, John Mearsheimer, leading American realist thinker, bluntly submitted that the United States cannot run the world by itself and that institutions like the UN are needed.[23] If this is so, the question is not whether, but what for is the UN needed in the field of international security.

At the strategic level, there is a consensus, including the sole superpower, that authorization of the UN SC, if not necessary, is at least much desirable for any international military intervention, peacekeeping included. At the operational level in missions labeled peacekeeping, strict adherence to the consensual peacekeeping prevail. But an unexpected and undeclared divorce from these was taking place at an obscure front in the Congo at the end of 2005. UN and Congolese forces, acting in hot pursuit, killed about 80 rebels in a week south of Beni in the North Kivu district. Further, Congolese troops supported by the UN contingents retook nine localities in the Ituri district.[24] Not a single cornerstone of the consensual peacekeeping doctrine remained in place in that operation. Consensus of the parties, impartiality of the UN troops, and the restriction of use of force to self-defense—all these principles were overturned. Strangely enough the edifice of peacekeeping did not go tumbling down in the UN HQ or anywhere else. It remains to be seen whether these events are an isolated incident or a quiet test of a new policy. But with even NATO having troubles in staffing its noncombat mission in Afghanistan, the later, if ever true, does not seem to have much chance. Availability of men ready to take risks under an international flag is at the roots of a success or a failure of any meaningful reform of peacekeeping.

Urquhart, remembering the remorse, felt by anyone involved, for the failure to stop the genocide in Rwanda in 1994, rallies for giving the UN a real muscle by creating a volunteer-based rapid reaction force, permanently at the disposal of the SC. One of the UN peacekeeping architects, who was in the past against a permanent UN Force and peace enforcement by soldiers under the Blue Flag, clearly recognizes now that a changed nature of challenges require changes in response.[25] Alas, his voice sounds like a call in the wilderness.

Conceivably there are also other new avenues for peacekeeping. An opportunity for opening an entirely new space for deployment of the Blue Helmets might had been lost during the countdown to the invasion of Iraq. While even the supposedly solid intelligence can turn out to be mistaken, the temptation to avert the danger of an imminent attack by a preemptive strike is great and the risks of inaction incalculable. Tedious and often-obstructed work of arms inspectors could had been supported by the UN international troops protecting the inspectors, aggressively supervising suspicious sites, and ready on coercive action in emergency. Their presence would amount to a preventive international occupation, leaving only the trappings of sovereignty intact. According to a publication in a usually well-informed German weekly, a project along these lines was supposedly considered by the German and French authorities before the invasion of Iraq.[26]

A permanent UN rapid reaction force and a preventive UN occupation are—by current political standards—unrealistic, to say the least. But reality is not a fixed commodity. It is rather a moving target defined by our priorities and perceptions. Any idea about coordinated air attacks on World Trade Center and Pentagon was utterly unrealistic—until it was proven otherwise by a bunch of obscured fanatics. These attacks transformed the reality radically but the matching adjustments of international security strategy are yet to come about.

In face of increasing global threats the UN may either take part in formulation of new strategies and their implementation or opt out by clinging to flawed concepts and practices. But doing business as usual seems to enjoy continuing support of the membership of the organization and of influential international policy makers. That support is qualified only by the recognition that high-risk operations should be performed by coalitions of the willing (under authorization by the SC) instead of by the Blue Helmets. As we are witnessing in Afghanistan, that qualification does not prevent problems experienced in the UN-led operations to appear in the new context. Continuation of business as usually is therefore the most likely scenario for the peacekeeping theatre.

A few years ago a prominent member of the UN Secretariat advanced a fitting comparison of the peacekeeping to other public services. It is clear, he said, that if the world wants the UN to serve, even occasionally, as a fire brigade, it will have to do better than the present system, under which the fire breaks out, the aldermen on the Security Council agree it needs to be put out, and the fire chief is then sent out to hire firemen, rent fire trucks, find hoses of the right length, and look for sources of water to put into them while hoping that, when he has what he needs, there will still be enough survivors to rescue.[27] But the otherwise accurate description invites an essential supplement: the firemen may use the water hoses only in self-defense, when their own pants catch fire. Despite the calamities suffered and contrary to declarations of readiness to change, the old paradox seem to keep all actors in the peacekeeping theatre in a lock: the firemen brigade refrains from making any use of the water hoses in order not to fan the flames; the peacekeepers do not make use of their arms because they do not want to inflame wars. So, the UN either leaves wars and other violent crises alone so that they can burn themselves out, or, when in place already, keeps a safe distance from fire and reports on the outcome.

Thus, global policing of this imperfect world is practically left to the United States with an occasional input from UK and France, the later mainly in emergencies affecting their former colonies. It is only too obvious that the scope of such policing must be severely restricted by political and material constraints. In absence of any meaningful input from the UN or from any other unlikely party stepping into its boots, the global insecurity may only grow more intractable than before.

Until the political elite, the international media, and the public take a genuine interest and learn to detect and repudiate the real substance of the present peacekeeping policies and practices, the chances for change are negligible.

STRUCTURE OF THE BOOK

Chapter 1 is an inquiry into the theoretical background for peacekeeping that is but one of tools in the arsenal of tools for conflict resolution. But, according to A.B. Fetherston, in essence, we are still largely in the dark in terms of improving analysis, effectiveness, and success of peacekeeping. That is the case, he said, due to the lack of theoretical underpinning for the field.[28]

The UN military contingents alone do not provide for a quick fix-up of violent conflagrations. To meaningfully contribute to conflict resolution or, less ambitiously, to its management or containment, the Blue Helmets have to be credible and effective. But views on what for they appear in distants land with their guns differ widely. There is no clear answer from the UN still and an emerging consensus on placement of peace enforcement in the gray area between peacekeeping and war fighting does not inform the policies and practices of international military interventions yet.

Chapter 2 analyzes the responsibilities of the main actors in running the peacekeeping operations and shows how these were discharged.

The Security Council, empowered by the UN Charter to decide on matters of peace and war, resembles a security organ of a world government that neither exists nor will exist in a foreseeable future. The Council launches UN peacekeeping operations under its exclusive discretion. Whether it deploys international contingents on a successful mission to Namibia or on a misconceived one to Somalia, or does nothing to effectively intervene in a much bloodier civil war in Sudan, there is no official scrutiny. More often than not the emphasis in the Council is on political correctness of resolutions with scant regard to the realities on the ground. In the case of ex-Yugoslavia the sheer volume of the Council's official pronouncements amounted to a political pornography: more than seventy resolutions have been issued in 3 years and largely ignored.

Peacekeeping operations are authorized by the Council either under Chapter VI or VII of the UN Charter (see Appendix) and the latter are commonly but inaccurately labeled peace enforcement missions. It may be recalled, that the Council authorized the use of force in the first UN operation in the Congo without evoking Chapter VII.[29]

The Secretary General of the United Nations and his staff, the UN Secretariat in short, function as the executive arm of the Security Council. The Secretariat is a bureaucracy, only more so because of its international composition and unaccountability. Convinced of its impartiality, for half of the century it portrayed itself steadfastly as a neutral technical force simply following orders by the SC or other intergovernmental UN bodies. But Annan, the first UN Secretary General elevated from among the UN bureaucrats, made a dramatic and unexpected turnabout. In a clear break with the long tradition of the UN infallibility, the repenting now SG exposed serious mistakes and errors of the Secretariat in failed peacekeeping missions in Rwanda and ex-Yugoslavia.[30] Alas, neither of these groundbreaking reports seemed to attract the attention they deserved and the UN peacekeeping rules remained unchanged.

The troop-contributing governments' role in the peacekeeping theatre is threefold. As members of the Security Council and/or of the General Assembly, they bear the responsibility for the actions of the organization. Outside these assemblies, they represent sovereign states, capable and willing to criticize these actions and the organization itself. Finally, they can and more often than not they do meddle in the conduct of the missions by instructing their national contingents over the heads of the UN command. Real motives and implications of governmental decisions concerning contributions to the UN peacekeeping operations remain often obscure not only to the public opinion, but also to the political elite.

It is the military men of all ranks that carry the burden of their governments temporarily disowning them, of the ambiguous marching orders of the SC, and of the fuzzy policies of the UN Secretariat. But it is the commander of the UN Force who has to translate the mandate into the rules of engagement for his men and to decide if and how they should defend themselves and their mission. Despite all limitations, his and his men's attitudes make a difference to the outcome of their mission.

The case studies in Chapters 3 to 9 show how peacekeeping worked in the past. The nineteen missions described are representative in size and kind of the totality of the sixty peacekeeping operations undertaken by the UN from the first mediating and monitoring mission in Palestine in 1948 through 2005 (thirteen were launched in the 40 years prior to the end of the cold war in 1989 and forty-seven since).

This book covers the region of Middle East, five countries (the Congo, Namibia, Somalia, Cambodia, and Rwanda), and a federative state under dissolution (ex-Yugoslavia). An exception from the country-by-country presentation was made for the Middle East, which became a formative ground for the UN peacekeeping doctrine and policies. Three operations are ongoing in that region yet and the UN continuing military presence there for about half of a century allows to assess its effects from a historical perspective. The featured operations range from a simple monitoring of cease-fires or armistices to securing and supervising elections, protecting humanitarian missions, and nation building. Both of the only two cases in which the peacekeepers went to war—in the first and second operation in the Congo and in Somalia—are included, and also the extremes of the peacekeeping experience are reflected in the most successful operation to date in Namibia and in the tragic failure of the mission to Rwanda. The aggregated total maximum strength of the UN contingents deployed in the operations featured in this book was over 160,000 of military and police personnel compared to uniformed personnel of 71,554 deployed worldwide in sixteen missions in 2005.[31]

In reconstructing origins, records, and results of these operations, I focused on the impact that the guiding principles of UN peacekeeping doctrine had on the outcome of the operations. In analyzing the anatomy and functioning of the operations, I particularly highlighted the performance of the troops in regard to the right to use of force to self-defense of themselves and of the mandates, their ability to move freely, and the impact of an authorization to act under provisions of Chapter VII of the UN Charter. I also tried to shed light on considerably varying interpretation of these principles by UN civilian and military leaders. The conflicts themselves, and their historical background, are described only to the extent necessary for understanding the environment in which the international troops deployed.

The concluding Chapter 10 reflects on prospects for change. The international response to the ongoing genocide in Darfur (Sudan) does not leave much hope for a substantial reform of UN peacekeeping. Should it be undertaken, however, the UN has to refrain from recycling the stereotypes about what its peacekeepers should do in favor of declaring what they can achieve. For a clear break with the past, the term "peacekeeping" should best be dropped out from the political discourse. "Peace support operations" or PSO seems a suitable candidate to replace it. All PSO, except the observatory missions, should be deployed under the provisions of Chapter VII of the UN Charter. New avenues for deployment of international troops should be explored with a preventive deployment given a priority.

The present system of troop contribution on call does not work for missions of high risk. The alternatives seem to be limited to recruitment of UN volunteers to be permanently at the disposal of the SC and to employment of corporate armies. But in the present political climate none of these alternatives seems to have chances of approval. Therefore demilitarization of the UN by restricting it to military observer missions might be a lesser evil than the protracted and ill-fated deployment of armed but helpless contingents.

Since the prospects for a renewal or a reinvention of the role of the UN in promotion of peace are bleak, the responsibility for what is going to happen in the international security environment rests with the members of the organization directly. But even the only one of them who is capable of worldwide deployment of troops would benefit from sharing the burden with a more efficient organization.

1

Script

PEACEKEEPING OPERATIONS always evaded an easy grasp. In the twilight zone between war and peace they often reflected the shortcomings of what is usually called the peace process and also the confusion emerging from diverging views, attitudes, and motives of different participants. The difficulty in defining peacekeeping increased when the operations evolved from patrolling of demilitarized buffer zones to deployment in complex emergencies of components such as civil administration and police, electoral units, and humanitarian agencies. The term has become too large a concept to be precisely and coherently described.[1] Continuous labeling of peacekeeping as a contradiction of peace enforcement only added to these difficulties. After a long period of adherence to the strictly consensual theory of peacekeeping, major players in the peacekeeping theatre and the academia embarked on searching for an adaptation of the theoretical framework to the realities of the prevailing conflicts. In the process the very term "peacekeeping" began to be redefined or even to fade away. Since there is no clear consensus on the new terminology yet, I use both that old term and the new designations as they appear in described contributions and events.

Peacekeeping under the UN umbrella relates to Chapters VI (Pacific Settlement of Disputes) and VII (Action with Respect to Threats to the Peace, Breaches of the Peace, and Acts of Aggression) of the UN Charter (see appendix). But the term is never mentioned in the Charter, and the UN Secretary General Dag Hammarskjold used to refer to peacekeeping as "Chapter Six and a Half" operations. That no UN organ ever defined peacekeeping was not necessarily a problem. Lack of an official definition could have been an advantage, allowing to tailor the missions in keeping with the nature of the conflicts. Urquhart considered the first peacekeeping mission in Egypt in 1956 to have been a face-saving operation of a unique kind.[2] Yet, the UN chose to codify the principles of consent of the parties to the conflict, impartiality, and use of force in self-defense only as a doctrine which it has subsequently applied indiscriminately. As a result, international military contingents have deployed with the same face-saving principles, even when one of the faces to be saved was that of a genocidal killer, as it happened in Rwanda in 1994. These principles are clear only at the first sight.

Consent of the parties to the conflict, except in increasingly rare classical intrastate conflicts, is a legalistic instrument which ignores dynamics of conflicts and difficulties in identifying the parties in intrastate confrontations. Consent of today may turn into a hostile denial tomorrow, and seeking consent of various warlords might provide them with legitimization and prestige, without bringing about other results.

Impartiality is an abstract political term, prone to differing interpretations. It is arguable whether any action by the UN forces, short of mediating, monitoring, and reporting, can be deemed impartial. UN troops escorting a humanitarian convoy to a besieged town, contrary to appearances, are not impartial. Furthermore, impartiality is in practice constantly confused with neutrality, which is inherent for the humanitarian organizations like International Committee of Red Cross (ICCR) or UN High Commissioner for Refugees (UNHCR), but not for armed contingents.[3]

Non-use of force except in self-defense is the sole principle directly related to armed contingents and is the most ambiguous. According to the UN interpretation, self-defense includes armed response to forceful actions of the warring parties preventing the peacekeepers from discharging their mandate. It boils down to nothing less than a blanket authorization to use force in defense of the mandates, thus. But as if an effort to offset such a conclusion, the Secretariat pronounces every use of force other than in self-defense to constitute peace enforcement which is inconsistent with peacekeeping and should be avoided at any costs: "The logic of peacekeeping flows from premises that are quite distinct from enforcement and the dynamics of the latter are incompatible with the political process that peacekeeping is intended to facilitate. To blur the distinction between the two can undermine the viability of peacekeeping operation and endanger its personnel."[4] The distinction looks good as long it is not exposed to the logic of war, the only logic to which the warring parties normally subscribe. Is removing by force of an illegal roadblock to enable the progress of a UN convoy an act of self-defense against an obstruction in discharging a peacekeeping mandate or an offensive action in peace enforcement? The UN distinction between the defensive and offensive use of force is blurred at the outset.

In theory these ambiguities disappear in case of operations authorized by the UN Security Council under provisions of Chapter VII of the UN Charter under which the troops are routinely authorized to use "all necessary means." But in practice little or nothing changes because the Secretariat, the troop contributing governments and the military in the field tend to adhere to the minimalist inter-pretation of the mandates as they please. For several months in Sarajevo (Bosnia) the UN troops were not allowed to target snipers indiscriminately killing civilians and UN soldiers, because targeting the killers would involve search operations, which would be incompatible with self-defense.

The Secretariat produced three major reports on questions related to the peacekeeping. In the report "An Agenda for Peace" the UN Secretary General Ghali admitted in 1992 that when other actions failed, military option to restore peace is essential to the credibility of the United Nations. But what he proposed was hardly a workable solution. Special peace enforcement units different from forces acting under the article 43 of Chapter VII of the Charter would be called to respond to "outright aggression, imminent or actual." It amounted to more confusion by dividing the UN peace enforcers into two categories.[5]

The "Agenda" did not go well with the member governments and after the disastrous experience of Somalia it was practically dead. The Security Council formulated a new set of criteria for launching new peacekeeping. The main concern was now ". . . whether reasonable guarantees can be obtained from the principal parties or factions regarding the safety and security of the United Nations personnel." The wording of the document implied that "personnel" includes both civilians and military.[6] The role of the UN peacekeepers as good weather soldiers had been confirmed, thus. It was probably a first official confirmation of a reversal in a traditional role of military men. Those who were expected to fight and protect were now to be deployed only under conditions that would assure their own safety and security.

On the occasion of the Fiftieth Anniversary of the United Nations in 1995 Ghali presented a Supplement to the "Agenda." In a full turnabout, the Secretary General (SG) declared that neither the Security Council nor himself had the capacity to deploy, direct, command, and control peace enforcement except perhaps on a very limited scale. Commenting on the operations in Bosnia and Somalia, Ghali stressed that "Even though the use of force is authorized under Chapter VII of the Charter, the United Nations remains neutral and impartial between the warring parties, without a mandate to stop the aggressor (if one can be identified) or impose a cessation of hostilities."[7] Neutrality and impartiality were, wrongly, equaled again.

It took Annan, Ghali's successor, to admit in his 1999 report on the fall of Srebrenica that with the end of the cold war and the ascendancy of irregular forces, the old rules of the game did not hold.[8] But the "comprehensive review of the whole question of peacekeeping operations in all their aspects" commissioned by the Secretary General, in the aftermath of Srebrenica, to a panel chaired by Lakhdar Brahimi not only did not revise the existing peacekeeping rules, but also reiterated them. The report introduced a new classification of UN peace operations that entail three principal activities: conflict prevention and peacemaking; peacekeeping; and peace building. It was refreshing to read that no failure did more to damage the standing and credibility of UN than its reluctance to distinguish victim from aggressor or that the United Nations military units must be capable of defending themselves, other mission components, and the mission mandate or that the peacekeepers—troops or police—who witness violence against civilians should be presumed to be authorized to stop it, within their means, in support of the basic United Nations principles. The Panel also proposed several administrative and operational improvements. But in regard to the peacekeeping doctrine and strategy, the report concluded flatly: "The Panel concurs that consent of the local parties, impartiality and use of force only in self-defense should remain the bedrock principles of peacekeeping."[9] That conclusion did not prevent it from recognition that no amount of money or resources can substitute for significant changes that are urgently needed in the culture of the organization. But also no amount of tinkering with administrative and institutional improvements can substitute for clarification on the profound strategic confusion about the role of the military component of the UN peace operations. Brahimi's report failed to bring it about.

The question of peacekeeping was not ignored in the wider context of the UN reform. But a high-level panel appointed by Annan in 2004 to elaborate recommendations on the UN response to "Threats, Challenges and Changes" conspicuously failed again in coming up with a reappraisal of the UN doctrine and policy in regard to deployment of military contingents.[10]

Lacking clear strategic guidance from the UN, the military leaders in the field are on their own in translating Security Council's mandates into operational plans and rules of engagement (ROE) for their troops. Precisely little is known about the latter because the UN Secretariat considers ROE confidential documents, not available to the public. But the rare insight into the ROE for UNPROFOR (United Nations Protection Force) in ex-Yugoslavia and for UNAMIR (United Nations Assistance Mission for Rwanda) in Rwanda is disturbing. In case of UNPROFOR the rules contained vast restrictions that made mockery even of the right of the UN soldiers to self-defense when under attack. In case of Rwanda they authorized use of force to prevent crimes against humanity, but these were deliberately not applied.

While the UN continues to cultivate ambiguity as to the role of the military component in its peace operations, the last decade brought up a vast body of important theoretical contributions on the subject. A need for better correlation between the research on peace operations and on conflict prevention, containment, management, and resolution was universally recognized.

Proposals for new typology proliferated. Typically a stratification of peacekeeping into different generations or categories is presented along with drafts of adjusted theoretical frameworks and definitions. Ramesh Thakur and Albrecht Schnabel identify six generations of peacekeeping operations: "... traditional peacekeeping-pending peace, non-UN peacekeeping, expanded peacekeeping–peace reinforcement, peace enforcement, peace restoration by partnership, and multinational peace restoration–UN state creation. . . . "[11] By inclusion of peace enforcement operations into a broader category of peacekeeping, these writers, associated with the UN University in Tokyo, exemplified the persistence of theoretic and semantic difficulties in defining what peacekeeping actually is.

But these difficulties notwithstanding a consensus seems to be emerging on a doctrine for the middle-ground or gray-area operations, beyond the traditional peacekeeping but short of all-out war. A newly defined active impartiality or impartial peace enforcement is at its core. Peter Viggo Jacobsen, John Gerard Rugie, and Phillip Wilkinson offer particularly pertinent insights into that emerging consensus. In doing so they draw on the national military doctrines of France, Great Britain, and the United States for peace support operations, all reflected to some extent in the respective NATO's doctrine. While differing in scope and details, on the basics of the new doctrine these writers are unanimous.

First, to achieve its aims the international force must be credible. When in doubt, a force capable of using both carrots and sticks to promote consent must be deployed to deter noncompliance, and if necessary to enforce it. A relatively modest-sized force may be more successful in achieving deterrence than a much larger force in obtaining compliance. Second, force may be used to coerce or compel but not to defeat a belligerent. Compliance at the tactical level should be enforced, but enforcing it at the strategic level should be avoided. General Rose is quoted saying that hitting a tank is peacekeeping but targeting a command center is war. But at the high level of the spectrum it might be virtually impossible to distinguish the actions necessary in gray-area operations from the war-fighting in all respects except their political and military aims. Third, development of a successful strategy for conflict resolution is a joint political and military effort. The best the military can achieve alone is the containment of the conflict.[12]

But there are also dissenting voices. Jerzy Ciechanski argues that forcible UN peacekeeping will be inevitably ineffective and, therefore, also in the light of legalistic considerations, use of Chapter VII of the UN Charter by the Security Council is a mistake.[13] More convincingly and from a different point of view Mats Berdal claims that by identifying peace enforcement as an act distinct from war-fighting, advocates of the so-called gray-area option are allowing governments to avoid hard decisions about the implications of deploying military personnel in combat capacities. He also quite rightly maintains that doctrinal revisions might be needed but it is more urgent for the political decision makers to rethink the requirements for the effective use of force (that is to think of what military force can achieve as opposed to what it can do).[14]

Berdal's argument exposes the weakness of any doctrine based on deployment of armed forces in hostile and volatile environments under constraints of a static model, designated as a gray-area operation. While appropriate at the outset, such a designation may turn obsolete when conflicts escalate to such an extent that a gray-area turns black. The problem is not much different from earlier concerns about the mission creep and the traditional peacekeeping operations escalating into peace enforcement. But escalation and other surprises are inherent in the business of war and peace, and operations performed under a doctrine of active impartiality are not an exception. While the related risks cannot be discounted, their presence does not necessarily disqualify the doctrine.

It might have been expected that tectonic shifts in the international security environment caused by the global terrorism's attacks on New York and Washington, DC, on September 11, 2001, would lead to increased commitment to effective peacekeeping in distant lands. Surprisingly, the opposite is true, as if the protracted war-fighting in Afghanistan and Iraq by the U.S.-led coalitions exhausted the available potential of political will and military readiness of those involved and discouraged the rest. Several analysts assess that the overall effect of September 11 is a decreased interest of major players in peacekeeping operations.[15] If the lack of commitments to intervene for averting the threats of growing world disorder may be surprising, the scarcity of theoretical contributions suggesting changes in peacekeeping related to war on terrorism is not. While terrorism is a method applied by shadowy groups that do not control any territory, peacekeeping is concerned with restoration of law and order in territorial units. But the importance of effective peacekeeping on territories affected by and prone to exponents of global terrorism, such as Afghanistan, cannot be overestimated.

John Mackinlay maintains that Bin Laden attacks on the United States pushed military doctrine writers across the page to writing another chapter on confronting insurgency in complex emergencies. For too long, western armed forces were held in the mental straitjacket of fundamentalist writers on peacekeeping, who insisted on its rigid separation from other military missions—he says. Consequently, confusions of definition followed with military staff colleges explaining post-cold war contingencies as peace enforcement, peace building, peace making, and so forth while the military task had more in common with counterinsurgency. That is the experience of the past to which the leaders of most peace operations need to turn now. Combating the insurgency against the British in Northern Ireland, which by 2002 took 34 years to achieve an acceptable level of personal security, and the combating of the insurgency in Malaya in the 1950 are on the record, appropriately. But Mackinlay's invoking the experience of the Kosovo intervention as a turning point away from the simple containment operations of the past is loaded with an unintended historical irony. NATO undertook the bombing campaign against Yugoslavia without the UN authorization in a declared effort to prevent persecution of the Albanian majority of the province. In doing so it directly supported the insurgent Kosovo Liberation Army (KLA). KLA was the first insurgency movement ever enjoying a massive close-air support.

Mackinlay suggests a model of three phases for deployment in a complex emergency: intervention, stabilization, and garrisoning the conflict zone. The overwhelming military force needed in the first phase is scaled down in the second. Civilians' representatives take over in the third phase while some military units focus on counterinsurgency tasks. The writer reminds that no insurgency was ever defeated by military means alone. Among proposals for improving the intervention model, Mackinlay, with a view to the differences in the nature of insurgencies, calls for a better definition of the adversary. "*It may be necessary to confront or even destroy the insurgent movement*, or its members may become the nucleus of a new government" (italics added)—he says.[16]

Here the difference between gray-area operation and war-fighting may be gone and we are clearly back to the language of Chapter VII of the UN Charter which calls for a definition of an aggressor and provides for armed forces to deal with him. In that sense Mackinlay spelled out what Berdal was implying in his concerns about political leaders avoiding hard decisions and choices. It might be pertinent to recall that running a limited warfare for return of peace and order by means of a minimum and proportional use of force against spoilers, as opposed to fighting a war to destroy an enemy or conquer territory, is an older invention than peacekeeping. According to a British Army's manual of 1923 "British soldiers have constantly been reminded that their task was not the annihilation of an enemy but the suppression of a temporary disorder, and therefore the degree of force to be employed must be directed to that which is necessary to restore order and must never exceed it."[17]

Despite declarations to the contrary, the theoretical framework for the UN-led peacekeeping operations remains informed by the misleading triad of consent, impartiality, and use of force in self-defense only. Outside of the UN system major Western military powers have their own doctrines that, to some extent, converged into NATO's directives for peace support operations. The former are unlikely to make use of them in conflicts remote from their national interest and the alliance is far from being ready for a forceful out-of-area deployment yet.

The script for international peacekeepers is far from being clear, thus. As a flurry of debates, contributions, and lessons learned seminars on the past experience show, there is no lack of competence and expertise on the subject. But the political will for change is missing. Peacekeeping is not insulated from perceptions of the international system that generates them. And in that system, as Urquhart says, national self-interest and short-term thinking seem to have now overcome practical idealism and a sense of common purpose.[18] That is the very underlying reason for the persistence of the stereotypes and doctrinal constrains related to consensual peacekeeping. These stereotypes provide a window dressing for a reluctance if not a refusal to forcefully intervene for restoration of international peace. Not diminishing the importance of the theoretical debates and frameworks, the basic cure for the peacekeeping ills is to be sought in the political realm.

Main Actors

THE MAIN ACTORS in the peacekeeping theatre are the UN Security Council, the UN Secretariat, the troop contributing governments, and the military personnel in the field. Recently, regional organizations, military alliances, and coalitions of the willing also appear on the ground under a UN authorization. The outcome of the UN peacekeeping operations depends on the performance of each one of these actors and on the ability of getting their act together. Matters related to conflict resolutions occasionally appear on the agenda of the UN General Assembly, but whatever measures the Assembly chooses to apply, they remain on paper if not translated into implementing actions of the Security Council and/or the Secretariat. Such was the fate of the partition plan for Palestine in 1947–1948. This chapter looks into the impact of these main actors on the outcome of peacekeeping operations, without loosing from sight the subjective factors involved. Peacekeeping, neither clearly defined nor transparent enough, is an area where individuals in leading positions enjoy a potential freedom of action much larger than commonly recognized.

THE SECURITY COUNCIL

The United Nations came into being largely by the initiative and determination of an American President, Franklin Delano Roosevelt, who wanted the allied powers to take a collective responsibility for international peace.[1] The UN Charter adopted in San Francisco in 1945 came close to Roosevelt's vision. The five Big Powers—China, France, the UK, the USSR, and the United States—became permanent members of the UN Security Council, which is invested with the primary responsibility for the maintaining international peace and security in accordance with the purposes and principles of the Charter. Ten additional members sit on the Council elected by the General Assembly for 2-year terms.[2] The Charter obliges all members of the organization to accept and to carry out the Council's decisions. No other international body, ever, had been equipped with powers to decide on war and peace whenever and wherever it considered the latter threatened. It came, thus, closer than anyone wished to admit, to assuming the security function of a world government.

But the Council's constitution was based on the illusory assumption about the wartime alliance of the Big Powers to last indefinitely. It did not and the members of the Council, first and foremost its permanent members, considered the United Nations to be no more as an additional means of their national diplomacy. This attitude became evident during the Palestine crisis in 1947–1948, when the western permanent members were not able to arrive at a common policy.

The Big Powers' dominance in the Council is assured by the voting procedures prescribed in the Charter. Each of the members has one vote, but decisions of the Council on matters other than procedural require an affirmative vote of nine members, including the concurring votes of the permanent members. An opposition of any of the latter effectively blocks an action by the Council, even if all other members of the Council vote affirmatively.

Marginalized during the cold war, the Council adopted a more active stance when it had ended. Both its survival and later activism confirmed in a way the frequently heard cliche, according to which should the United Nations not exist, it would have to be invented. As the Big Powers do not accept its supranational powers and make use of the Council when its suits their national interests, another cliche of a toolbox comes to mind. The failures of the SC were not caused by the widely criticized veto institution, but by the Powers' commitment to their own interests. Gunnar Myrdal quite rightly observed that

> ... the entirely negative device of the veto has been the one and only important rule of the Charter which has been really operative; and its observance prevented the United Nations from disaster. Without the veto, the organization would have been in danger of breaking up as soon as a really serious question was at stake.[3]

In absence of a grand political consensus, except fighting the wars against aggressors in Korea in 1950s (with the Soviet Union's delegate absent at the crucial meeting) and in the Gulf in 1991, the Security Council never performed the function of a world's gendarme prescribed to it in the Charter. But the reality of international relations leaves the wide field open for selective pinprick peacekeeping interventions. Their number and destination is a function of a consensus in the Council and of the availability of means. It may be deplorable that there was no intervention in the civil war in the south of Sudan, with hundreds of thousands killed, uprooted, and starving, while international troops enforced a regime change in Haiti in 1994, but this choice represented a consensus reached within the Council.

When a conflict finds its way to appear on the Council's agenda its first resolution usually expresses concern, supports diplomatic efforts for a political settlement, urges all parties to abide strictly by cease-fire agreements, and asks the SG to report as soon as possible on the course of possible further action. It is on his recommendation that the Council may launch a peacekeeping mission. Three factors are decisive for an intervention to be effective—speed of deployment, relevance of mandate to the realities of the conflict, and adequacy of means employed. An insight into failed peacekeeping missions shows the Council rarely meeting these requirements.

The Council was not unaware of its own shortcomings. In 1994 already, its President declared that "... the Security Council is conscious of the need for the political goals, mandate, costs, and, where possible, the estimated time frame of the UN peacekeeping operations to be clear and precise, ..."[4] But the small, brutal wars in Sierra Leone, Congo, and Liberia of the last few years showed the UN peacekeepers again overwhelmed by events, unable to control these conflicts, and sometimes just fighting for life. The Council's assuming responsibilities in a growing number of conflicts does not make its task easier. In 2001 alone, it adopted fifty-two resolutions dealing with missions to Afghanistan, Angola, Burundi, Congo, Cyprus, Eritrea and Ethiopia, Iraq and Kuwait, Macedonia, the Middle East, Sierra Leone, Western Sahara, and with terrorism. In 2005 it was seventy.

A serious political debate about the SC's performance is substituted on one hand by academic considerations and on the other by generalizations about the failures or (rarely) about the successes of international community and of the United Nations. Urquhart was probably right in saying that only a devastating international crisis would change SC's ways.[5] Short of such a catastrophe it is probably unavoidable that the political process at work in the Council will more often then not lead to compromises resulting in delayed, weak, ambiguous, or unrealistic mandates and/or inadequate means for peacekeeping missions. But mandates of complex missions may have to be articulated in general terms by the force of circumstances. Such was the case in Somalia, where the Unified Task Force (UNITAF) was mandated "... to help to create a secure environment for the delivery of humanitarian aid," and under Chapter VII of the Charter "to use all necessary means to do so."[6]

What is most disturbing though is the proliferation of obviously unrealistic mandates and turning blind eye to disasters unfolding in the field. In the 60 years' long history there is not a single case of the Council calling anyone to account for failures in the operations it mandated. Routinely appreciation is expressed for the performance of the international personnel and troops, whatever are the results of the mission, while all the blame is assigned to the unruly and ungrateful parties to the conflict.

In the wake of the U.S.-led war with Iraq and in the framework of recent discussions on the ever-recurring theme of the UN reform, the SC becomes again the subject of controversies. While supporters of the war see the Council sinking into irrelevance after refusing to endorse the invasion of Iraq, opponents of that invasion maintain that it had proved its independence as world body legitimizing the use of force in international relations. Since the Council survived bitter ideological divisions of the cold war, in time it will probably find a way to heal the deep rift about Iraq also. But the damage done affects the very cornerstone of the foundations of the UN, which was from the outset a reliance on the soft and hard power of the United States. The effective role of the Council hinges on the political and strategic relations between Washington, DC, and the Glass Tower in Manhattan. Since the United States covers 25 percent of the cost of every peacekeeping operation, that relationship also affects the scope of these missions more then anything else.

Following the UN Millennium Summit, the High-level Panel on Threats, Challenges and Changes chaired by the former PM of Thailand, Anand Panyarachun,[7] recommended to make the Council more representative by its enlargement. In the model "A," which gained more traction, the Council grew from 15 to 24 members and the number of permanent members from 5 to 11. Main contenders for the new permanent seats are Germany, Japan, India, and Brazil, and the issue becomes hotly debated in and outside of the UN assembly halls. There is no disputing that the composition of the Council is outdated but the debates on the extension managed only to resurrect national and regional rivalries. The proposals are shelved for a not foreseeable time. The extension of the Council would improve its political image but carries considerable risks. Reaching agreement on the scope and mandates of the peacekeeping missions will be certainly not easier in a body counting 24 instead of 15 members. The principle of universality is at odds with the principle of efficiency.

Significantly, what the extended Council should do and how it should work did not take much place in the reform debates. A proposal on that subject by a group of small countries—Switzerland, Costa Rica, Jordan, Liechtenstein, and Singapore—was met with very little interest.[8]

SECRETARY GENERAL AND HIS STAFF

The UN Secretariat translates the SC mandates into directives for action by the contributing countries and by the military men in the field. Not unlikely to relations between any legislature and executive, the Secretariat interpretation of the mandates can make a difference to what really happens. According to a former U.S. representative in the SC, "Improvisation has been chosen as a single word to evoke the problems of peacekeeping management. A kind of programmed amateurism was showing across the board, including the near total absence of contingency planning for hastily recruited, ill-equipped and often unprepared troops and civilian staff."[9]

But not unnaturally, staff members of the organization from the SG to the minor official in the field tend to defend its performance in peacekeeping, even in face of almost universal consensus as to the failure of certain operations. The standard explanations offered run on variations of the two palliatives: the UN cannot be any better than its members, and the UN and its peacekeepers are being blamed for failures to act in a way which would exceed their mandates. In short the UN is being used as a scapegoat for those who restrict its actions. The first palliative is untrue for two reasons: firstly, because it assumes that an organization equipped with a vast, privileged bureaucracy has no identity, attitudes, and interests of its own, and, secondly, because it assumes existence of a fictional overall quality of its membership. Obviously enough, China, Denmark, Iraq, and Nauru do not have many qualities in common, but are members of the UN and it is the Secretariat's unenviable task to find for them, and for the rest, a common denominator whenever a consensus is necessary. The other palliative about the mandates and means is half-true, because the Secretariat has a record of steadily indulging in minimalist interpretations of the mandates.

Both of the palliatives serve a function, however. The responsibility for the outcome of the operations is not with the UN Secretariat or with the peacekeeping troops. And if this is so, whatever the UN did may amount to a success. Few months after the massacres of Srebrenica, and after winding up of the operation in Bosnia, the most outspoken among the UN leaders, Ghali, confided to German public that the UN did a formidable work in ex-Yugoslavia. While humiliations of UNPROFOR in ex-Yugoslavia were nothing else than part and parcel of the peacekeeping script—he added—Mogadishu and Sarajevo, as minor incidents, received excessive attention. Half a year later yet, addressing the public in the same country, Ghali confirmed his stand: UN did not fail in ex-Yugoslavia, but suffered from contradictory mandates and lack of means.[10]

The SG was firmly on his ground: no UN organ ever defined peacekeeping and the only script that exists is the Secretariat's own interpretation and that originates from guidelines for the United Nations Emergency Force's (UNEF) operation at the Suez Canal. The roots of a consensual peacekeeping, as an extra UN Charter instrument, are in the Middle East where, in 1948 yet, the United Nations abdicating from peace enforcement in Palestine put on a mantle of a neutral mediator instead.

The new paradigm seized the United Nations with a remarkable ease. No Secretary General, until Boutros Boutros-Ghali, deviated from the neutralist current and some embraced it eagerly. Dag Hammarskjold, in spite of stumbling into a war in Katanga, thought that any idea of a stand-by UN intervening military force was quite unsound.[11] His successor, U Thant, went further and maintained, in relation to the conflict in Cyprus, that it would be "a little insane for the UN Force to set about killing Cypriots, whether Greek or Turkish, to prevent them from killing each other."[12] For Kurt Waldheim even a British offer to add aircraft for strengthening the deterring capacity of the UN Force at the same island during the Turkish invasion in 1974 was unacceptable.[13] Javier Perez de Cuellar maintained that use of force by the peacekeepers amounted to breaches of impartiality with devastating results for the missions.[14] Probably the most opportunistic among the

UN leaders, Ghali managed to champion in public both for and against peace enforcement. Talking in 1993 about the UN troops combating the forces of General Aidid in Somalia, the SG said: "We have to be in position to apply military force. The force for peace."[15] Two years later he simply declared that he was always against peace enforcement, thus indirectly admitting his opposition to the Charter of the organization he headed.[16] Proving that it was not a slip of tongue, Ghali pronounced, in an official publication, the UN "a neutral intervening force and honest broker."[17] The UN members either did not notice or did not care. There was no support for a different United Nations.

After the spectacular UN failures in Rwanda and ex-Yugoslavia, Kofi Annan's courageously attempted to break with the prevailing pacifist culture of the organization. Following the publication of reports admitting errors in not confronting the perpetrators of genocide and massacres in these countries, Annan voiced his discontent with the state of affairs in the UN peacekeeping in public. "We have in the past prepared for peacekeeping operations with a best-case scenario: The parties sign an agreement, we assume they will honor it, so we send in lightly armed forces to help them," said the SG and added that ". . . the time has come for us to base our planning on worst-case scenarios: to be surprised by cooperation, if we get it. And to go in prepared for all eventualities, including full combat, if we do not."[18] The artificial distinction between peacekeeping and peace enforcement, so often invoked earlier, did not have place in Annan's sober and accurate assessment of what needed to be done now.

Alas, 3 years later, the organization continued "business as usual." In 2003, in the Ituri Province of the Democratic Republic of Congo, where 60,000 people have been killed and half a million displaced since 1999, the UN performed a lesser scale replay of its performance in Bosnia and Rwanda. The UN promised to secure a zone vacated by units of the Ugandan army, but sent only 712 Uruguayan soldiers who were allowed merely to guard UN property and escort relief workers. Tribal militias attacked both the UN and each other, and committed atrocities against civilians. The UN area commander was stabbed and the peacekeepers did nothing to stop the massacre of 400 people in Bunia. Ultimately the Uruguayans were rescued by a French short-term expedition, authorized by the SC. Since then the operation showed a bumpy record of alternating between more humiliations and retaliatory actions.[19] At the beginning of 2006 eight Guatemalan UN soldiers of that mission were killed in an ambush by members of the Lord's Resistance Army infiltrating from Uganda.[20]

The ongoing official debates on UN reform expose a strange paradox: the more elaborate the analyses and other contributions on the necessity of a new security consensus in the post-9/11 world, the less of substance is on offer. A report by the UN High-level Panel on Threats, Challenges and Changes provided a compelling case for a broader, more comprehensive concept of collective security, but fell short of articulating it.[21]

Chapter IX of the report "Using force: rules and guidelines" reaffirms that the SC remains the sole source of legitimacy of resorting to force in international relations but its decisions should be made on solid evidentiary grounds, and for the right reasons, morally as well as legally. In considering whether to authorize the use of military force the Council should adopt and apply basic criteria as proposed by the Panel. Nothing in that chapter distinguishes the potential use of force in war or in peace enforcement or peacekeeping operations and much of its content relates to war fighting between countries rather than to more limited operations. But in an important and new contribution the Panel states that "We endorse the emerging norm that there is a collective international responsibility to protect, exercisable by the Security Council authorizing military intervention as a last resort, in the event of genocide and other large-scale killing, ethnic cleansing or serious violations of international humanitarian law which sovereign governments have proved powerless or unwilling to prevent."[22]

It is an excellent norm, even when it neglects governments vicious enough to exterminate own citizens, like it happened in Rwanda and like it as is happening in Sudan. But who should the Council dispatch to intervene under that emerging consensus? Are these missions in the realm of peacekeeping or out of it? Is the old UN mantra about the contradiction between peacekeeping and peace enforcement valid still and if not by what it should be replaced?

Alas, the report in its chapter "Peace enforcement and peacekeeping capability" does not provide answers. The Panel recognizes that "discussion of the necessary capacities has been confused by the tendency to refer to peacekeeping missions as Chapter VI (of the UN Charter) operations and peace enforcement missions as Chapter VII operations. But such "characterizations are to some extent misleading" and therefore "it is now the usual practice for Chapter VII mandate to be given in peacekeeping and as much as in peace enforcement cases." Thus, the distinction between these operations is upheld even when they are deployed under the same Chapter without any definition of what that distinction entails. The doctrinal confusion remains in place. The sole reference in the Panel's report to the daunting confusion on what the peacekeepers are entitled or obliged to do with their arms is a remainder that differences between Chapter VI and VII mandates can be exaggerated. Consequently—the Panel explains—"there is little doubt that peacekeeping missions under Chapter VI have the right to use force in self-defense—and this right is *widely understood* (italics added) to extend to 'defense of the mission.' "[23] So much for the clarification of the most controversial issue in the present doctrine and practice of peacekeeping.

The real challenge, in any deployment of forces of any configuration with any role—the Panel continues—is to ensure that they have an appropriate, clear, and well understood mandate and the necessary resources to discharge it. But even when the common understanding of mandates was a major problem in the past, no suggestions to decrease risks of misunderstanding are offered. Equally, in terms of availability of resources, the Panel merely appeals, primarily to the developed countries, to put more forces at the disposal of the UN. A warning is attached, to this invitation for Annan to continue circulating with a begging bowl, that in the absence of a substantial increase in the numbers of available military personnel, UN peacekeeping risks repeating some of its worst failures of the 1990s.

Most disappointing in the Panel's report is a total absence of new ideas on potentially most promising preventive deployment of the Blue Helmets. Out of 320 paragraphs of the report a single one deals with this issue of an immense potential. In that single paragraph national leaders and parties to the conflict are encouraged to make use of preventive deployment.[24] But deterring of a would-be aggressor will be most effective when troops are deployed on his territory and it is an illusion that an invitation from him would be forthcoming.

The much publicized Panel also proposed several improvements in the existing institutional arrangements, such as the badly needed reform of the discredited UN Human Rights Commission or the less obviously needed establishment of a peacebuilding commission. Why did it conspicuously fail in bringing more clarity into the theoretical and practical framework of peacekeeping? It may be an educated guess that in that sector the report presented results deemed palatable to the sponsors and recipients—the UN Secretariat and the member governments. Such an attitude in committee work is not uncommon in the corporate world.

There is evidence of a deep commitment of influential members of the Secretariat to the neutralist and pacifist understanding of the UN role in peacekeeping in the past. Ghali's declaration to the effect that the UN was authorized to use force in Bosnia under a humanitarian mandate was indirectly contradicted by Shashi Tharoor, an officer in charge of the ex-Yugoslavia desk in the UN Secretariat.[25] Both before and after the surrender and massacres in Srebrenica, Tharoor insisted that the proper reading of the resolution of the SC authorizing the use of "all necessary means" in deterrence of attacks on safe areas prove "... that UN troops have indeed done precisely what they are authorized to do." He added that "... we were deployed to help extinguish the flames of war, not to fan them" and stressed that the Security Council never used the words "protect" or "defend"; therefore, the UN was simply expected to deter attacks on these areas through mere peacekeepers' presence.[26] But the last UNPROFOR commander in Bosnia, General Rupert Smith, rightly submitted that "To deter someone is to alter, or frame, or form his intentions. That intention is formed by the prospect of what will happen if he does not go into the direction you want him to go. If you are going to deter by your presence, then you are not going to deter."[27] Tharoor, an Indian writer and diplomat prior to joining UN, also said "Words can save. Words can kill."[28] The interpretation by the UN Secretariat of the word "deterrence" was an accomplice in Srebrenica killings.

Some of the UNPROFOR's staff members confessed their strong moral doubts about what they were doing in Bosnia or whether they should in fact have remained there at all.[29] But no one left except the former PM of Poland, Tadeusz Mazowiecki, whom Ghali appointed UN Special Rapporteur on Human Rights in ex-Yugoslavia. In his open letter to Ghali, Mazowiecki explained that after the surrender by the UN of Srebrenica and Zepa he recognized the futility of his work and did not want to contribute any more to the pretences of defending human rights.[30] Tharoor continues his career in the UN.[31]

Michael Barnett discussing Rwanda and David Rieff discussing Bosnia offer conflicting explanations of the commitment of the Secretariat to organizational loyalties prevailing over the purposes and principles of the UN Charter.[32] The former attributes it to a noble concern for the organization's survival, the latter to parochial interests under a fig leaf of the humanitarian assistance.[33] But neither claims that the attitudes of the leading members of the Secretariat, whatsoever their motivation, contrasted with those prevailing among the member governments the servant of whom the Secretariat is.

TROOP CONTRIBUTING GOVERNMENTS

Motives of the governments in joining the UN peacekeeping vary widely. Following impulses of international solidarity is a common declared motive, but following national interests, giving their military an opportunity to exercise, earning money from the UN for services might be for many a more plausible description. The later is especially true for poor and newly emerged countries, even if proving political correctness in their case is also an important factor. Obviously, material contributions and professional level of troops from particular countries vary also widely and, practically, there is a "division of labor" under which the United States may be providing an airlift for the operation to which Ireland contributes a well-equipped infantry battalion and Bangladesh another one, but not equipped. These disparities, reinforced by language problems, not uncommon in other military coalitions, make clarity of mandates, of strategy, and of rules of engagement even more important than in case of a single-nation operation. But even the permanent members of the SC are not free from confusion about peacekeeping.

Commenting on casualties among members of the French contingent of the UN Force in Lebanon (UNIFIL), the PM of France, Jacques Chirac, said in 1986: "Our soldiers courageously serve an organization, which, unfortunately, did not rise up to the level of the responsibilities it pretends to assume."[34] But the vulnerability of the UN mission of Lebanon originated in its utterly unrealistic mandate, established by the Security Council with the affirmative vote of France, which she repeated twice each year ever since.

In 1995, after the fall of Srebrenica, the President of France, Jacques Chirac, echoed the PM and accused the UN for making peacekeepers accomplices of Bosnian Serbs' barbarity. He also accused the Western democracies for behaving more or less as Neville Chamberlain and Edouard Daladier did when faced with Hitler's threats against Czechoslovakia in 1938.[35] It was rather astonishing to hear these condemnations coming from a country that had the strongest national contingent in ex-Yugoslavia and three consecutive UN Commanders on the ground, including General Bertrand Janvier during the fall of Srebrenica.[36]

But the fall out of the misshapen UN missions in the 1990s brought about reappraisals of the peacekeeping policies and doctrines. In the United States,

Britain, and France new political guidelines and doctrinal approaches had been formulated with a view to avoid the mistakes of the past.

The United States had seldom been a troop contributor for the UN missions in the strict sense, but for obvious reasons of its political, economic, and military weight, its position and views on international peacekeeping operations have a dominant if not a defining role. After the debacle of the United States' confused participation in the adventure of the UN Mission in Somalia (UNOSOM II), the administration issued new policy directives. Presenting the "Policy on Multilateral Peace Operations," the U.S. Permanent Representative to the UN, Madeleine Allbright, reminded that while some Americans see UN peacekeeping as a dangerous illusion, others consider it the linchpin of world peace. Her administration had a more balanced view. She said: "We see UN peacekeeping as a contributor to ... our national security strategy ... as a way to defuse crises and prevent breaches of peace from turning into larger disasters. It lends global legitimacy to efforts to mediate disputes, demobilize armed factions, arrange cease-fires and provide emergency relief." The value of UN peacekeeping does not depend on how many missions are attempted but on how well each mission is conducted, said Allbright, and added: "... no new UN peace operations has yet been proposed formally for Burundi, Sudan, Nagorno–Karabah, Tajikistan, Afghanistan, or Sierra Leone despite the terrible violence that has occurred in each. This reflects not callousness on the part of international community but rather a recognition of the limits of what UN peace operations can achieve in the absence of a demonstrated will on the part of contending factions to choose negotiations over force of arms."[37]

"As in recognition of these limitations, 2 weeks earlier, she voted in the Security Council for a radical reduction of the number of the UN troops in Rwanda amidst war and genocide. Now, proposals for new peacekeeping operation should be examined under a set of questions to be answered in positive; will UN involvement advance U.S. interests? Is there a real threat to international peace and security? Does the proposed mission have clear objectives? If the operation is a peacekeeping—as opposed to peace enforcement—is a cease-fire in place, and have the parties to the conflict agreed to an UN presence? Are the financial and personnel resources available? Can an end point be identified? What happens if we do not act?" Allbright also made clear that the United States reserved its right to freely choose the form of intervention: "We may act through the UN, we may act through NATO, we may act through a coalition ... or we may act alone." As to the possible future participation of the U.S. troops in the UN peacekeeping, General Wesley Clark clarified the question; the President will never relinquish the command of the American troops, which, however, under certain circumstances, can be put under a foreign operational control.[38] Peacekeeping was going to be more credible, cost effective, and professional.

In France, a report on the politics of intervention by Jean-Bernard Raimond, MP and former Minister of Foreign Affairs and Chairman of an Inquiry, presented in February 1995, contained ten conditions for military interventions, based upon the Inquiry's understanding of the role of France in the world and on its history, her military means, and on the values in which she believes. In its main purpose, the French policy, as the U.S. directive, confirmed the primacy of national interest. But two other important policy guidelines differ with the United States in a significant way. On one hand United Nations authorization prior to undertaking any military intervention is sought, but on the other the option of a UN leadership of the operation is excluded. While the United States allowed putting American soldiers under a foreign operational control, France would not participate in peacekeeping operations deployed under Charter VII of the UN Charter unless they are placed under French national, under third parties, or multinational command—but in no case under a UN command.[39] But at the time of the presenting of the report the French contingents of UNPROFOR were under the command of the United Nations Peace Force's (UNPF) in Zagreb, led by the French General Janvier.

Significantly both the new American and French policy guidelines continued the distinction between peacekeeping and peace enforcement as the UN did, without clearly identifying what such a distinction entails.

In contrast, U.K. addressed the main theoretical issue of the peace support operations head-on. The British assumed that neither "peacekeeping" nor "peace enforcement" are terms adequate to describe what is required from the troops deployed in areas of armed conflagration. Thus, a third category of operations had been introduced, called "wider peacekeeping" (WPK). But as Rod Thornton explained, its purpose was not as much guidelines for the future, but a justification for the Army's restraint in Bosnia: it was needed to explain why the mission could not go beyond escorting convoys. After criticism within the British military establishment, the WPK had been rejected and replaced in 1998 by a new doctrine of Joint Warfare (JWP 3–50, Peace Support Operations). It stressed closer coordination with civilian agencies, a need for "carrot-and-stick" approach and upgraded the use of force from "minimal" to "judicious." But the criticism did not abate, and it had been pointed out that "the risk no longer lay in getting into a bloodbath, but in creating an image of an emasculated NATO and an emasculated British Army; an army that had once looked with pride on its ability to deal effectively with peace operations . . ."[40]

The British concept, according to Jacobsen, corresponded with the French new approach, but was more cautious. The French introduced a new category of "peace restoration" operations in the middle ground between peacekeeping and peace enforcement, and a new concept of an "active impartiality" which allows for the use of force in defense of the mandate and of the civilians. The troops should enjoy, to the extent possible, undisputed military superiority and be capable of imposing compliance with UN resolutions, including operations under Chapter VI of the Charter. An "impartial peace enforcement" was deemed justified in peace support operations as opposed to "partial enforcement" exemplified by the Gulf War.

The British adopted the French approach to gray-area operations, whereas the force would also use limited force if necessary to protect the population and the mandate. The Americans, according to Jakobsen, adopted the same approach in their manual FM 100–20 on Stability and Support Actions, and he concluded that a consensus was emerging among the three Big Powers on use of force in gray-area operations. Jacobsen's claim that the new consensus informs current practice and that everyone is embracing it sounds overoptimistic, though.[41] Whatever the degree of convergence between the American, British, and French military doctrines for "peace operations," a political will to deploy robust UN peace operations is missing, still.

While the western Big Powers distanced themselves from contributing to operations unrelated to their national interests, some of the lesser powers and staunch supporters of the UN peacekeeping attempted to improve the UN capabilities. The Dutch, Canadians, and Danes initiated studies on improvement of the sole existing institutional instrument for a rapid deployment of UN troops, the UN Standby Arrangements System (UNSAS).

UNSAS is a database that, in theory, allows for deployment of military and other assets indicated by the governments as available to peacekeeping operations at 7, 15, 30, 60, or 90 days notice. The database included in 2000 about 150,000 personnel from 88 countries, out of which only 31 have concluded memoranda of understanding, which defined their responsibilities.[42] But that instrument is far from reliable. None of the 19 approached governments that have undertaken to provide troops on request agreed to contribute to the reinforced UN Mission in Rwanda (UNAMIR) in 1994.

As a result of the combined efforts of a few engaged governments a UN Standby Forces High Readiness Brigade (SHIRBRIG) functions within the framework of UNSAS now. But its deployment is restricted to consensual Chapter VI operations. That excludes complex emergencies such as in Afghanistan, in the Congo, or in Darfur.

The UN commander in Bosnia in 1994, General Rose, recalled that "the plea most frequently made to me by visiting heads of states, foreign secretaries, defense ministers and military chiefs of the troop contributing nations was not that the UN should use more force but that it should use less. They were conscious of their responsibility to get their young volunteer peacekeepers home alive."[43] How to reconcile such legitimate concerns with the UN responsibilities for international peace and with a declared readiness of the troop contributing countries to support it remains an open question.

NATO AND OTHER SECURITY COUNCIL'S AUTHORIZED CONTRACTORS

The British and French who were major contributors in the past large UN operations are now likely to appear in the peacekeeping theatre in another role. The former rescued a hapless UN peacekeeping mission from collapse in Sierra Leone and the latter went to the Ivory Coast, separating belligerents in a civil war and preparing ground for a UN peacekeeping mission.[44] Both countries are former colonies of Britain and France, respectively.

In comparison to earlier interventions of the ex-colonial powers in Africa undertaken merely to evacuate expatriates, these new operations mean progress. The UN leadership seems to welcome the new trend. Jean-Marie Guéhenno, the UN Undersecretary General for Peacekeeping Operations, submitted that when the world's most capable militaries deploy in support of UN peace operations, "it might sometimes have to be . . . a short, sharp injection of force, followed by an early exit."[45] Subcontracting of the operations by the UN Security Council to single powers, multinational coalitions of the willing, or to military alliances is the trend. It happened in Bosnia, Kosovo, Macedonia, East Timor, and Afghanistan already. But a closer look at the performance of the multinationals, as opposed to single power's interventions, reveals problems disturbingly similar to these experienced by the Blue Helmets.

In November 2003 the SC established that 2 years after the U.S.-led coalition Enduring Freedom drove out the Taliban regime, and despite the presence of International Security Assistance Force (ISAF), "insecurity caused by terrorist acts, factional fighting, and drug related crime remained the main concern of Afghanistan today."[46] One of the reasons for that lack of security was the restriction of ISAF to patrolling Kabul. On insistence of the Afghan government, the SC, by resolution 1510 under Chapter VII of the UN Charter, extended its mandate by authorizing the multinational force to take "all necessary means" in support for the security in the country. NATO, in the midst of an identity crisis, took over the command of ISAF.

But commencing its first out-of-area operation the Alliance opted for a minimalist interpretation of what enhancing security in Afghanistan entails. It deployed outside of Kabul initially only in a PRT in Kunduz.[47] In February 2004, 200 German soldiers arrived there and 300 more were expected later. The lightly armed team left the armored personal carriers in Kabul. "Less arms, more safety," said their commander. Contacts established with 150 local persons—added he—should be helpful in strengthening political structures and in creating a civil society. To the amazement of some of the Afghans, the soldiers of ISAF did not intend to interfere with drug cultivation or traffic because they were not authorized to do so by the *Bundestag* (the German Parliament). Moreover—according to a German aid organization—burning of the poppy fields would bring nothing because they are cultivated under armed supervision of men deployed by the authorities on whose goodwill the PRT depends in its efforts to help stabilizing the region. Early February 2004 seven people were killed in Argo, which lies in the PRT area of operation, in fighting between the militias of the district chief and the police chief over the control of the local narcotics trade.[48] The local political structures call not so much for strengthening but for a regime change. But this is not in ISAF's brief.

Jaap de Hoop Scheffer, the Secretary General of NATO declared at the outset of his tenure that, if we want to win the war on terrorism, we must win the peace in Afghanistan. But, a few weeks later, he complained about the lack of troop contributions because of force protection presenting a continuous problem.

Scheffer maintained that no NATO country can be expected to approve request for more troops unless there is no clear assurance on who will come to the assistance of troops in extreme circumstances.[49] The mightiest military Alliance's difficulties in assembling troops for a mission of a high political priority testify both to a weakness within and to a radical shift in understanding what the soldier's profession is about. It is evident now that the lack of boots in the field where the ground is hot is not solely a United Nation's problem.

Two years later, Scheffer, who is Dutch, still pleaded with his own parliament to approve a deployment of 1,200 Dutch peacekeepers in the insurgent-infested southern Afghanistan. But now he came up with a different question: "You should not say, sorry, it is too dangerous. We will not go. That is an argument I do not buy. What do you have armed forces for?"[50] Eventually, the Dutch, along with the British and Canadians will go, extending the NATO's military presence in Afghanistan from 9,000 to 15,000.

A comparison with the capabilities deployed by the Alliance in the European backyard of Kosovo exposes the hollowness of claims to a priority attributed to the mission in Afghanistan. Its state of 2 decades of anarchy, civil war, and disintegration into warlord fiefdoms, almost completely destroyed administrative and physical infrastructure, its difficult terrain and its role as the largest producer of opium in the world—if not as the past and potential future hub of international terrorism—call for a mandate and size of a force much stronger than for Kosovo. But despite acting under Chapter VII of the UN Charter, ISAF has no authority to act on its own and is restricted to assisting the Afghan authorities. NATO sent to Kosovo as of June 1999 about 50,000 soldiers. According to Winrich Kuehne's calculations Afghanistan has about thirteen times the population of Kosovo, thus an equivalent force would be about 650,000. A similar calculation based on the size of the territory produces even more astonishing numbers. With Afghanistan about 600 times larger than Kosovo, the equivalent force of ISAF would be more than 5 million.[51] What these figures seem to suggest is not only a neglect of an efficient operation in Afghanistan, but an overkill deployment in Kosovo.

As the resurgent Talibans are back and in control of almost a third of the country, Afghanistan is still a project in progress.[52] But building ISAF's presence around the PRTs seems to expose a disturbing similarity to the UN traditional peacekeeping by symbolic contingents under minimalist mandates.

Peacekeepers in other NATO-led operations encounter problems in facing violent opposition. In a most brazen armed challenge to a Western peacekeeping force since the lost battles in Somalia in 1993, the Bosnian Croat combined forces of nationalist politicians and organized crime succeeded in humiliating Stabilization Force's (SFOR) soldiers in Bosnia and Hercegovina in 2001. Opposing a seizure of a bank suspected of criminal acts, Croatian mobs launched assaults in four cities. SFOR retreated in humiliation, after returning boxloads of sensitive bank documents to rioters in exchange for the release of hostages they were holding in the Grude branch of the Hercegovacka Banka. The French General Robert

Meille authorized the use of deadly force to free the hostages but the Spanish and Italian commanders of the Quick Reaction Forces, garrisoned nearby in 30 armored vehicles, refused to intervene, citing rules of engagement established by their own governments.[53]

There are other players subcontracting in peacekeeping operations for the UN under the SC authorization, but it is doubtful whether their members are willing to put their soldiers in harms way. If a statement by the German Minister of Defense may indicate a trend, the opposite is true. Franz Josef Jung initially rejected the UN request for the European Union's Rapid Reaction Force (to which Germany contributes 1,500 soldiers) to support the United Nations Mission in the Congo (MONUC) in protecting the first free elections in that country in decades, as envisaged in April 2006. What his army needs—as the result of years-long reforms and after the demanding overseas assignments of the recent times—is not new missions but a return of calm, the minister explained. Such attitudes do not bode well for the Congo where, according to Amnesty International, the monthly toll of victims of violence, expulsion, and hunger is 31,000. Since 1996 almost 4 million people perished.[54]

GENERALS AND PRIVATES

Summarizing the experience of the first peacekeeping operation in Egypt in 1956, U Thant recognized that "the ... military man was faced with a concept of soldiering which is entirely foreign to anything taught to him in national service. The soldier is trained basically to fight. In UNEF, he was ordered to avoid fighting in all circumstances, and, indeed, to seek to prevent it."[55] An intensive promotion of the merits and universality of the nonviolent military interventions, modeled on that operation but divorced from realities of other conflicts, succeeded in creating a virtual reality in which soldiers serving under the Blue Flag might be requested to forsake not only their professional attitudes but also common sense reflexes and simply human impulses.

In Somalia, the German military contingent of UNOSOM was prohibited from using arms, self-defense including, and moved around only under protection. The Germans driving in armored personnel carriers have been protected by Italians, driven in open trucks with their naked backs exposed to the sun.[56] In Rwanda, a journalist reported, "the Blue Helmets have had helplessly to look at women being raped, children taken on bayonets and men castrated. Humiliated by the contempt of the warmongers and depressed by the suffering of the natives, the UN soldiers had to follow their orders." In an apparent show of disgust with these orders some of the UN–Belgian soldiers, upon their return from Kigali, at the airport in Brussels, had thrown off their blue berets on the tarmac and put them to fire.[57] The Rwandan experience proved evidently to have corruptive effects on the reporter, who did question neither legal nor moral responsibility of those who allegedly ordered these soldiers to passively witnessing atrocities.

It is difficult, if ever possible, to identify dominant trends in behavior of the military men serving under the Blue Flag. Their attitudes varied between the national contingents and even more so between individuals and many suffered from their experience. A military physician from the University of Oslo recorded frequent mental disorders among the Norwegian UNIFIL soldiers back from the mission in Lebanon, which, compared to Rwanda or Bosnia, was a kindergarten.[58]

As one of the UNPROFOR's Bosnia Commanders remembered, "A French lieutenant stood all night in front of a Serb T-55 tank, refusing to give up the weapons put under the UN control (in an exclusion zone around Sarajevo) . . . and telling the Serbs that they would not only have to kill him but the whole of his platoon to gain the weapons. At dawn the Serbs left empty handed and had not returned. At another site guarded by a Ukrainian platoon, they had been able to take a tank without any resistance."[59]

But it was the attitudes of the UN military leaders which could make more difference to the outcome of the mission. There is no better opportunity to see how much varied their attitudes, views, and actions as to refer to testimonies of the UN commanders in ex-Yugoslavia, the largest, most confused, but best-reported UN peacekeeping operation.

The French commander of UNPROFOR in Bosnia, General Philippe Morillon, was determined from the outset to not applying any force in discharging his mandate. When Security Council authorized it in getting the humanitarian aid through to the besieged population centers, he declared that "There is no intention to force our way through any blockade" and added that there was no military solution except 100,000 deaths and absolute catastrophe.[60] Upon signing an eighteenth cease-fire in Bosnia on November 10, 1992, Morillon took off his flak jacket, invited the press, and declared the war over. But he signed the nineteenth cease-fire 1 month later.[61] When the Serbs killed Bosnia's Deputy Prime Minister Hakija Turajlic while inside of a French armored personnel carrier (APC), Morillon's only reaction was an appeal condemning the act and a call for restraint and peace. He excused the unit involved, despite findings of a special UN inquiry to the effect that UNPROFOR's standing operating procedures on never opening the doors of APC to foreign forces were violated.[62] In the main, Morillon was right. The UN soldiers were allowed to use force only in self-defense and they were not shot at, but Turajlic who happened to be sitting in their vehicle. A few years later and out of Bosnia, Morillon confessed that his understanding of the role of the UN military was wrong: "It was not until the Bosnian drama and the fall of Srebrenica, that it become clear that the need to protect one's own soldiers cannot be the sole reason for the deployment of armed military units."[63] Some of the French knew it already, but not under his watch. In May 1995, when the Serbs overrun the UN held Vrbanja bridge in Sarajevo, the French counterattacked and retook it at the cost of two own fatalities and fourteen wounded. The French, who accounted for 12 percent of the total UNPROFOR strength, suffered 27 percent of its casualties.[64]

General Francis Briquemont of Belgium, Morillon's successor, confronted with the obviously insufficient mandate and with the mission rules and practices of which contradicted his professional integrity, was not ready to follow them. He resigned his assignment after half a year. Testifying before a Commission of the French National Assembly, Briquemont said that the humanitarian mandate given to Morillon instead of enforcing respect for Bosnia's independence was a deliberate act of cultivating ambiguity, only confounded by multiplication of resolutions by the SC. He deplored sending soldiers into a conflict without a clear mandate and sufficient means, the disturbed relations between the civilian and military leadership of the mission, the poor quality and unreliability of certain national contingents, and also a formidable confusion of military and political objectives between UN and NATO.[65] The general considered the UN on a wrong course and did not want to be a part of it.

The British General Michael Rose, who succeeded Briquemont, was ready to work within the script and means available. Determined to achieve the overriding objectives that were the delivery of humanitarian aid and facilitation of a negotiated settlement of the conflict, he also recognized that to this end the use of force not only could not be excluded but was at times necessary.[66] The contribution of one of the most decorated and experienced Britain's soldiers brought the subject of peacekeeping beyond recycling of the stale mantra on noncombat use of armed forces. In a war zone, according to Rose, "a UN peacekeeping mission needs to be equipped with the forces' structures, command disciplines and military technology of war, if it is to survive." The war machine is indispensable, but it should be utilized for achieving peacekeeping objectives and not for winning a war. Therefore, the general says, "The central lesson . . . is that a careful balance has to be struck between military enforcement measures and the need to continue the principal mission. . . ."[67]

A NATO general, O. Kandborg, came to similar conclusions and recommended that, in peacekeeping operations, there should always be the capability to escalate from Chapter VI to Chapter VII (of the UN Charter).[68] Thus, according to these military leaders, peace enforcement or coercive actions are part and parcel of peacekeeping. Those who would wish to uphold the artificial divide might as well heed General Rose's view on the meaning of an authorization to use "all necessary means," included in an SC resolution. "To this question there is no simple answer as it is impossible to draw a clear line between the permissible use of force in a peacekeeping mission and an act of war."[69]

The successor of General Rose in Bosnia, General Smith, exposed even more assertive stance in confronting the aggressive Bosnian Serbs. In doing so he continuously irritated the UNPROFOR's chief political officer in Sarajevo, who, echoing the sentiments of Tharoor, kept telling the general "If you want to fight a war . . . do it under a UK flag or NATO flag, not under the UN flag."[70]

Whatever the attitudes of the military leaders are, the rank and file is guided by rules of engagement (ROE). But the UN military leaders who openly criticized several aspects of their own assignment were remarkably silent on the ROE they produced themselves.[71] The lecture of a document issued March 24, 1992, revised July 19, 1993, and signed by the UNPROFOR Commander, General Jean Cot, reveals, that its authors followed U Thant's guidance for peacekeepers to avoid fighting in all circumstances. The document composed in the form of prohibitions and permissions with annexes makes a difficult reading even for an experienced reader. Prohibitions prevail and, typically, the response allowed to a "Hostile Act (with Use of Fire) is to take immediate protection measures, observe and report. Warn the aggressor of intent to use force and demonstrate resolve.... Warning shots are authorized.... Report action taken. If the hostile act does not cease and life is threatened, option B (opening fire) can be ordered by troop commander. Retaliation is forbidden, and the UN Forces must cease-fire when the opponent stops firing."[72] Bruce Berkovitz rightly concluded that the hostile forces could ratchet their provocations to just under the threshold beyond the troops could use force and therefore these rules were not allowing the mission to be carried on effectively and at an acceptable level of risk. There is no mention whatsoever on using force in case of restrictions encountered in discharging the mandate and humanitarian convoys are not mentioned at all. But on protected and safe areas the ROE are unexpectedly clear: UNPROFOR personnel may use their weapons "to resist deliberate military or para-military incursions into them." Hence, ROE equaled the famous "deterrence" of the SC resolution 836 to an authorization to resist incursions by force.[73] General Cot's ROE amounted to an instruction for a self-defeat when attacked.

But confusion about the mandates and restrictive ROE notwithstanding, while some military leaders professed having their hands tied up by higher orders and instructions, others, like Bob Stewart and Alistar Duncan, British colonels who served in Bosnia, felt the opposite. Talking to Malcolm Riffkind, the British Defense Secretary, Stewart explained that he never did concern himself with worries about the mandate and *he looked at problems in simple terms whether an action was essentially right or wrong* (italics added). Similarly, Duncan assumed considerable latitude in discharging his mandate: "My task was to provide an escort to the convoys.... In addition, we were to provide assistance to endangered people as required. That was all. There were no further close directions from the UN or from the British Government or Military. Strange though it may seen, I was quite delighted with that, because *my hands were entirely free to deal with the problem as I saw fit* (italics added)."[74] In other words, as Brendan Simms wrote, these officers were plucking from the often-contradictory SC resolutions on Bosnia their own mission's statement.

Whatever are the attitudes of the men in the field, the outcome of the mission is a result of the interplay of all main actors involved. But it is the military that pays the price in blood. The subsequent chapters show what was achieved at that price in the largest UN peacekeeping missions.

Betrayal in Palestine and Its Legacy (Middle East)

IN 1945 the United Nations proudly pronounced itself determined to save succeeding generations from the scourge of war. Its Charter equipped it with an arsenal of tools needed to pursue such a lofty, almost utopian, goal. In 1947–1948 the Middle East and Palestine offered the UN the first major opportunity to employ these tools and to test the organization's credibility. The results were negative: instead of preventing the local conflict from escalating, the UN helped to turn it into a major international conflagration. By introducing for a territory engulfed in a civil war a partition plan without the intention of enforcing it, the UN made an international war for Palestine inevitable. It also failed in bringing this war to an end, despite the deployment of several military missions in the Middle East theatre. The partition of Palestine is an ongoing process, leaving Israel without internationally recognized borders and the Palestinians without a state of their own. The Arabs and Israelis feel the consequences daily and with them the rest of the world.

This chapter sheds light on the circumstances and results of the UN military presence in the region, which became a continuous testing ground for the exercise of peacekeeping. Out of the six UN peacekeeping missions undertaken in the region, three are ongoing.

MISHAPPENED MANDATE AND A FAILED TAKEOVER

On Friday May 14, 1948, the British High Commissioner of Palestine, General Sir Alan Cunningham, left Jerusalem without anyone in attendance but his soldiers, who left soon thereafter. Jerusalem, the cradle of Judaism and Christianity, holy for centuries to Muslims as well, was about to change hands again. But the new master, the United Nations, was neither present on the ground nor prepared for the takeover. The organization, which accepted the responsibility for Palestine after the surrender of the mandate by the British in 1947, left the territory's fate to be decided by the struggle between the Arab and the Jews. It was a sorry end to the hopes aroused only 30 years earlier when the first Christian army since the times of the Crusaders had arrived at the gates of Jerusalem. On December 11, 1917, another British general, the commander of the Egyptian Expeditionary Force, Sir Edmund Allenby, promised order and equal treatment for all communities present in Jerusalem.[1]

Initially, both the Jews and the Arabs of Palestine looked up to the British as liberators from the Ottoman rule. But the efforts of the British Military Administration to maintain a peaceful equilibrium between the two increasingly hostile peoples did not bear fruits. Not even the most benevolent administration could have overcome the underlying ambiguities and contradictions of British policy toward the territory. Arthur Koestler described Lord Balfour's declaration of 1917, which promised a National Home to the Jews of Palestine, as one of the most improbable political documents of all times, because one nation solemnly promised to a second nation the country of a third. Other British politicians, rallying for Arab support in the fight against the Ottoman Empire, suggested prospects for an independent Arab Kingdom, which was to include Palestine.

The creation in April 1920 of the British Mandate for Palestine on behalf of the League of Nations and the replacement of the Military by a Civil Administration did not arrest the growing tide of conflict. During the first year of the Mandate riots broke out, Jews and Arabs were killed in a pattern that would repeat itself ad nauseam. The end of World War II in Europe only intensified the hostilities and increased the British costs of policing the territory. The main reason for this deterioration was the determined effort of thousands of survivors of the Holocaust to reach the land of the Jewish National Home and the growing impatience of Jewish organizations intent on establishing a Jewish state. The British maintained strict immigration quotas and turned overcrowded rickety ships bringing refugees away from the shores of Palestine. Upon arrival to the Promised Land people saved from Hitler's gas chambers were sent to detention camps in Cyprus and Mauritius. It was a bitter irony that the very power that had announced its intention to establish a Jewish Home added now to the monstrosity of Holocaust another cruelty. Terrorism by Jewish extremists intensified in response, culminating in July 1946 in the bombing of the British administration's headquarters that was in the King David Hotel. Ninety-two people—Britons, Arabs, and Jews—died. The extremists, who included two future Israeli Prime Ministers—Menahem Begin and Yitzhak Shamir, pursued a "blood and fire" policy to get the British out.

Unable and, perhaps, unwilling to check the increasing disintegration of its mandate, the Government of His Majesty, in the throes of a serious post-war economic crisis, criticized from all quarters for the creation of the problem and its handling, on April 2, 1947, requested the Secretary General of the United Nations to place the question of the future government for Palestine on the agenda of the General Assembly. Sir Alexander Cadogan summarized the British position simply. "We have tried for years to solve the problem of Palestine," he said. "Having failed so far, we now bring the question to the United Nations, in the hope that it can succeed where we have not."[2] The British washed their hands off Palestine. No one had any idea how the UN could proceed to a success, but it approached its task eagerly and vigorously.[3]

In the same month yet, diplomats gathered at the special session of the United Nations Assembly at a converted skating ring in Flushing Meadows, not far from New York, and appointed a Special Committee on Palestine (UNSCOP). As a result of its work, the Committee failed to reach unanimous conclusions and two conflicting proposals emerged. The majority (seven members) recommended partition of Palestine into an Arab and a Jewish state bound together in an economic union. Jerusalem would be initially governed separately as a UN Trusteeship and its future decided later. Three members of the Committee recommended a single federal state and one abstained from voting. The principle of partition clearly prevailed in the face of fierce opposition by most Arab countries. The plan did not differ much from two earlier British proposals prepared during the Mandate.[4]

On November 29, 1947, at a stormy Session of the General Assembly of the United Nations the partition plan was adopted in resolution 181 by a vote of 33 to 13 with 10 abstaining, Britain among them. The majority included the United States, the Soviet Union, and the countries of Western and Eastern Europe. The walk-out of the representatives of Egypt, Iraq, Saudi Arabia, and Yemen immediately followed the vote. In Jerusalem, the news from the UN was greeted with public jubilation by the Jews and hostile silence or isolated attacks on Jews by the Arabs.[5]

The decision on the partition plan inflamed a smoldering conflict between Palestinians Jews and Arabs. More and more people died in armed attacks and counter-attacks. The figures published by the British on January 9, 1948, showed 1,069 Arabs, 769 Jews, and 123 Britons killed in the 6 weeks following that decision, with some 50 people killed every day in Jerusalem alone. Civil unrest had become a full-scale civil war.

With signs of an imminent British withdrawal the fighting intensified. Volunteers from neighboring countries infiltrated to fight on the Arab side, but politically and strategically the Arabs were disunited. On April 5, 1948, when the Palestinian charismatic commander Abdul Kader al-Husseini visited Damascus with a plea for arms and ammunition he was flatly refused.[6] After he was killed later in the battle for the Jerusalem–Tel-Aviv highway, many of his followers left the battlefields. The Jews took Haifa and Jaffa. Arab villages, conquered by Jews, were leveled to the ground and their inhabitants expelled. Others left the land on their own. The first Palestinian exodus began. Whether it was a result of what would be now called ethnic cleansing is a subject of controversy between scholars and writers.[7]

The General Assembly resolution on partition provided also for the establishment of a new Palestine Commission, which was supposed to take over administration from the Mandatory Power and to establish in the Jewish and Arab independent states Provincial Councils of Government that would gradually receive full responsibility for the territory. Its mandate also included the super-vision of the erection of the administrative organs of central and local govern-ments, the creation of an armed militia and the creation of an economic union between the two states—a tall order for a territory consumed by hatred and fighting.[8]

Lie called the members of the new Palestine Commission "five lonely pil-grims." The representatives of Bolivia, Czechoslovakia, Denmark, Panama, and the Philippines met at Lake Success on January 9, 1948. The commission's means were not proportionate to its task. Its predicament became visible when the repre-sentatives of Great Britain, the Arab Higher Committee, and the Jewish Agency were invited to join its deliberations. The British appointed Sir Alexander Cado-gan and the Jews Moshe Shertok, but the Arab Higher Committee cabled Trygve Lie on January 19, 1948, that "it determined to persist in rejecting partition and in refusing recognition of the UNO resolution in this respect, therefore it was unable to accept invitation." Later, the Higher Committee said that ". . . it would never submit or yield to any Power going to Palestine to enforce partition. The only way to establish partition was to wipe them out—man, woman and child" (the Committee meant the Arab population of Palestine).[9]

Nor were the British cooperative; they did not agree for the Commission to proceed to Palestine earlier than 2 weeks before the date of the termination of the Mandate and to progressively turn over authority to the Commission but only abruptly and completely on May 15. Only the Jews cooperated. The Jewish Agency had already indicated that it would accept partition even while claiming that the plan demanded territorial sacrifices from them.[10]

It became obvious that there were no chances for the Commission to discharge its mandate without enforcement. In a special report of February 16 to the SC on the problem of security in Palestine, the Commission noted that Arab interests both inside and outside Palestine were engaged in a deliberate effort to alter by violence the settlement recommended by the UN Assembly. Armed forces from surrounding Arab states had already begun infiltration of Palestine. In the view of the Commission, a basic issue of international order was involved. A dangerous and tragic precedent would have been established if force, or the threat of the use of force, was to prove an effective deterrent to the will of the United Nations. Unless an adequate non-Palestinian force was provided for keeping order after May 15, the period immediately following the termination of the Mandate would be a period of uncontrolled, widespread strife and bloodshed in Palestine, including the city of Jerusalem. Such a result would have been a catastrophic conclusion to an era of international concern for the territory.[11] The representatives of five small countries stated plainly what was at stake.

The UN Secretary General dealt with the crisis with an extreme restraint and reluctance. He produced a statement for the SC referring to a sufficient degree of agreement reached earlier for the establishment of a United Nations emergency international force that would be more than adequate to cope with any Palestinian challenge. Lie stressed that the UN could not permit violence to be used against its decisions and organs and that if the moral force of the organization was not enough, physical force would have to supplement it. But that statement was never presented, because he considered submitting it hazardous and wanted to sense better the trend of the Council's discussion and action. Not without a hint of satisfaction, he later recalled that the caution proved to be well justified. After an impressive presentation by the SC's Chairman, Karel Lisicky of Czechoslovakia, of the dramatic Palestine Commission report on February 24, 1948, the British representative Arthur Creech Jones said that His Majesty's Government could not promise the kind of cooperation now requested. In view of the earlier British pronouncements it was not surprising. A surprise came from the U.S. representative, Warren Austin. He now claimed that the SC could take action to maintain international peace, but lacked the power to enforce partition or any other type of political settlement.[12] From now on it became clear the Americans had washed their hands off Palestine, too. Without them and without the British there was no hope anyone would act.

But on March 19, the American representative—in reverting to an earlier pro- posal by Australia—performed a complete reversal of the original U.S. position. The United States now believed that a temporary United Nations Trusteeship for Palestine should be established and that the partition should be suspended. Instead of embracing the American proposal as a way out of the impasse, Lie took the American reversal as a personal rebuff and did nothing to support it.[13]

On April 10, the Palestine Commission reported that the armed hostility of both Palestinian and non-Palestinian Arab elements, lack of cooperation by the Mandatory Power, the disintegrating security situation in Palestine, and the fact that SC did not furnish the Commission with the necessary armed assistance, made it impossible for the Commission to implement the Assembly's resolution on the partition of the territory.

The SC repeated its call for a truce and by the resolution of April 23 established a Truce Commission, composed of the consular representatives in Jerusalem of Belgium, France, and the United States. A Spanish diplomat Pablo de Azcazarte was appointed its Secretary.

The second special session of the General Assembly on Palestine opened on April 16, and debated for a month. It refrained from taking any action and rejected the Trusteeship proposal, even after the Americans announced that they would be prepared to assign troops to enforce it. It now was the United Nations that washed its hands of Palestine. On May 14, 1948, by resolution 186, the Assembly relieved the Palestine Commission of its responsibilities and created the office of the UN Mediator for Palestine. The few diplomats who believed that the UN decisions were serious enough to be enforced disappeared from the picture. The Mediator was empowered to use his good offices with the local and community authorities in Palestine to arrange for the operation of common services necessary to the safety and well-being of the population of Palestine; assure the protection of holy places, religious buildings and sites in Palestine; and promote a peaceful adjustment of the future situation of Palestine.

The UN's new course was a very different one from that envisaged by Brian Urquhart, then a promising young UN diplomat and an aide to Lie:

> In 1947 we were naively optimistic—recalled he—as to what could be done about this most complex and tragic of historical dilemmas, where two ancient people were in an equal, but deadly competition for a small, but infinitely significant piece of territory, a struggle made crucial by Hitler's annihilation of the Jews of Europe on the one hand and the emergence of Arab nationalism on the other. British must be enabled to relinquish the Mandate for Palestine with dignity. The Jewish refugees from World War II must be allowed to settle. The Palestinians' interests and rights must be protected. . . . The international community, through the United Nations, must restore peace and execute the plan. In our innocence, none of these things seemed to us impossible.[14]

On his arrival on May 14, 1948, to Jerusalem from Amman, Pablo de Azcazarte, the Secretary of the newly created Truce Commission, witnessed these expectations unraveling: "The High Commissioner and the Chief Secretary had left Jerusalem that morning . . . in this almost clandestine manner twenty hours before the official expiry of the mandate . . . I had always counted on the British trying to hold off as long as possible (especially in Jerusalem) the chaos, which must inevitably follow their departure. . . . The time had come for the plunge into unknown."[15]

In fact it was not so unknown. In the void created by the British withdrawal and the UN absence, the war could only intensify and there were parties eager to quickly filling this void. At 4.40 a.m. on May 14, 1948, David Ben Gurion, the Chairman of the Jewish Agency, read out a Declaration of Independence and announced the establishment of a Jewish State. In another reversal of its policy, the United States immediately recognized the Provisional Government as the de facto authority of the State of Israel. It was the personal decision of the U.S. President Harry Truman, taken against the advice of his main international policy advisers who saw in support of the Jewish case a danger to American interests in Arab countries.[16] The first recognition de jure came later from the Soviet Union.

On the same day in Egypt a very different announcement was drafted. When the SC met on May 15, it had on its table a blunt cable from the Egyptian Minister of Foreign Affairs, reading that "Egyptian armed forces have started to enter Palestine to establish security and order . . ."[17] The invader presented himself in writing. But the only statement made by the SG about his role in Palestine in May 1948 was that "I have dispatched an advance party of the Commission to Jerusalem. . . . The conditions in that city gave me serious concern for their personal safety, and I took all possible measures to ensure that they were safely evacuated."[18]

Reduced to the role of passive observer of the violent disintegration of a country, which he had called not long ago yet "the sacred trust," the last British High

Commissioner, General Cunningham, closed a chapter of history in embarking by ship to Britain on May 14, 1948. Surrendering the Mandate amid chaos and violence, the British repeated the gesture of Pilate in the same city 2,000 years ago. They knew well what they were doing. But by taking over responsibility for the Mandate, the United Nations apparently did not.

At the SC meeting in the afternoon of that day, as Arab troops crossed the frontiers, the representative of the United States did not say a word. For Lie there seemed to be a conspiracy of silence in the Council (with the exception of its Soviet member), reminiscent of the most disheartening head-in-the-sand moments of the Chamberlain appeasement era.[19] It took the Council 2 weeks to adopt a resolution calling for a truce and threatening to apply sanctions to a party refusing to comply. Both Arabs and Jews accepted the demand.

Count Folke von Bernadotte, a member of the Swedish Royal Family, appointed Mediator for Palestine by the Security Council, negotiated terms of the truce and its supervision. But the truce, which took effect on June 11, had been broken by July 9 already. Renewed fighting lasted for another 8 months, interrupted by several short-lived and never strictly held cease-fires.

On the battlefield, to the surprise of many, the Jews—better organized and fighting according to strategically sound plans—stood up well to the Arab onslaught. The only real setback for Jewish forces was the surrender, after heavy fighting, of the Jewish Quarter of the Old Town of Jerusalem to the Arab Legion. The main losers of the war were Arab Palestinians, who left the country by the tens of thousands, either expelled by the Jews or desperate to escape the war. Jews had nowhere to go.

Bernadotte established his headquarters at the Greek island of Rhodes and shuttled from there in a white plane, with big "UN" letters on its wings, between the capitals of the belligerents. Military observers assisted the Mediator, all of them officers delegated on the UN request by members of the Truce Commission— Belgium, France, and the United States. They were unarmed and wore their national uniforms with white-blue armbands to mark them as UN personnel.

On September 17, Bernadotte was assassinated when on his way by car to visit the Israeli military governor of Jerusalem. A French colonel, Andre-Pierre Serot, was also killed. The murder was committed by the Jewish terrorists, members of the Stern Gang. In spite of numerous arrests of suspected terrorists by Israeli authorities, the killers have never been apprehended.[20] Ralph Bunche, then the Secretary's General Personal Representative, took over Bernadotte's work.

During his short-lived mission, the first UN Mediator had not been impressed either by the policies or by the practices of the organization he served. Bernadotte considered the partition plan for Palestine an unfortunate decision and held the view that "The United Nations showed itself from the worst side. It was depressing to have to recognize the fact that even the most trivial decisions with regard to measures designed to lend force to its words were depending on the political calculations of the Great Powers."[21]

As by 1949 the Israelis had reached most of their military objectives and the Arabs had lost their hopes for a military victory, Bunche could negotiate an armistice. By the end of July 1949, bilateral Armistice Agreements between Israel and Egypt, Israel and Lebanon, and Israel and Syria had been concluded, including establishment of demarcation lines between the belligerents. The partition of Palestine was now a fact accomplished by military force; it had nothing to do with the plan for a Federal State of Palestine adopted by the United Nations. The territory of the former British Mandate was divided between Israel, Egypt, and Jordan. Israel annexed 2,555 square miles, about 50 percent more than envisaged by the partition plan; Jordan annexed 2,200 square miles; and Egypt the Gaza Strip, about 135 square miles. Jerusalem was divided between Israel and Jordan. The Palestinian Arabs were not a party to any settlements and hundreds of thousands of them left the country, leaving everything behind and joining those refugees who left during the war already.[22] Israel paid for its right of existence with the lives of 6,000 of her citizens (4,000 soldiers and 2,000 civilians) and the enmity of the Arab world. The Arab losses have been probably much higher.[23]

The British Commander of the Arab Legion, Glubb Pasha, commented afterward:

> This chain of tragic events shed light on the enormous fault of the United Nations, who voted for a partition plan without providing deployment of an international force for its implementation. Should a neutral army have been introduced to Palestine in the spring of 1948, the Israelis would not undertake to occupy all of the country, the Arab States would not intervened, the Palestinian question would not concern the whole of the Middle East.... Finally, Jerusalem would remain under international control.[24]

The first Secretary General of the United Nations was of a different opinion. Lie maintained that "Ultimately, the Security Council did solid work to bring peace to Palestine."[25] History proved Lie wrong because the Agreements contributed to no more then few years of absence of war and 60 years after his judgment there is no peace in Palestine. Glubb Pasha's was perhaps overoptimistic, but, most likely, deployment of a neutral international army would make a great difference. Extremists from both camps were bound to oppose it, but an all-out involvement of Arab states against the UN would be most unlikely. A measure at least of an internationalization of Jerusalem was not an unrealistic prospect because of the Jewish initial, if reluctant, support for the idea. In 1950, there were even segments of Jewish population of the ancient city who preferred an international rule in Jerusalem to that of an Israeli government.[26]

UN OBSERVERS CORPS: A PRESENCE AT ANY PRICE

On August 11, 1949, the Security Council terminated the office of Mediator for Palestine and the Truce Commission became known as the United Nations

Truce Supervision Organization (UNTSO). No single resolution established the UNTSO's mandate and its tasks were defined case by case. It was responsible for demarcating armistice lines, mediating the differences between the parties, establishing demilitarized zones, deterring an arms build-up, facilitating the exchange of prisoners, and investigating complaints of violations of the Agreements. The last task fell to the responsibility of the Mixed Armistice Commissions (MAC) working under Chairmen appointed by the United Nations. Three demilitarized zones were established; in the El Auja area on the Israeli side of the demarcation line with Egypt, near Lake Tiberias between Israel and Syria, and on Mount Scopus in Jerusalem.[27]

From the outset severe understaffing diminished the potential impact of the new organization. UNTSO took over the military personnel employed by the Mediator for Palestine, but their number was slashed by 95 percent, from 572 to 21. Seven Belgians, 7 Frenchmen, and 7 Americans were expected to supervise armistice agreements involving 5 countries and hundreds of miles of cease-fire lines and demilitarized zones.

The example of the Jordanian–Israeli MAC demonstrates the scale of the understaffing. Its five observers based in Jerusalem had to cover a 350-mile stretch of the demarcation lines, as well as to attend two or three weekly meetings between the local Jordanian and Israeli commanders, investigate the complaints concerning violations of the Armistice (roughly one on each day), and respond to urgent occasional calls for arrangement of a cease-fire.[28]

The observers lacked support from the parties involved and had to deal with growing tensions between the belligerents. There were constant obstructions of the freedom of movement of the UN observers and continuing petty harassment. The UN restricted itself to lodging protests, which were usually ignored. No party of the conflict had ever properly marked the demarcation lines on the ground, leaving space for conflicting interpretations. Moreover, the observers lacked the ability to check the cross-border infiltrations and raids from both sides.[29]

By early 1955 commando raids on Israeli civilians by the Palestinian *fedayeen* supported by Egypt had become frequent and provoked Israeli retaliatory attacks. Innocent victims on both sides became a sad reality. In September 1956, Israeli forces occupied the demilitarized zone of El Auja, which was the site of MAC and prohibited the Egyptians from access to the area. For all practical purposes the Commission was dead. But it moved to Egyptian-controlled Gaza and, despite the absence of any Israeli cooperation, continued to examine complaints submitted by Egypt.[30] The Israelis could have been encouraged in the takeover by the earlier experience from Mount Scopus in Jerusalem. Contrary to a signed agreement, they had never allowed the UN to take over the control of the zone and even prevented the UNTSO's Chief of Staff from entering it.[31]

The Israel–Syria MAC was virtually paralyzed by complaints from both sides. By October 1966 it had registered 35,488 Israeli and 30,600 Syrian complaints. It ceased to meet regularly in 1951 and its last emergency session was held in

1960. The other two Commissions, those for Israel–Jordan and Israeli–Lebanon performed only a little better but survived until the outbreak of the 1967 Six Days' War.

Dag Hammarskjold, who succeeded Lie, did not accept the Israeli unilateral denunciation of the Armistice Agreement with Egypt after the outbreak of the Suez Canal War in 1956 and requested UNTSO to maintain its structures. Neither did he recognize the later renunciation by Israel of the other agreements. Since these did not provide for unilateral termination, Hammarskjold's position was legally correct. However, the continued deployment of UN military personnel in the field despite the fact that it was not recognized by one of the parties to the conflict meant the introduction of a make-believe element into the presence of the UN in areas of armed conflagration. Flying the flag for its own sake became a priority, recognized by Hammarskjold's successors to the detriment of the credibility of the UN ever since.

Notwithstanding full-fledged Arab–Israeli wars in 1956, 1967, and 1973, the organization established for supervision of a truce continued to function and even flourished by acquiring more personnel and deploying at new places. In the war of attrition between Egypt and Israel along the Suez Canal in 1969–1970, UNTSO observers were sitting duck not only because they were under crossfire, but because both sides deliberately targeted them.[32] At present the UNTSO observers are on loan to UNIFIL in Lebanon and to UN Disengagement Observer Force on Golan Heights (UNDOF), which allows to keep up the UNTSO facades in Jerusalem, Beirut, and Damascus.

UNTSO unequivocally failed in fulfilling its function of maintaining the cease-fire lines and preventing incursions across the international frontiers; "the parties to the conflict were not prepared to cooperate with the UN observers, the demarcation lines were not clearly marked, and the observers were not equipped, politically or militarily, to deal with the type of confrontations that developed in the demilitarized zones."[33] The only tangible effect of UNTSO's deployment was monitoring and reporting from the conflict areas done at the sacrifice of lives of 44 personnel as of February 28, 2006. UNTSO's experience exposed the SC and the Secretariat's powerlessness in face of deliberate obstruction of the missions and direct attacks on UN personnel. The offending parties did not suffer any consequences from their actions incompatible with their obligations as UN members and with the specific agreements concerning the mission. UNTSO also showed that it was easier to launch a mission than to wind it up.

EGYPT: TWO UNITED NATIONS EMERGENCY FORCES AND THREE WARS

In the summer of 1956, as Palestinian raids on Israeli-held territories and Israeli retaliatory attacks became increasingly frequent, the Arab–Israeli conflict took on new dimensions. President Nasser, the charismatic dictator of Egypt, nationalized the Suez Canal and imposed restrictions in the Gulf of Aqaba for

Israeli shipping. The conflict threatened to grow into another full scale Arab–Israeli war with a risk of an open East–West confrontation.

While the main shareholders of the Canal—Great Britain and France—strongly supported Israel, Nasser was determined to settle accounts with her. On October 25, 1956, he concluded agreements with Syria and Jordan on forming united military command. Three days later, on October 29, Israeli forces launched three-pronged attacks toward El Arish, Ismaila, and the Mitla Pass. On October 31, working with Israel on a prearranged plan, British and French forces attacked Egyptian targets from the air and parachuted troops in the area of Port Said and at the northern end of the Canal.[34] What Hugh Gaitskell, the leader of the opposition in the British House of Commons, called an act of disastrous folly, produced an unprecedented shock and disbelief at the UN, from which even the British and French delegates to the UN were not free. It was in this atmosphere that the first Emergency Special Session of the General Assembly opened at 5 p.m. on November 1.

Before the Emergency Session has begun, the Canadian delegate, Lester Pearson, approached Dag Hammarskjold to suggest that a deployment of a United Nations Force might become necessary. The SG was initially skeptical, but the idea was supported by the British and French governments, under fire also from public opinion in their own countries. Ultimately, on November 4, the Assembly requested Hammarskjold to submit within 48 hours a plan for the setting up of an emergency international force to secure and supervise the cessation of hostilities. He began to work on the report before lunch the next day and by 2.30 morning finished what Urquhart called ". . . a conceptual masterpiece in a completely new field, the blueprint for a nonviolent international military operation."[35]

The first UN deployed international force was to enter Egyptian territory with consent of the Egyptian Government in order to help maintain order during and after the withdrawal of non-Egyptian forces. In Hammarskjold's concept "The force would be more than an observer corps, but in no way a military force temporarily controlling the territory in which it was stationed. . . . Its functions . . . could cover an area extending roughly from the Suez Canal to the Armistice Demarcation Lines."[36] Hammarskjold's recommendations were endorsed by the General Assembly and the UNTSO Chief of Staff, General E.L.M. Burns from Canada, was appointed the Chief of Command of the first United Nations Emergency Force.

The response to the UN request for national contingents to serve with UNEF was surprisingly good. Twenty-four countries offered to send troops; Hammarskjold selected ten from countries impartial to the conflict. At the outset, the new Force was 6,000 men strong but gradually reduced and stood at 3,378 men at its conclusion. It included contingents from Brazil, Canada, Colombia, Denmark, Finland, India, Indonesia, Norway, Sweden, and Yugoslavia. One of the practical problems to be resolved was the identification of the troops. Fortunately, there were large quantities of American helmets readily available in Europe and spraying them blue was no problem. Thus were the Blue Helmets born.[37]

The unique international situation at the time of the Suez crisis made nearly everyone welcome the Blue Helmets. The Soviet Union faced serious challenges to its domination in Eastern Europe and was not eager to get actively involved in the Middle East. The United States wanted to stay out, and the British and the French governments anxiously looked for a way out of their ill-advised adventure without loosing face. Finally, Egypt knew that the UN was its only hope for averting a disastrous military defeat.

UNEF was a departure from the United Nations policy of not employing any armed personnel. Understandably, the new policy, as expressed in the guidelines for UNEF, was not free from ambiguities. The rules of engagement (ROE) of the first UN armed contingents ordered the UNEF's soldiers not to use force except in self-defense. They were not to initiate the use of force; they could only respond to an armed attack on them, even if this meant refusing an order from the attacking party not to resist.[38,39] The intention of this diplomatic, rather than military, wording was quite clear; arms were not to be used for carrying out the UNEF's mandate.

The spirit of the guidelines was in accord with Hammarskjold's pacifist sentiments and intentions. But it was not so to the man chosen to command the Force, the Canadian General E.L.M. Burns, who requested a strong force, containing heavy armor and fighter aircraft capable of carrying out operations of war. That request was turned down, as were his later requests for authorization to fire on infiltrators in the Gaza Strip. His argument that the Israelis had been accustomed to pushing UN military observers around and that an emergency force which could not use its weapons would be little more than a corps of observers was in vain.[40]

Israel never agreed to a UNEF presence at her side of the frontlines and therefore it was deployed on the Egyptian side along the Armistice Demarcation Line in Gaza and the international frontier in the Sinai Peninsula. While it was unable to eliminate infiltrations, its presence helped to avoid major clashes.

The situation was different in the Israeli–Syrian and Israeli–Jordanian sectors. Since the establishment in 1964 of the Palestinian Liberation Organization (PLO) and its main group Al-Fatah, Palestinian raids and acts of sabotage against Israel became more frequent and so were the Israeli retaliatory actions.[41] In early 1967, tensions between Israel and Syria were mounting and Nasser, with his army generously reequipped by the Soviets, was persuaded that a Syrian–Israeli war was imminent. For the second time in a decade, he decided that the hour of revenge by the Arab world against its Israeli enemy was near, so UNEF's presence in the Egyptian controlled Sinai became awkward.

It was ten o'clock at night, Cairo time, in Gaza on May 16, 1967, when the Egyptian Brigadier Mokhtar handed General Rikhye, UNEF Commander, a communication signed by the Chief of Staff of the United Arab Republic (UAR), General Fawzi. It read:

> I gave my instructions to all UAR Armed Forces to be ready for actions against Israel, the moment it may carry out any aggressive action against any Arab country. Due to

these instructions, our troops are already concentrated in Sinai on our eastern borders. For the sake of complete secure [*sic*] of all UN troops which install observation posts along our borders, I request that you issue your orders to withdraw all these troops immediately . . .[42]

Brigadier Mokhtar verbally requested the immediate withdrawal of the UN units from El-Sabha and Sharm el Sheikh. Rikhye replied that he did not have the authority to withdraw on any order other than that of the UN SG. He also said that as long as UAR troops did not attempt to use force against UN personnel, there would be no clashes. But Rikhye's own instructions to UNEF's Yugoslav commander in Sinai issued on the same day were tantamount to authorizing surrender. Colonel Prazic was told that "they must . . . not be involved in any incident with the U.A.R. forces and certainly should not, under any circumstances, resort to use of force in the event they were evicted from their post."[43]

His attitude was confirmed in a cable he received next day from U Thant who told him to do what he reasonably could to maintain the position of UNEF without, however, going so far as to risk an armed clash. In his memoirs Rikhye maintained that he was determined not to withdraw from a single UNEF position, unless he was forced out of it. But this is precisely what happened. Before he received U Thant's order for withdrawal on May 18, Egyptian troops forced UNEF's soldiers to leave El Sabha, the camps El Kuntilla and El-Amr, Sharm el-Sheikh, and an observation post at Ras el-Nasrani.[44]

Neither the UN documents nor Rikhye in his memoirs mention any use of force by the Egyptian side in the process of evicting UN soldiers from their positions and it is obvious that they would, if there was any. It follows that the UN soldiers obeyed Egyptian orders before getting an instruction for withdrawal from New York.

In Egypt the circumstances of the decision on UNEF's withdrawal were not clear. The first message to General Rikhye demanded a withdrawal from the Armistice line in Sinai but did not address the UN presence in Gaza and Egypt as such. The ambiguity continued thereafter. Neither Nasser's adviser on foreign affaires, Dr. Mohamud Fawzi, nor members of the government were informed about that decision which Fawzi later called a gross miscalculation based on gross misinformation. It was most likely taken personally by two leaders: President Nasser and Field Marshall Amer. The latter, initially not aware of all intricacies involved, issued instructions to intercept Brigadier Mokhtar on his mission and to request him to await further communication. But it was too late and the Brigadier delivered the order to General Rikhye before any counter-order could have been issued. The attempt to alter the course of events failed.[45]

Urquhart rightly maintains that Egypt's request for UNEF's withdrawal was in accordance with the relevant agreement. He also called the very idea of a resistance to the Egyptian Army, some 80,000 strong, by the tiny, symbolic UN Force hypocritical and escapist nonsense, still remarkably prevalent in Western folklore.[46] But it is improbable that the Egyptians would open fire on UNEF when confronted with a resolute opposition. Even a token opposition before the official request for the withdrawal of UNEF was submitted to U Thant on May 18 could have probably opened some space for negotiations and changed the course of events.

A few days later Nasser announced the closure of the Strait to Israeli shipping. Under the existing circumstances, the point of no return from war was reached. U Thant's attempt to relocate UNEF into Israeli-controlled territory was promptly and flatly rejected even while Tel-Aviv tried to persuade the United Nations not to follow Nasser's demands for withdrawal.

In the early hours of June 5, Israeli planes struck and destroyed the bulk of the Egyptian Air Force on the ground. The third Arab–Israeli war had begun and was again fought in Gaza, Sinai, and the Golan Heights, on the West Bank of the Jordan, and in Jerusalem. Again underestimated by the Arabs, Israel succeeded on all fronts and conquered new territories. The war was over in 6 days. On June 28, the Israelis announced that Jerusalem was reunited. The old conflict assumed new dimensions. The Israeli action was the first exposure of a logic, which— in contradiction to the UN Charter—attributes the right of States to use force preemptively.

In the aftermath of the Six Days' War, U Thant and the United Nations were widely and fervently criticized for withdrawing UNEF and thus allowing the outbreak of the war.[47] However, it became clear that the mere presence of the UN troops, without the backing of the SC for sufficiently punitive actions against the offending parties would deter neither the Arabs nor the Israelis from pursuing their goals by military means. It was tragically manifested during the first days of the war in the Gaza Strip when, caught in the cross fire, 15 UNEF soldiers were killed.[48]

No new UN mission was proposed after the withdrawal of UNEF I. Calm lasted in the Suez Canal sector until early 1969, when the fighting broke out again and continued until August 1970. It was full-fledged warfare, except that the positions of the adversaries did not move. On several occasions, the Secretary General appealed for an end to this war of attrition, but without any effect. UNTSO observers, targeted by both sides, were duly monitoring and reporting on the developments. It took United States political involvement to negotiate a cease-fire. The fighting stopped on August 7, 1970. For about 3 years.

Kurt Waldheim, appointed Secretary General of the United Nations in 1972, recalled that looking back, it seemed strange that no one had heeded the Egyptian and Syrian-declared intentions to regain the territories occupied by Israel in 1967. Golda Meir, the then Prime Minister of Israel, 1 month before the outbreak of the war told Waldheim that if only the United Nations would refrain from interfering in the affairs of the Middle East, in 2 or 3 years the Arabs would be prepared to recognize the State of Israel and to concede it the borders which it believed essential to its security.[49]

In 1967 the Israelis took the Egyptians by surprise, but it was now their turn to be surprised. Nasser's successor, Anwar Sadat, ordered his army to cross the

Suez Canal on October 6, 1973, celebrated as Yom Kippur by the Israelis, leaving behind UNTSO observers, two of them killed in the crossfire. The fighting on the Egyptian front soon spread to Golan Heights in Syria.

The Americans airlifted emergency supplies of arms to the Israelis, who quickly recovered from the first shock and drove back through the Canal, cutting off the Third Egyptian Army in Sinai and threatening the Port of Suez. Now, the Egyptian Ambassador to the UN, Ismail Meguid, requested that UN observers step in and stop the Israeli advance. As Sadat called for Soviet and American intervention, neither wanted to get drawn into it directly. Few days later, on October 20, King Faisal from Saudi Arabia announced oil embargo on the United States and the Netherlands. British documents declassified 30 years later revealed that the Americans seriously contemplated invading Saudi Arabia and Kuwait in response to the embargo. The conflict dimensions were changing.[50]

After 2 weeks of confusion, the famous rounds of Henry Kissinger's shuttle diplomacy brought about a consensus in the SC. On October 22, it adopted resolution 338 calling for an immediate cease-fire and asking the SG to dispatch observers. It also called for an immediate beginning of the implementation of resolution 242, which requested the Israeli withdrawal from the territories occupied in 1967. But the cease-fire, accepted by both sides, did not work.

Following much diplomatic wrangling, the SC agreed on October 25 to deploy UNEF II. Waldheim nominated UNTSO's Chief, the Finnish General Ensi Siilasvuo, to be UNEF's Interim Commander. Austrians, Finns, and Swedes from the United Nations Peacekeeping Force in Cyprus (UNIFICYP) were dispatched within 24 hours. Ultimately, contingents from thirteen countries participated in UNEF II—Sweden, Austria, Finland, Australia, Ghana, Nepal, Ireland, Peru, Panama, Indonesia, Senegal, Canada, and Poland. Its maximum strength was 6,973 men; at the time of its withdrawal it was 4,031; 120 observers from UNTSO assisted the Force.

The essentials of the peacekeeping guidelines for UNEF II, written 17 years after those of UNEF I, remained unchanged. But direct responsibility for the Force was shifted from the SC and General Assembly to the UN SG, the principle of equitable geographical representation in the composition of the Force introduced, and the term of self-defense newly formulated. From now on it would include resistance to attempts by forceful means to prevent it from discharging its duties under the Security Council's mandate. This last qualification is crucial and largely overlooked, because it gave the UN Forces a blanket authorization to use force in defense of the Security Council's mandates. Approved by the Council on October 27, 1973, these guidelines have been considered since then as a standard for new UN operations.

The mandate of UNEF II was supervision of implementation of an immediate and complete cease-fire in positions occupied by the respective forces on October 22, prevention of the recurrence of the fighting, and cooperation with the ICRC in its humanitarian activities, cooperation with UNTSO, and supervision of the implementation of the disengagement agreements.

UNEF II was deployed in the buffer zone between the two armies. Its check-points, observation posts, and patrols remained until the withdrawal following an American-sponsored peace treaty between Egypt and Israel in July 1979. On November 19, 1977, President Sadat of Egypt brought to Jerusalem a totally un-expected message: peace between Arabs and Israel was possible and necessary. During his 3-day visit he addressed the Knesset where he received a standing ovation. He later visited Yad Vashem, the museum of Holocaust, where he signed the guest book with the inscription: May God guide our steps toward peace.... [51]

All parties to the Yom Kippur war suffered heavy losses. It was with a shock that Israelis learned that 2,676 members of the Israeli Defense Force (IDF) were killed. They had not suffered such losses since the war of independence in 1948. They also lost 420 tanks and 106 aircraft. The Arab losses were even higher. The Egyptians lost 8,000 and the Syrians 3,500 men. The Arab side lost also 1,280 tanks and 454 aircraft, including 22 Iraqi planes.[52] These figures, explain in part why there has not been another all-out Israeli–Arab war. But an absence of war is not peace.

UNEF II did its job well and its deployment helped to avoid the Soviet–United States confrontation.[53] But the nonrecurrence of fighting was a result of diplomacy, of coincidence of the superpowers interests, and of Sadat's courage. Should any of the adversaries decide to attack the other, the Force would just be overrun, as UNEF I was before and other UN Forces have been since.

SYRIA: GUARDING A BUFFER ZONE—UNITED NATIONS DISENGAGEMENT OBSERVER FORCE

Syria's Golan Heights, occupied by Israel as a result of the 1967 Six Days' War, are of a paramount strategic importance to both countries. Syrian guns placed there can dominate the plains of northern Israel, but Israeli tanks deployed on the Golan Heights are only 50 miles from the Syrian capital of Damascus. The Syri-ans, in concert with the Egyptians, attacked the Israelis on October 6, 1973. As on the Egyptian–Israeli front, the surprise Syrian assault resulted in some territorial gains, but the Israeli counterattacks pushed the Syrians back and pursued them along the road toward of Damascus, retaking the town of Quneitra (occupied by them as a result of the Six Days' War in 1967) on the way and occupying a salient as far as the village of Saassa. The cease-fire ordered by the SC took effect on October 24, but it did not last long. The Syrians rejected negotiations and hostil-ities continued, culminating in a heavy battle for Mount Hermon in April 1974, retaken by the Israelis at the cost of twelve Syrian and fifty-one Israeli soldiers killed.[54]

Claiming that until now the deployment of UN peacekeepers had been little more than a substitute for a political solution of the Arab–Israeli conflict and a confirmation of Israel's territorial conquests, Syria's President, Hafez el-Assad, did not want UNEF II to extend its operation into his country.[55] Eventually, he accepted UNDOF established by SC resolution 350 on May 31, 1974. It deployed immediately with contingents borrowed from UNEF II, coming initially from six countries: Austria, Canada, Finland, Iran, Peru, and Poland. Its strength grew to 1,331 men in 1991. Established for 6 months the Force remains in the field, its mandate repeatedly renewed by the SC every year since then.

The Force's mandate is to ensure the observance of the cease-fire; to supervise the absence of military forces in the area of separation, and to oversee restriction of arms and personnel in the Syrian and Israeli areas of limitation, and to facilitate the implementation of Security Council resolution 338 which called for a political solution of the conflict.

Although UN sources report that both sides regularly restrict UNDOF's movements, on the whole it has encountered no serious difficulties. The Force Commander invariably protests the restrictions, which apparently settles the matter for the UN.[56] Both sides appear to be satisfied with UNDOF's presence and until a political settlement is achieved or until another war comes, it is likely to stay where it is, at their sufferance and UN cost. Thirty-two years of the UN presence in Golan Heights proved to be not long enough for politicians to find a resolution of the conflict.

LEBANON: MUDDLING THROUGH IN A COUNTRY TORN APART-UNITED NATIONS INTERIM FORCE[57]

Lebanon is a small country wedged between Syria and Israel, on the Mediterranean Sea. It is a conglomerate of four major communities divided by religion and clan loyalties. Maronites are Christians; its Druze, Sunni, and Shi'a are Muslims. The delicate political balance that maintained a precarious internal peace in this the multiconfessional society was challenged by the rise of Arab nationalism in the 1950s. In 1958 the Christian-dominated Lebanese government alleged that the United Arab Republic (Union of Egypt and Syria) was involved in gross interference in the domestic affairs of the country, infiltrating weapons and people in support of extreme opposition groups.

On Lebanon's request, the United Nations Observation Group in Lebanon (UNOGIL) was established in June 1958, but only after a civil war broke out in May and the president of the country, Camille Chamoun, approached in vain the United States regarding possible intervention. UNOG II's mandate was straightforward—"to ensure there is no illegal infiltration of personnel (or) supply of arms or other material across the Lebanese borders."[58] Twenty-one countries contributed military personnel to UNOGIL. At its peak in September, the Group consisted of 214 observers, with aircraft and helicopters at their disposal. Not more than a month after UNOGIL's deployment, U.S. marines stormed a shore in Beirut; the British joined later. The UN mission withdrew, accomplishing nothing. Merely some of UNTSO observers, a remainder of the long defunct Israeli–Lebanon Armistice Agreement, carried on.

Until the early seventies, Lebanon enjoyed calm along its borders with Israel. But as the PLO, forcibly expelled from Jordan in 1970, set up its headquarters in Southern Lebanon, the fragile balance of power among the Lebanese unraveled. A civil war broke out in April 1975 and ended, at least on paper, in October 1976 with the introduction of the Arab Deterrent Force into the country. The force, nominally under the command of the Lebanese president, was actually controlled by the Syrians. In March 1978, a PLO raid on the Haifa–Tel Aviv road took the lives of 39 Israeli civilians and left dozens wounded. In retaliation, Israeli forces entered Lebanon on March 14–15 and in a few days occupied the entire area south of the Litani River, save for the city of Tyre, a Palestinian stronghold.

As an alternative to restraining the Israelis, the United States launched the idea of introducing a peacekeeping mission. There were strong misgivings at the UN as there was no government authority in Southern Lebanon, the PLO was responsible to no one and the Israeli sponsored Christian militia under the command of Major Saad Haddad was capable of disrupting any peace process. To complicate matters further, the terrain of the area, hilly and ravenous, ideal for guerillas, was difficult for conventional forces.[59]

The fate of UNTSO observers illustrated conditions in the country. They had been subject to widespread harassment, obstruction of movements, and outright robbery by various armed groups and factions. Between October 1975 and February 1978, UNTSO lost 124 vehicles in stealing or hijacking. One of the UNTSO members lost five vehicles in 4 months.[60]

But all misgivings about launching a peacekeeping mission were pushed aside under pressure from the United States and the UK. On March 19, 1978, the SC called for strict respect of the territorial integrity of Lebanon, for a cease-fire, and for the withdrawal of the Israeli forces. It also established the UN Interim Force in Lebanon (UNIFIL) "for the purpose of confirming the withdrawal of the Israeli forces, restoring international peace and security and assisting the government of Lebanon in ensuring the return of its effective authority in the area, the force to be composed of personnel drawn from Member States."[61] Established for a period of 6 months it is still there in 2006.

In spite of the differing circumstances of the mission and a much broader mandate, the guidelines for the force were the same as those applied to UNEF II: consent, impartiality, and self-defense. UNIFIL began its deployment with contingents transferred from UNEF II and soon reached the target of 4,000 men, later reinforced to 7,000. General Emmanuel A. Erskine of Ghana became the force's commander. Apart from the Israelis, UNIFIL faced the main factions in Southern Lebanon, the PLO and Lebanese Christians who had their own military forces at disposal. Neither PLO and its military wing El Fatah nor the South Lebanese Army (SLA) under the command of Major Haddad controlled all armed militias present in the area. The Lebanese Army was merely a token presence, and the government in Beirut was haphazard. The IDF moved in and out of Southern Lebanon at will. None of the parties present on the ground could agree on the same definition of UNIFIL's area of operation, so it was never properly defined.

As a result, the Force was deployed as permitted by the circumstances of the day and the disposition of the parties concerned.[62]

By April 1978, the Israelis had withdrawn from about half of the occupied territory and UNIFIL took over the positions evacuated by the IDF. Checkpoints, observation posts, and patrols were set up to prevent infiltration by any armed elements. But neither PLO nor Haddad's forces were inclined to cooperate.[63] In the next stage of withdrawal the Israelis vacated the territory to Haddad's militia instead of to the UNIFIL. This led to counterattacks by the PLO and to attacks on UNIFIL by both sides. Attacks in May left 3 French soldiers dead and 14 wounded, including the commander of the French battalion. Harassment by the SLA was also common, and moreover it conducted raids into the UNIFIL area of operation, abducting people and blowing up houses belonging to suspected PLO members or sympathizers and establishing its own positions. PLO also was encroaching.[64] Negotiations to remove the infringing positions did not bring any results. UNIFIL was unwelcome to anyone in arms in Southern Lebanon.

There was apparently no obstructions, harassments, or attacks on the Force disturbing enough to provoke the SC to resolutely react in defense of its own decisions and the men it had sent out into harms way. After heavy shelling of UNIFIL headquarters in Naqoura by SLA, the Council satisfied itself with a resolution condemning the act. In another incident, when three Nigerian UNIFIL soldiers were killed, it took it 5 days to issue a condemnation, largely because the U.S. ambassador to the UN, Jean Kirkpatrick, opposed the resolution for 4 days long on account that it mentioned Israel in its text.[65]

UNIFIL was on its own, and could only muddle through, oscillating erratically between combat actions and pathetic humiliations from which even the Force's Commander was not saved. In May 1979 Erskine faced an angry crowd of Haddad's supporters, was manhandled, and lost his badges of rank and the Blue Beret in the process.[66] Whatever was left of the credibility of UNIFIL disappeared with the general's dignity.

Not all of the general's troops were passive. Norwegians and Fijians were among those more assertive and had fewer problems in their areas of operations.[67] But no amount of resolve of some of the national troops or even of all of them could have saved a drifting operation not equipped for its task. UNIFIL was unable to control infiltration into the area of its operation nor shelling, raiding, and other hostilities by all parties to the conflict. A steady deterioration culminated in an all-out assault by IDF ground and naval forces on Palestinian positions in July 1981. Another wave of heavy retaliatory Israeli air attacks on targets in Lebanon followed in 1982.[68]

When the new UNIFIL's Commander William Callaghan met General Rafael Eitan in the morning of June 6, the Israeli Chief of Staff told him that the IDF would launch a major military operation into Lebanon within the hour and they expected not to be obstructed. Callaghan protested, instructed all his contingents to block the advancing forces, to take defensive measures, and to keep their positions unless their safety was seriously imperiled.[69] As promised, the Operation Peace for

Galilee started at 11.00 hours. Two IDF mechanized divisions entered UNIFIL's area with full air and naval support and progressed along three axes into Lebanon. Only two cases of token resistance by Dutch and Nepalese soldiers were reported. Other troops apparently waved the Israelis through.[70]

By June 8, the UNIFIL became the first UN mission operating in a country occupied by a foreign army. The Israelis moved fast and with full force, causing a large number of casualties and massive destruction. A member of the Israeli forces invading from the sea remembered that

> The invasion has begun and it was surreal, like going on a pleasure-cruise.... Then we came up from the beach on the main road, and what we saw stopped us in our tracks.... There were a great many dead.... They lay among the wreckage of their vehicles, the young and the old, the crippled and the fit, men, women and children together, never knowing what hit them.... During the night our paratroopers had helicopters in to secure the beachhead. In the pitch dark, unable to see what was coming at them, they'd poured round after round into anything that moved.[71]

On June 11, 1 day after the Israelis had engaged the Syrians at the outskirts of Beirut, a cease-fire was announced but the hunt for the Palestinians continued. On June 18, the Israelis entered the center of Beirut and encircled a few thousands of PLO fighters still there. The Israeli Air Force struck relentlessly, up to 4 hours without intermission. Ultimately, as a result of a deal negotiated by the special emissary of President Reagan, Philip Habib, Arafat left for Greece and the PLO completed its pull out from Beirut on September 1.

UNIFIL had been completely sidelined. The Lebanese government invited the United States, France, and Italy to send forces to stabilize the situation. It believed that these major Western powers would bring about what they were not able to get from the United Nations—the release of their country from military occupation by Israel and Syria. The multinationals duly arrived, some, like the French, on loan from UNIFIL. But they left Beirut by September 10, having accomplished nothing.

Four days later a bomb placed at his headquarters killed the Lebanese president. The next day, the IDF returned to West Beirut. A day after, the Phalangists—the Christian militia—massacred inhabitants of the Palestinian refugee camps in Sabra and Shatila, including women and children. The Israelis looked away and the SC protested for the record. The Lebanese decided to ask for the return of the multinational force and it came back by the end of September.[72]

The massacre in Sabra and Shatila shocked the world and many Israelis as well. On September 25 in Tel Aviv, 400,000 people took part in the largest demonstration ever held in Israel. An official inquiry strongly criticized Defense Minister Ariel Sharon for having allowed the Phalangists to enter the refugee camps and called him to draw personal conclusions. Sharon resigned from the post of the Minster of Defense, but remained member of the cabinet as Minister without a portfolio.[73]

In the following months, attacks on the Israeli occupying forces increased in Southern Lebanon as civil war in Beirut intensified between Lebanese fractions. The multinational forces were seen as a party to the conflict, and on April 18, 1983, a bomb destroyed the American Embassy in Beirut, killing 63 people, including 17 Americans. In mid-September, U.S. battleships bombarded positions of antigovernment forces around Beirut, openly taking sides. On October 23, a truck bomb exploded in a suicidal crash into a U.S. Marine barracks, killing 241 Americans while a parallel attack took the lives of 58 French servicemen. Everyone now wanted to get out of Lebanon, except UNIFIL. The SC was regularly extending its mandate, unchanged.

UNIFIL's functioning on territory under the Israeli control brought about a radical shift in its relations to the main parties to the conflict. It recognized the right of the IDF as an occupying army and of its surrogate force SLA (when in conjunction with the Israelis) to carry on military operations. The right of the Lebanese to resist the occupation was also recognized. But on one hand UNIFIL restricted it in practice by exercising control and confiscation of arms from the local civilians and on the other, when locals did attack IDF/SLA, the Force did not intervene, except to protect its own personnel and noncombatants.[74] In effect UNIFIL had violated its own mandate and became a spent and useless force.

Analyzing the UNIFIL's future in 1991 Marianne Heiberg saw three options: withdrawal, reduction, or major reinforcement. Her arguments for withdrawal were most convincing. First—argued she—the operation is too costly. UNIFIL ties up enormous assets consuming some two-thirds of all funds for UN peacekeeping. Moreover, in many respects it has lost sense of mission, became over-bureaucratic, administratively wasteful, and inefficient to the extent that may have irreversibly undermined its military and political credibility. UNIFIL's role in providing security and assistance to the local Lebanese population was commendable, but in light of the human catastrophes that loom in the Horn of Africa and elsewhere, this role cannot be assigned a sufficiently high priority.[75] Four years later, a study requested by the UN SG did offer neither alternatives to the existing concept of the mission nor changes in its composition.[76]

During the Operation Peace for Galilee, PLO ceased to exist as an organized presence on the territory, but tens of thousands of Palestinians remained in the Tyre pocket in official and unofficial camps. A new force appeared on the stage—Hizbollah. Having links to Iran, Hizbollah was, if anything, more secretive, militant, and fundamentalist than the PLO. It targeted all Israelis, soldiers and civilians alike, whenever and however it could.[77] Lack of a political solution and impotence of UNIFIL contributed to the rise of an organization more militant, as the PLO was crippled by the Israelis.

In April 1996 Hizbollah began to increase the number and viciousness of its attacks. Towns in Galilee were repeatedly shelled and it also struck elsewhere. The Israelis struck back with a new blitzkrieg that lasted 3 weeks. Thousands of Lebanese left their homes, and more then 150 were killed. As usual, UNIFIL reported the attacks and tried to protect civilians.

On April 18, IDF shelled UNIFIL's base at Quana, killing more than 100 Lebanese civilians seeking shelter there. The Israelis reacted to the outcry in the international media by explaining the shelling as a result of a mistake by an artillery officer who was responding to Hizbollah's firing rockets from the vicinity of the UN base. While a UN report prepared by a Dutch general contested that claim, Israel and the United States denounced it. A spokesman for the Israel Foreign Ministry retorted: "They accuse us of cold-blooded murder, but they do not take a moral stand on what Hizbollah did."[78]

Hizbollah's choice of launching the rockets from its mobile units at the immediate proximity of the UN compound could indeed be an attempt to provoke the Israeli fire. But the UNIFIL Commander, General Stanislaw Wozniak of Poland, said: "renewed launching of rockets from the vicinity of UNIFIL's compounds cannot be excluded."[79] It follows that, while resolving nothing, the UNIFIL's presence might bring about more risks and suffering.

During the period from its inception in 1978 to February 28, 2006, it absorbed more than half of the fatalities suffered by all United Nations peacekeeping operations in the Middle East since 1948. The muddling through, to which it was condemned by its utterly unrealistic mandate, took the lives of 257 members of the Force, compared to the total losses of the UN Forces in the Middle East amounting of 503 personnel.[80] To avoid such a costly failure the UN had either to give the mission an executive authority in Southern Lebanon, to reduce its mandate and composition to an observer mission, or to withdraw. It did neither.

In 2000, as a result of the growing domestic opposition to its ineffective presence, Israel unilaterally withdrew from Southern Lebanon, leaving the ground to the triumphant Hizbollah. On July 31, 2001, the SC decided to cut the number of troops and, after 23 years of endorsing a futile operation, asked the SG to present plans that could reconfigure the Force to an observer mission.[81]

Apart from proving the futility of an ill-conceived UN operations, Lebanon offered devastating arguments against deployment, outside of the UN framework, of hastily improvised multinational forces, armed with everything but a clear and feasible political objective.

EMERGING PATTERNS

The number, size, and longevity of the UN peacekeeping operations in the Middle East made it the formative ground for shaping of the UN peacekeeping missions. Distinct patterns which emerged there were to appear at other peacekeeping theatres in the future.

Whether at the level of the General Assembly in New York or of an observation post in Sinai, United Nations' decisions and personnel were trampled upon at without any consequences for the offenders. The partition plan for Palestine overthrown by force, the unarmed observers sitting duck for both the Egyptians and Israelis fighting at the Suez Canal war of attrition in 1969, and the UNIFIL soldiers killed in Lebanon are cases in question. The UNEF I soldiers evicted by the Egyptians from their positions in Sinai, the Indian soldiers killed in Gaza in the Israeli assault in 1956, and UNIFIL's positions overrun in the Israeli invasion of Lebanon in 1982 are other examples of irrelevance of the UN military presence in face of determined belligerents.

Keeping up the flag became a priority in observer missions even whereupon it did not signal anything else than the organization's impotence. The Secretariat's decision to leave the UNTSO machinery intact after the withdrawal of Israeli participation in the Armistice Agreement structures was later imitated by the UN Military Observer Group in India and Pakistan (UNMOGIP), continuously deployed after India withdrew her recognition in 1972.

UN engaged in three largely successful conflict containment operations, UNEF I and II and UNDOF. All of them came into being under convergence of interests of the Big Powers, which sought to avoid a direct East–West confrontation in the Middle East. But the UN withdrew UNEF I hastily under a political pressure, making the outbreak of a new war in 1963 more likely. UNDOF's presence in the Golan Heights between Syria and Israel since 26 years illustrates in turn a paradox. An effective containment operation not followed by equally effective diplomacy takes off the urgency from a political resolution and is likely to petrify the conflict. The Israelis reached their strategic goals in Golan and the Syrians recognized having no chances for a military comeback. The UN became a guardian of that stalemate. But it is only an expression of a wider stalemate in the Arab–Israeli conflict and of the marginalization of the world body.

The uninterrupted military presence of the United Nations in Middle East did not prevent either a succession of Arab–Israeli wars or the political stalemate from continuing. The roots of the failures in the Middle East are in the betrayal of trust by an absentee United Nations in Palestine in 1947–1948. Upon leaving Jerusalem on May 14, 1948, the last Chief of the British Palestine Government, Sir Henry Gurney, put the keys to his office under the doormat.[82] That bitter gesture testified both to the failure of Britain and that of the United Nations. It is far from certain that the young world organization would succeed where the British failed, but chances were not negligible, especially in Jerusalem, where an internationalization of the Holy City seemed a feasible option. The UN never recovered the keys to Palestine left by Sir Gurney and the consequences are being felt not only by the Israelis and Arabs, but by the rest of the world, still.

The next chapter shows how, without changing the tune, Hammarskjold, the same UN Secretary General who had established the first peacekeeping operation in Egypt, created an operation of a different type. Powerful outside interference, immaturity of the local leaders, and his own inconsequence deprived him from having succeed. But the Congo adventure had shown that there were alternatives to the UN's position of bystander or pushover. Opting for such an alternative the organization annoyed almost everyone and its Secretary General lost his life.

Stumbling into War (The Congo)

THE UNITED NATION'S OPERATION IN THE FORMER BELGIAN CONGO (Operation des Nations Unies au Congo), or ONUC, resulted from a decolonization gamble that went wrong. The Belgian government wrote its script, but the Congolese nationalists sought to rewrite it from the outset. Both were overwhelmed in the course of the play, which came to involve super and colonial power and multinational economic interests.

The Congo was caught in the wave of decolonization of the late fifties, but on the whole African continent there was no other colony less prepared for independence. With a territory the size of all Western Europe, the Congo had a population of 14 million people split into 200 tribes. Without the colony's 100,000 Belgians it had no governing class capable of a takeover. The number of indigenous graduates at college level was about one per million in 1960, the year of independence. Rich in minerals, particularly in the province of Katanga, the country was run by Belgian civil service officials and Belgian and multinational companies; law and order was maintained by the 25,000 strong *Force Publique* in which the highest rank available to a Congolese was that of sergeant. Belgian control did not prevent the spread of nationalism, which was as inflamed as uninformed. After riots in 1959 the Belgians initiated a process leading to a largely improvised independence. Two competing nationalist leaders were elected in June 1960 to represent the new state: Joseph Kasa-Vubu became President of the Republic and Patrice Lumumba its Prime Minister. They signed a treaty of friendship, assistance, and cooperation with Belgium on June 29; the country became independent the day after. The treaty, never ratified, provided for a barely disguised Belgian control. It proved to be a bad miscalculation. The Congolese members of the Force Publique, now renamed the Congolese National Army

(ANC) rebelled against the Belgian officers in Leopoldville and the rebellion spread quickly to the rest of the country. Within 10 days the Congo collapsed into nearly total anarchy. The rebel soldiers supported by excited mobs, attacked Belgians and other foreigners all over the country, looting, raping, and killing. When the Belgians ordered the troops out of the bases in Kamina and Kitona to restore order and protect foreigners, the Congolese accused Belgium of wishing to recolonize the country.[1]

Kasa-Vubu and Lumumba then turned for help to the United States. The Americans were not interested and advised the Congolese to address the United Nations. They did so, submitting a request for UN assistance on June 10. As the matter was taken up at UN Headquarters in New York, on June 11, Moise Tshombe unilaterally announced independence for his breakaway province of Katanga. The blow was severe because Katanga accounted for about 80 percent of the total Congo export revenue. Belgian and other foreign interests openly supported Tshombe's action. On June 12 the Congolese asked repeatedly for UN military assistance in the form of troops from neutral countries to repel external aggression and not solely to restore order.[2] In the absence of an immediate UN reply, Kasa-Vubu and Lumumba panicked. On June 14 both leaders asked the Soviet Union for help and received a favorable reply from Nikita Khrushchev. They did not know that Hammarskjold had that same day obtained an authorization from the SC for a major operation in the Congo. East–West rivalries raised the stakes in the conflict. This chapter shows how the UN tackled the task amid the challenges of an escalating conflict and what were the results of the first peacekeeping operation that stumbled into war.

UNITED NATIONS ENTERS A DECOLONIZATION GAMBLE

Hammarskjold, the visionary Swedish diplomat, was aware of the complex political setup and of the looming threat of a confrontation between the super-powers. In the Congo he saw an opportunity for the United Nations to assert itself as the world authority in controlling and resolving major international conflicts. It was his determination, personal commitment, and effort, which launched the clumsy ship of the world organization full speed into the stormy and uncharted waters of the Congo. He knew how to start the big gamble, but could not have known when and how it would end. The SG entered the game and played alone, apparently misunderstood even by his close associates, only to perish in a flying accident never sufficiently explained. It was a tragedy that his commitment and talents were applied and, ultimately, laid waste in what he himself called a political bordello with a clutch of foreign madams.[3]

Initially the two superpowers welcomed the opportunity to avoid a direct confrontation and supported the UN efforts. Using his powers under Article 99 of the Charter, the SG convened the SC to consider the course of action to be taken. He had lost no time in the few preceding days. According to Thomas

Franck "it is fair to say that the Secretary General essentially wrote the Congolese request, conceived the UN response ... prompted the resolution by which he was empowered to act, and helped ensure its adoption."[4] Hammarskjold kept the Council in session from 8.30 p.m. to 3.25 a.m. the following day and, as soon as his proposals were accepted, he proceeded to his office with one of his closest aides, Urquhart, and started calling all over the world for troops, supplies, aircraft, and staging areas. Instructions were drafted and structures of the mission set up before even giving it a name. Three hours after the Council adjourned, and before the Secretary General and his assistant went for breakfast, ONUC was already under way.[5]

The first troops arrived from Tunisia aboard an U.S. military aircraft in Leopoldville on the evening of July 15, less than 2 days after the resolution of the Security Council. It was possible thanks to the high prestige the UN under Hammarskjold's leadership enjoyed, and to a personal involvement of the Tunisian representative to the UN, Mongi Slim, who called the President of his country, Habib Bourgiba, at 4 a.m. on July 14 from the SG office. By contrast, in the 1990s, deployment of UN peacekeeping contingents within 2 months of its authorization would have been heralded for a great success.

Resolution 143 of the SC adopted at Hammarskjold's proposal called upon the Government of Belgium to withdraw its troops from the Congo and authorized the SG "to take the necessary steps, in consultation with the Government of the Republic of Congo, to provide the Government with such military assistance as might be necessary until, through that Government's efforts with United Nations technical assistance, the forces might be able, in the opinion of the Government, to meet fully their tasks."[6] Both superpowers voted in favor of the resolution, no one opposed it, but there were three abstentions: China, France, and the UK. Hammarskjold's mandate was broad, vague, and open-ended. Significantly, the resolution did not mention Katanga, which had declared independence 2 days before.

The UN was breaking a completely new ground. It was its first operation to provide military and technical assistance to an amorphous government under conditions in which law and order collapsed. In his arsenal of interventionist tools, Hammarskjold had only the principles tailored hastily 4 years earlier for the face-saving operation in Egypt. Ultimately, these principles became the cover for a massive involvement in Congolese internal affairs under a disguise of nonintervention.

WHOSE LAW AND ORDER?

Hammarskjold's guidelines for ONUC emphatically stressed that "although it might be considered as serving as an arm of the Congolese Government for the maintenance of law and order and protection of life, the Force was necessarily under the exclusive command of the United Nations, vested in the Secretary General under the control of the Security Council.... The Force ... could not be permitted to become a party to any internal conflict."[7]

The build-up of this neutral force proceeded remarkably well; within a month the ONUC could deploy 14,500 men in military contingents from Ethiopia, Ghana, Guinea, Ireland, Liberia, Mali, Morocco, Sudan, Sweden, and Tunisia. At its peak the operation totaled about 20,000 of troops and 2,000 civilian staff. More than thirty countries contributed military personnel; among the larger contributors have been India, Indonesia, Malaysia, Nigeria, and United Arab Republic. Ralph Bunche was nominated Special Representative of the Secretary General and Chief of Staff of UNTSO, the Swedish General Carl von Horn, became the Force's commander. Before von Horn's arrival in Leopoldville, the British General Alexander seconded by the Ghanaian government asserted himself as de facto Commander and managed to restore an uneasy order in the European sector of the city. On Bunche's orders he also took over the radio station and power stations.

To von Horn, Bunche interpreted the Security Council's mandate loosely as follows: the ONUC was to replace the Belgians rapidly, then replace the unreliable ANC troops, curb their undesirable activities, and gradually transform them up into a reliable force. von Horn was to secure ONUC freedom of movement throughout the country, and even though Lumumba had appealed for the Soviet help, von Horn was to prevent any unilateral interference. His task boiled down to taking over the responsibility for law and order in the country, both from the remaining Belgians and from the rebellious and disorganized units posing as the Congolese army. For a force, which was supposed not to interfere in the internal affairs of the Congo and not to use military force, except in self-defense, it was a creative interpretation of the mandate.

The ambiguities of the mandate, the sheer size of the country, bad communications between Leopoldville and remote duty stations—compounded by a lack of an effective central authority—all left the local UN commanders more or less on their own. Where the mere show of military force was not enough, some resorted to less conventional means. The Moroccans were successful in putting down a local rebellion using a venerable black goat to lead their battalion. On another occasion, a Moroccan sergeant, restored order in Thysville at the cost of one Congolese killed. Initially court-martialed and sentenced to death in Morocco, he was later pardoned by King Hassan and awarded a medal.

By July the Belgians had withdrawn from much of the Congo, but not from Katanga, or from their military bases and the first 2 months were a relative success, except for Katanga, which the UN contingents did not enter. It was largely to the credit of General Alexander, who managed to persuade the ANC Commander, a young General M'Polo, elevated to this position after a 18-day career as Minister of Youth and Sports, to order his troops to hand over their arms to ONUC. The order was not universally obeyed, but it took a lot of the heat off the UN Force and simplified their task enormously. But not for very long.

A relatively minor incident prompted Lumumba to declare that he would not allow the disarming of ANC troops any more. With support of von Horn, General Alexander went to New York, to persuade Hammarskjold that only through the complete disarming, disciplining, and retraining of the ANC was there the slightest hope for the Congo. von Horn remembered, "His proposals made extremely sound sense and would have been unhesitatingly adopted in any normal army. Unfortunately, we were not any army; we were a United Nations Force in which logic, military principles—even common sense—took second place to political factors."[8] Alexander's mission was in vain. Disarming the ANC was out of question; orders were issued to return to the ANC the arms and equipment they have had voluntarily handed over to ONUC, instead.

But ANC was more a collection of disorganized armed groups torn by tribalism and a menace to law and order and to political stability than a national army. The reversal of it disarmament was done in order to maintain the facade of noninterference in the internal affairs of the Congo. In response to the accusations from the Soviets and from Lumumba, that the ONUC had refused to advance into Katanga to end Tshombe's secession, the Secretary General replied, "I do not believe personally that we help the Congolese people by actions in which Africans kill Africans and Congolese kill Congolese." But it was exactly as a result of this pacifist policy that Africans and Congolese died in horrifying numbers. Many lives might have been saved, had the UN not evaded its responsibility for maintaining law and order in a country that had not yet come into existence. The first 2 months showed that the enormously difficult task was not beyond the organization's capacity. But it was beyond its political constraints.

Leaving the ANC troops at large and refusing to move into Katanga triggered a chain of events which dramatically changed the attitude of the Congolese toward the UN mission, led to an open civil war between the Congolese factions, and indirectly to the death of Lumumba and Hammarskjold. Ultimately, the ONUC could not avoid armed confrontation in Katanga either and, UN contingents, which toward the end of the operation comprised in Katanga about 70 percent of the total strength of the ONUC, suffered fewer casualties than the UN troops in the rest of the Congo, where they tried to avoid military confrontation.

PREVENTING GENOCIDE AND PERMITTING MURDER

On September 6, 1960, Leopoldville radiobroadcast the dismissal of Patrice Lumumba by President Kasa-Vubu from the post of Prime Minister of the Congo Republic, ostensibly for having plunged the country into civil war. The President went home, telephoned the UN for protection, and was given a detachment of Moroccan troops. Half an hour after the Kasa-Vubus pronouncement, Lumumba went on the same radio station, dismissed Kasa-Vubu as the head of state, and called on the people to defend him and the country.

At an emergency meeting in the UN mission headquarters in Leopoldville, Andrew Cordier, who had replaced Bunche, did not waste time on deliberating the UN's impartiality and noninterference in internal affairs. Acting swiftly, he closed all main airports except to UN traffic and suspended all broadcasting. This was disadvantaging the Lumumbist faction, because Kasa-Vubu could use the radio station in Congo–Brazzaville, just across the river. But, unlike Lumumba, he did not dispose of any aircraft. Surrendering the new state's sovereign rights, Kasa-Vubu requested the UN Force to take over responsibility for the maintenance of law and order throughout the whole territory.[9] From now on, it was up to the UN to determine what actions were to be taken to this end. But whenever the UN opted for inaction, the principle of noninterference in internal affairs of the country was invoked.

The dismissal of Lumumba split the country further and intensified the disorder. The consequences of the split echoed in the United Nations assemblies, where East and West took opposing sides. The East with the majority of the newly independent states supported Lumumba; the West supported Kasa-Vubu and a new Congolese player who shortly was to appear on its side.

Amid the confusion prevailing in Leopoldville, Colonel Mobutu, deputy commander of ANC, decided to move his whole family for safety to the house of the UN General Kettani, Lumumba's military adviser. A week later Mobutu appeared at ONUC's headquarters in civilian clothes and announced his intention to resign from the army. He was urged to stay on for the good of the country.[10] The advice has been taken perhaps too seriously and 2 days later Mobutu announced over the newly reactivated Leopoldville radio, that he had neutralized the Chief of State and was taking over the government. His first move was to close the Soviet and other Eastern Block embassies.

There were now four rival political factions in the country: Mobutu in Leopoldville; Antoine Gizenga, Deputy PM in the government of Lumumba who, acting on his behalf, established another government in Stanleyville; the secessionist regime of Albert Kalonji's in southern Katanga and southern Kasai; and Moise Thombe's regime in the rest of Katanga, with its capital in Elisabethville.

Given the new situation, Hammarskjold asked the SC for instructions, but did not receive any. The question was referred to an emergency session of the UN General Assembly, which did not admit to the Assembly Hall either of the two Congolese delegations present in New York, one appointed by Kasa-Vubu and the other by Lumumba. Later, at the fifteenth regular session, convened in September–December 1960, the majority of the Assembly, under a strong American pressure, voted to seat Kasa-Vubu as head of the Congolese delegation. Twenty-three heads of governments and fifty-seven foreign ministers took part in this Assembly session, which became a political circus paralleling the violent and bloody farce going on in the Congo itself. It was during that session that Krushchev banged his shoe on the pulpit and even the UN insiders could not resolve the question whether he had used one of his own shoes, borrowed one from his Foreign Minister Gromyko, or brought an extra shoe to use expressly to bang.[11] The UN and Hammarskjold personally were fiercely attacked by the Eastern Bloc and nonaligned countries for not supporting Lumumba and, eventually the Soviets called for Hammarskjold's resignation. Strong criticism came from the other side too, for not recognizing Mobutu's Council of Commissioners.

In the Congo, ONUC civilian and military personnel became the target for increasing harassment, hostility, and attacks from all of the Congolese factions resulting in considerable casualties. The factions were supported by outside forces that supplied arms, which the UN Force could not intercept.

The SG instructions left a wide margin of freedom for ONUC's leadership and local commanders in regard to the maintenance of law and order, but, despite the increasing violence and chaos, Hammarskjold was adamant in his refusal to allow any use of force which could have been interpreted as partisan, also in Katanga.

Frustrated by the UN's passivity, Lumumba embarked on a new and tragic course of action. He airlifted ANC units into Kasai Province to prepare an offensive against Katanga. Dispatched without any plans or logistic support, the troops had to live on what they could take from the land and its people. The people resisted and the secessionist movement of Albert Kalonji counterattacked, engaging the ANC which, supported by Lulua tribesmen, perpetrated horrifying massacres of Baluba civilians. The UN Secretary General was shocked by the reports of the atrocities, which he called an incipient genocide. His reaction was swift and clear. "Prohibition against intervention in internal conflicts," he said, "cannot be considered to apply to the senseless slaughter of civilians or fighting arising from tribal hostilities"[12] and instructed Cordier to authorize UN troops to use force in stopping of the massacres. In doing so, Hammarskjold did not seek the Security Council's approval. The massacres were stopped and ONUC launched a relief operation for 250,000 Baluba refugees. Hammarskjold's responses to the challenges in the Congo were those of a man of integrity, torn between deep moral convictions and professional diplomatic instincts. The moralist wanted to follow the ethic judgment without calculating political price, while the diplomat, estimating the price for preventing evil, resolved not to bear the costs. The Balubas had more luck than the Tutsis in Rwanda 30 years later, killed by thousands in the presence of the UN Forces.

It proved easier to save thousands of people in Kasai from the incipient genocide than the life of the man who invited the UN to his country. Following the Mobutu takeover, the UN placed Lumumba under protection in his house in Leopoldville, guarded by Tunisian and Moroccan troops. From there he issued inflammatory and contradictory statements, demanding on September 16 the total withdrawal of UN Forces from the Congo and a few days later agreeing with Kasa-Vubu in requesting further UN assistance. On November 27–28, a stormy night, when Kasa-Vubu was returning from New York to celebrate his victory in the General Assembly with a big banquet, a black car left Lumumba's compound. Without difficulty it passed through the inner ring of the UN soldiers who were instructed to protect Lumumba from intrusions, but not to restrict his movement. Requests by Kasa-Vubu and Mobutu for UN assistance in pursuing and intercepting Lumumba were, on Hammarskjold's instructions, rejected by his Special Representative in Leopoldville, Rajeshwar Dayal. Lumumba's personal request for a UN escort from Port Francqui to Mweka in northern Kasai was also rejected. On the morning of December 2, in Mweka, the Ghana platoon commander saw cars with ANC soldiers stopping down the road from his post and Lumumba being taken out of one, then kicked and slapped. The Ghanaian intervened to stop this, without realizing, apparently, that it might have been considered interference in internal Congolese politics. von Horn, received an immediate request from the Ghanaians for permission to take Lumumba in protective custody. The request was rejected by Dayal after consultation with UN headquarters in.[13] On the evening of the same day, an aircraft landed at the UN-controlled Leopoldville Airport. Lumumba was taken out with his hands tied behind his back. He was reportedly taken to the military camp at Thysville and later surrendered to his archenemy Tshombe. Lumumba was seen alive for the last time by Swedish soldiers controlling the airport in Elisabethville. He was blindfolded and savagely beaten. The Soviets accused the United Nations Command in the Congo and the SG of complicity in handing over Lumumba to Katanga. Indonesia, Morocco, and UAR immediately withdrew their military contingents from ONUC.[14]

On February 13, Godefroid Munongo, Katanga's Interior Minister announced the death of Lumumba. Addressing the Security Council on February 15, Hammarskjold decried the revolting crime against the principles for which this organization stands and must stand. The SG maintained that the UN had had neither the authority nor the means to prevent the tragedy. The claim about the lack of authority is arguable, but not about the lack of means. The Ghanaians who wanted to rescue Lumumba from his henchmen were capable but prevented from doing so. Arguably, Lumumba contributed much to his own demise and went terribly wrong in his demagogic and erratic leadership of a country prematurely born. But his fate recalls an image employed by Hammarskjold in an earlier speech about the UN's role in the Congo, delivered to the General Assembly in October 1960. "You try to save a drowning man without prior authorization and even if he resists you;" he said, "you do not let him go, even when he tries to strangle you. I do not believe that anyone would wish the organization to follow other rules than those you apply yourself when faced with such a situation."[15] Yet Patrice Lumumba's death resulted from the same Secretary General denying him the status of a drowning man. Ultimately the diplomat won over the moralist.[16]

THE LAST STRAW IN KATANGA

From the beginning of the UN involvement Hammarskjold understood that reversing the secession of Katanga was the key to any resolution of the conflict in the Congo and he consistently tried to pursue it, but without resorting to force. On August 9, 1960, the SC adopted resolution 146, calling upon Belgium to immediately withdraw. Authorizing an UN entry into the province, the Council reaffirmed the principle of nonintervention in the internal conflict.

Three days later, taking great personal risk, Hammarskjold landed in Elisabethville with two Swedish UN contingents. In an effort not to antagonize Tshombe, he refused to take with him any representatives of the Congolese Government and did not agree to meet Lumumba while in Leopoldville on his way.

When Bunche and Urquhart saw Lumumba in Leopoldville on the day of Hammarskjold's successful entry into Katanga, the Prime Minister imperiously demanded that the UN leave the Congo at once. Later he refused to see the SG on his way back from Elisabethville and there was no return possible to the difficult, but certainly not hostile relations that had earlier existed between him and the UN representatives.

Upon listening to Hammarskjold's account on the situation in the Congo following Lumumba's murder, the SC adopted in February 1961 resolution 161 authorizing ONUC to use force, but only as a last resort, to prevent civil war. It demanded the immediate evacuation of all Belgian and all foreign military and paramilitary personnel not under the UN command, as well as of all mercenaries. Finally, the Council urged the reconvening of the Parliament and taking of the necessary protective measures in this respect.[17]

The immediate result of the resolution was an increased hostility from the authorities both in Leopoldville and Elisabethville. Harassments and attacks on UN Forces multiplied. At the end of April, 44 members of the Ghanaian UN contingent in Port-Francqui were suddenly overpowered by ANC troops and massacred.

In Katanga the UN troops, acting under their new mandate stopped the advance of Tshombe's gendarmerie into the northern part of the province and established control over the contested area between Kabalo and Albertville.[18] But it was not sufficient for the new government under the leadership of the moderate Cyril Adoula, who pressed the UN to put an end to Katanga's secession. On the international stage, multiple calls for the UN to enforce the authority of the central government clashed with accusations that the UN was trying to destroy the only remaining oasis of law and order in the Congo. But Hammarskjold felt that the fate of the whole UN operation in the Congo and his own position hung on a progress in Katanga. Urquhart believed that after resolving the Katanga problem Hammarskjold would have resigned.[19]

Tshombe's separatist regime's existence depended entirely on foreign advisers, mercenaries, and finances but Hammarskjold tried in his precise instructions to the UN people in Katanga to end the secession by political means.[20] But in the rapidly shifting situation on the ground there was little chance for the Secretary General and his people in the field to share the same perceptions and views.

The first test of force in Katanga began on August 28, 1961, with the rounding up of foreign officers and mercenaries. The operation authorized by Hammarskjold and code-named "Rumpunch" was a success. The UN Force took over the radio station, the post office, the telephone exchange, and the headquarters of the gendarmerie in Elisabethville without meeting any resistance. Tshombe appeared amenable and, on request of the UN's Representative in Katanga, Connor Cruise O'Brien pleaded with his supporters on the radio not to oppose the UN. Over 80 mercenaries were intercepted and about 350 surrendered. But the rest, with assistance of some of the consuls from countries sympathetic to Tshombe's regime, went into hiding to plot the next move.[21]

UN representatives were taken in by the Tshombe's conciliatory stance. All positions briefly occupied by UN troops were quickly returned to the Katangese. Tshombe and his lieutenants realized, perhaps to their own surprise, that the swift UN action was not intended to put an end to the secession and so returned to their old tactics. Obstruction and harassment became the order of the day again, accompanied by even more violent propaganda against the UN over radio Elisabethville. In its opposition to the UN, the Katangese regime found encouragement in the neighboring Federation of Rhodesia and Nyassaland, Belgium, and the UK. Hammarskjold declared that only an open and clear instigation to civil war by the Katangese leaders would constitute a justification for UN Forces to intervene. While arguable in strictly legalistic terms, this interpretation of the UN mandate only added to the confusion regarding the UN's proper role.

While signs of another showdown begun to multiply in early September 1961, the key ONUC people, O'Brien, Mohmoud Khiary, and Sture Linner, developed plans to launch an operation code-named MORTHOR (a Hindi word for SMASH) in emergency. MORTHOR's main objective was to round up the remaining foreign mercenaries, to neutralize Tshombe, and to bring him and the representatives of the central government to the negotiating table. There was a flurry of cabled messages, proposals, instructions, and clarifications between UN Headquarters in New York and ONUC in Leopoldville. Concerned by these exchanges Hammarskjold, in a last ditch effort to resolve the problem of Katanga by political means, decided to travel again to the Congo, between September 13 and 18. In doing so he believed that no major action would be undertaken prior to his arrival to Leopoldville. The people in the field believed in turn that having obtained Hammarskjold's approval, they could activate the plan on their own assessment of the ever-shifting situation. The perspectives from the Glass Tower in New York and from the barracks in Katanga could not, and did not, coincide.

What followed was a chain of events that led indirectly to the death of the SG. Fighting broke out in Elisabethville, apparently provoked by Katangese mercenaries, on the early morning of September 13, as Hammarskjold was flying over the Atlantic. MORTHOR was activated immediately, but contrary to the previous operation, everything went wrong. UN troops, ill-prepared and under a weak commander, encountered heavy and effective resistance. In other locations, thinly spread UN troops found themselves on the defensive. The Katangese air force, consisting of one aircraft flown by a mercenary, inflicted heavy damage and disturbed the deployment of UN contingents.[22]

Overnight Hammarskjold's mission transformed from seeking a political settlement to attempting to achieve a cease-fire in an unfavorable military situation. The UN action provoked an outcry in countries sympathetic to Tshombe's regime, comparing it to Hitler's invasion of Poland. Hammarskjold, who learned about MORTHOR on the plane, defended the action and tried to rectify the balance of forces by calling on Ethiopia, India, and Sweden to dispatch aircraft to Katanga. Most importantly, and to the shock of O' Brien, the Secretary General decided, on short notice, to ask Tshombe for a meeting at Ndola in Rhodesia. O'Brien later compared Hammarskjold's trip to Ndola to Chamberlain's voyage to Munich.[23]

The plane carrying Hammarskjold and his team left Leopoldville on September 17 but never landed in Ndola, where Tshombe was already waiting. A few minutes before landing, the control tower lost contact with the pilot. The wreckage of the plane was located next day a few miles from the airport. The circumstances of the catastrophe, never properly explained, are described in the following section "Postscript—The Ndola Disaster."

Khiary, the chief of ONUC's Civil Operation, signed a cease-fire agreement with Tshombe on September 20. A protocol signed on October 13 prohibited both ONUC and Katangese troop movements. It was a tactical victory for Tshombe.

On November 24 the SC adopted resolution 169, condemning the secession of Katanga and authorizing the SG to use force to complete the removal of mercenaries. In response Tshombe launched a violent public campaign against the UN. His forces broke the cease-fire and openly attacked UN contingents and personnel. On November 28 a commando of the Katangese gendarmerie abducted Urquhart who replaced O'Brien and had him severely beaten and knocked unconscious. His life was saved just by chance. "Better beaten than eaten" was Urquhart's response to a question regarding how he felt afterward.

Urquhart was no less loath to use force than Hammarskjold and prevented his troops from reacting to Katangese provocations for several days. But a new showdown proved inevitable. As he remembered, "The last straw came on December 5 when the roadblock at the airport road was not removed as promised but reinforced during the night. I told Kimba (the man in charge on the Katangese side) that unless it was removed by noon, we would remove it by force. He stalled, and nothing happened, so at noon we moved in. The battle soon spread all over Elisabethville."[24] By December 19, the UN Forces were in control and Tshombe was prepared to negotiate with Adoula.

In August 1962, the new UN Secretary General, U Thant, presented a plan of national reconciliation, which was ultimately accepted by both Tshombe and Adoula. On Tshombe's part it was just another tactical maneuver. In December the Katangese started to shoot at UN troops again and on Christmas Eve shot down a UN helicopter. For a week ONUC Forces did not return fire, but then moved in, led this time by the Indian General, Dewan Prem Chand. UN Forces quickly cleared all Katangese roadblocks in and around Elisabethville and by January 21, 1963, ONUC was in control of all important centers. Tshombe was ready to end the secession. Representatives of the central government arrived in Elisabethville in February 1993 and the Katangese episode went to its end.

The ONUC was gradually dissolved and the operation, paid for with the lives of 250 men in Blue Helmets, terminated in June 1964. But the political chaos continued. Moise Tshombe became Prime Minister of Congo, only to be ousted by the experienced coup d'ètat instigator, Joseph Mobutu. In the fall of 1964 the Belgian paratroopers were back again, descending on Stanleyville in a rescue operation for European hostages who had been seized by rebel forces of a Lumumbist faction.

Given the circumstances of foreign intervention and domestic chaos with its bizarre mix of tragedy and farce, the first UN operation which went beyond the consensual peacekeeping was both a success and a failure. But important lessons on peace enforcement and nation building were neither absorbed nor officially formulated. The political costs of keeping Congo together apparently had been too high for the exercise to be repeated elsewhere. It took the UN 10 years to launch another peacekeeping operation and 35 years before it deployed another a mission in Africa.

The operation in the Congo remains an important and surprisingly valid illustration of a massive, if confused, UN intervention in an ungovernable country under the disguise of peacekeeping. Confronted with the realities on the ground the principle of nonintervention in the internal affairs found a creative interpretation. As a member of the UN staff in the Congo recalled:

> We brought the members of parliament back from all over the country, wherever they have fled into the bush, to their villages. It was not easy: some of them were really afraid, in some cases we used force. And when we had them in Leopoldville, Mohmoud Khiary put them in the old university and said: 'You are not getting out of here until you choose a government. No beer, no women, no exit.' And they did not believe him, until they looked out of the window and saw the UN troops rolling out the barbed wire. So they produced a list of ministers, and Khiary went through it with a great red pencil and crossed out three or four as Belgian agents. And sent it back, and they came up with some new names, and the Congo had a government.[25]

Preventing the country from disintegration by supporting its political institutions and ending the secession of Katanga was a major achievement of the mission. So was the protection extended to the Baluba tribe endangered with genocide. But the reversal of the disarmament of the disorganized bands masquerading for the Congolese National Army and abdication of responsibilities in preventing blatant violations of law and order, most evident in abandoning Lumumba to his henchmen, were the mission's serious failures that prevented it from bringing more stability to the country.

At the time of ONUC no one tried to differentiate between peacekeeping and peace enforcement yet. Resolution 161 of the Security Council authorizing the use of force in expelling foreign mercenaries did not invoke the Chapter VII of the UN Charter. Elaborate discussions on the meaning of the right to self-defense were equally unknown.

FROM CONGO TO CONGO AFTER FORTY YEARS

After 40 years the Blue Helmets are back in the Congo deployed in the United Nations Organization Mission in the Democratic Republic of Congo (MONUC). They arrived in the aftermath of a devastating civil war that involved since 1998 also intervening forces from Angola, Namibia, and Zimbabwe supporting the government and Rwanda and Uganda supporting the rebels. All seemed to be interested not so much in politics as in access to, and control of, the diamonds and other high-value commodities abundant in the unlucky country. MONUC, authorized in 5,537 strength by resolution 1291 of the SC of February 24, 2000, grew to 17,175 established in resolution 1565 of October 1, 2004. Its mandate restricted initially to monitoring the cessation of hostilities, disengagement of forces, and withdrawal of foreign troops developed later to include other functions, such as support of government operations to disarm foreign combatants.

But fighting continued in the eastern provinces, especially in Ituri and the Kivu as were massacres of civilians and attacks against UN Forces. In 2003 the Blue Helmets needed to be rescued by the Interim Emergency Multinational Force in Bunia (Ituri) deployed by the European Union (EU) with France as the lead nation. Forty years ago the UN was an important actor in the Congo but until recently MONUC was reduced to passive observer of the horrors unfolding around them. In an undeclared shift in its role it appeared in direct support of government forces pursuing and combating the rebels in 2006.

The next chapter presents an unusual success of another African–UN operation, undertaken in South-West Africa (Namibia) in 1989.

POSTSCRIPT—THE NDOLA DISASTER

A DC-6 B plane, the Albertina, flown by an experienced Swedish chief pilot, Captain Per Hollonquist, was boarded by Dag Hammarskjold and his team in Ndjili in the Congo and took off at 4.51 p.m. local time for Ndola in Northern Rhodesia. In the last message Albertina informed Ndola tower at 11.45 p.m. local time that it saw the airport lights and was descending. It never replied to the tower's later inquiries and never landed. The plane brushed the treetops on descent, touched the ground with its left wing, and burst in flames. Out of 15 people on board, 8 of them Swedes, 14 were killed on the spot, and 1 survived without regaining consciousness for 4 days.

The catastrophe provoked a number of theories on sabotage and attacks from the ground or air as its cause. Three independent commissions of investigation were established by the UN General Assembly, by the Federal Government of Rhodesia and Nyasaland, and by the Swedish Government. The commissions neither found evidence supporting any of these theories nor were able to exclude an outside interference. The incontrovertible fact that the plane was too low in avoiding the treetops suggested human failure. The other incontrovertible fact however was that no search or rescue effort was undertaken by the Rhodesian authorities for 15 hours from the time of the crash and it took 16 hours to find the wreck of the plane only about 9 miles away from the airport.

Two former senior UN staff members on duty in Katanga, George Ivan Smith and Connor Cruise O'Brien, in a letter in *The Guardian*, London, on September 11, 1992, appeared to shed a new light on the catastrophe. They maintained that the European industrialists who controlled Katanga had sent two aircraft to intercept Dag Hammarskjold before his meeting with Tshombe. These revelations prompted the Swedish Government to entrust Ambassador Bengt Rossio with a reinvestigation of the case. He dismissed the revelations of *The Guardian*, with some of the other old theories of sabotage along. But he did not find a plausible explanation for Rhodesia's striking indifference to the plane's vanishing from the air space. Rossio confirmed that the inaction at Ndola could have been interpreted as an indication that the authorities were aware of a planned assassination. But, in his rather benevolent view, it was extremely unlikely that the British, Rhodesian, or any other government would intentionally arrange for Hammarskjold's plane to crash. In fact the qualification of the behavior of the Rhodesian authorities for negligence amounts to an understatement. There were 18 Royal Rhodesian Air Force planes ready to take off anytime at Ndola, but the first was airborne many hours after the crash. The U.S. Air Attaché offered to conduct search with his DC 3 plane but was refused permission. The search finally launched by the Rhodesian Air Force was initially limited to the north and south of the airport, whereas the approach route of the plane was from the west where it was found later.[26]

Thousands of pages have been written about the catastrophe, but those who need to hide something in this case do not tell. With this reflection Bengt Rossio closed his report in an apparent belief of having the last word.[27] It was not so, however.

A few years after Rossio's report, another conspiracy theory was implied in a public disclosure of top secret South African documents by the Chairperson of the Truth and Reconciliation Commission, Archbishop Desmond Tutu, in Cape Town in August 1998. Documents purported to originate from an institution called SA Institute of Maritime Research, contained cryptic exchanges between undisclosed persons referring to the need of getting rid of Hammarskjold and to his travel by air. There were seemingly relevant and repetitious references to an operation code-named "Celeste" in these documents.[28] A follow-up of that disclosure was beyond the mandate of Archbishop Tutu's Commission, which was dissolved after completing its task. No other public information on the subject is known.[29]

Mission Accomplished (Namibia)

WHEN PALESTINE, the mandated territory of the League of Nations, was dropped by its British administration at the doorsteps of the UN, the organization did nothing to assert its transitional authority. UN dealt with the territory of South West Africa (SWA), another mandate of the League of Nations, in a radically different manner. Smacking of political fiction, the UN declared the territory to be under its direct responsibility and administration. The declaration ran squarely against the realities on the ground where the mandatory power exercised full control and did not intend to resign. Eventually, though, the UN brought the territory to independence under the name of Namibia in the most successful mission peacekeeping operation to date. For obvious reasons, the conflicts in Palestine and Namibia are not comparable, but the UN operation in Namibia testified to the organization's capability in peaceful resolution of a seemingly intractable armed conflict. This chapter shows what was the framework of the success and how it was implemented, including averting a catastrophe that loomed just at the beginning of the UN mission.

CONTESTED MANDATE

Namibia is a vast country about the size of Western Europe, but with only 1.5 million of inhabitants very sparsely populated. Much of the country is arid, including the Kalahari and Namib deserts. About half of its population lives in the northern part of the country, which offers better conditions for crops and vegetation. The indigenous population is a mosaic of several ethnic groups, of which the Ovambo and the Herero are the most numerous. A tiny, but economically powerful white minority consists mainly of descendants of German, British, and South African settlers and colonial administrators.

The German colony of SWA was occupied during the First World War by South Africa (SA), which was consequently given the responsibility for the territory under the League of Nations mandate. After the Second World War, South Africa contested the authority of the UN as a successor of the League of Nations and sought to incorporate the territory as its fifth province. In 1948 it gave the whites living in SWA direct representation in the SA parliament, while the indigenous population lived under harsh colonial rule. International Court of Justice (ICJ) opinions, submitted in 1950, 1955, and 1956, and a charge brought up in 1962 by two former members of the League of Nations, Ethiopia and Liberia, did not resolve the question of the territory's legal status.

Nationalists seeking self-rule or independence decided to take the fate of the country in their own hands. South West Africa Peoples Organization (SWAPO) was born, with independence from South Africa as its goal. In July 1966, SWAPO declared itself ready to achieve national liberation by armed struggle, if need be. A low intensity guerilla war began, restricted mainly to the northern regions of the country. Politically, SWAPO adopted an increasingly Marxist stance and attracted support from the Soviet Bloc.

Riding the waves of decolonization the UN General Assembly passed in October 1966 resolution 2145, which revoked the South African mandate and declared the Territory to be the direct responsibility of the UN. In May 1967, the Assembly approved resolution 2248, which established a UN Council to administer SWA until independence, with the maximum participation of the people of the Territory. In 1968, the Council adopted the name of Namibia for the Territory, as proposed by SWAPO and in 1971 the ICJ confirmed that SA must withdraw its administration and end its occupation. In 1973 the General Assembly created the post and office of the UN Commissioner for Namibia, and in 1976 recognized SWAPO as the sole and authentic representative of the Namibian people.[1]

South Africa continued to reject the UN involvement in Namibia's affairs and sought to preempt its actions by declaring that it also favored independence. In 1975, it convened in Windhoek a Constitutional Conference of the leaders of the homelands, and in 1976 an interim government was created as a first step toward independence. But the UN persevered, and in January 1976 the SC adopted resolution 385, declaring that holding free elections under UN supervision for the whole of Namibia was the only way to assure the Territory's independence.

The UN's unprecedented effort to create institutions similar to governments-in-exile was not mere political posturing. The office of Martti Ahtisaari, the UN Commissioner for Namibia, sponsored the "Nationhood Program for Namibia," under which studies and reports were elaborated to assist the future Namibian government and fellowships were organized for Namibian students to prepare cadres for the emerging country. Most importantly, by articulating a clear political goal and sticking to it, the UN changed political realities in and around the Territory without dispatching a single representative into the field. Namibia provided a stark contrast to the protracted UN missions in the Middle East and Kashmir, where showing the flag had for decades substituted for abandoned political goals.

UN efforts found powerful support among some of the Western members of the SC. Representatives of Canada, France, Germany, the UK, and the United States established a Contact Group to work with SA, SWAPO, and the African frontline states (at that time Botswana, Mozambique, Tanzania, and Zambia). At a round of negotiations of "proximity talks" held in New York, the group elaborated "A Proposal for a Settlement of the Namibian Situation" and presented it to the SC in April 1978.

A RESOLUTION MATURES AND BECOMES REALITY

The proposal's objective was Namibia's independence through free and fair elections. As a matter of political compromise, the elections were to be administered by South Africa even if its administration was considered illegal. But the process was to be held under the supervision of Special Representative of the UN Secretary General (SRSG), assisted by the United Nations Transition Assistance Group (UNTAG) with civilian, police, and military components. The transition would start on with a cease-fire between SA and SWAPO forces to be confined to selected bases. Adoption of a constitution for Namibia by the Constitutional Assembly, emerging from elections certified by the SRSG as fair and free, would end the process. That well-designed, coherent plan of action did not leave developments in the territory to chance. The Contact Group, somehow optimistically, expected to implement the plan by the end of 1978. It took 10 years more.

The SG appointed Martti Ahtisaari his Special Representative for Namibia and dispatched him in a survey mission to the territory. As a result a detailed plan on how to proceed was approved in resolution 435 by the SC on September 29, 1978.[2] But SA stalled, using two major issues as stumbling blocks: the bias of the UN toward SWAPO and the "linkage" of the withdrawal of Cuban troops from the neighboring Portuguese colony of Angola. SWAPO guerillas had found support and shelter among their brethren from Angola's governing, Marxist-oriented MPLA. In the civil war that ensued after the Portuguese left Angola in 1975, the MPLA received assistance from the Soviet Bloc and a direct support by Cuban troops invited by the new Angolan government.[3] South Africa and the United States supported the other factions. The military bases and training centers of SWAPO in Angola became subject to direct SA attacks. South Africa saw the armed emissaries of communism advancing to its own borders and was convinced that the Cuban presence in Angola and the withdrawal of the SWA administration from Namibia would expose it to a communist takeover. The political and military stalemate continued for several years. SA could neither defeat combined Angolan–Cuban forces nor eliminate SWAPO's guerillas in Namibia. But SWAPO could not defeat the powerful SA war machine either.

That stalemate was broken in 1988, when the South Africans for the first time took considerable casualties and material losses in a battle with the Cubans over the city of Cuito Cuanavale, only 30 miles from the Namibian border. At the same time, the Soviet Union began to reduce its support for potential satellites like Angola and for the independently minded revolutionaries from Cuba. The UN, the African frontline states, and SWAPO initially opposed any "linkage" between the Cuban presence in Angola and the struggle for Namibia's independence, but everyone had finally to recognize that such a link existed. After several meetings between SA, Cuba, and Angola and the two superpowers—but without SWAPO—the Geneva Protocol was signed in August 1988 on "Principles for a Peaceful Settlement in South West Africa." SWAPO informed the SG that it complied with the cessation of hostilities, effective August 10, 1988. Under the U.S. patronage an agreement was later reached to establish a tripartite Joint Military Monitoring Commission (JMMC), with U.S. and Soviet Union observers. The beginning of the "peace process" was set up on April 1, 1989.

The way had been paved for the implementation of resolution 435 but a controversy developed about the size of UNTAG's military component, a reduction of which the frontline states opposed despite the improved political climate. Ultimately a compromise proposal of the UN SG, Javier Pérez de Cuellar, was adopted for a force of three battalions with the strength of 4,650 and four other battalions remaining in reserve in their home countries. The Force would monitor the disbandment of the paramilitary and other nonregular forces in the Territory, the confinement of the South African Defense Force (SADF) and SWAPO in designated locations, and secure installations in the northern border areas. Some 200 to 300 military observers would perform surveillance of borders to prevent infiltration. The UNTAG police component was increased from 300 to 500 people. The SG also declared that the UN would refrain from attributing to SWAPO the status of the sole representation of the Namibian people.

On February 16, 1989, the SC passed resolution 632 enabling the implementation of resolution 435 in its original and definitive form as of April 1, 1989. But the controversy regarding the size of the UNTAG revived in the General Assembly and delayed the budget's approval until March 1. As a result, at the official beginning of the mission on April 1, only a part of its personnel had arrived.[4] SWAPO and SA accepted the formal cease-fire beginning at 04.00 hours GMT on April 1. About that time the war started again.

WAR ON THE FIRST DAY OF PEACE

On Friday, March 31, 1989, the South African Administrator General of South West Africa (AG), Louis Pienaar, hosted a dinner for senior SA and UN diplomats in Windhoek to celebrate the Territory's first steps on the road to independence. Present were the SRSG, Ahtisaari, who just arrived in Namibia, and the UN Forces Commander, the Indian general, Prem Chand, in the country for a few weeks already. The occasion turned out to be a working dinner. Before it even started, the main SA guest, the Foreign Minister Pik Botha approached Ahtisaari and gave him an information he had submitted earlier on the same day at the meeting of the South African, Cuban, and Angolan JMMC at Ruacana. It included detailed documents, showing where—contrary to the agreements reached—SWAPO units in Angola were still positioned below the 16th parallel, including some 150 SWAPO guerillas deployed about 10 kilometers north of the border and ready to move into Namibia. The Angolans and Cubans promised to look into the matter, but the South Africans were weary about the results, that being the twenty-seventh protest they had lodged since the signing of the tripartite agreement in New York.[5]

On the same evening Ahtisaari transmitted to UN headquarters in New York the information received and also contacted SWAPO. But it was too late to alter the course of events. According to the South Africans, SWAPO had begun to cross the river Kunene at the Angolan–Namibian border a few hours after the AG and his guests had been at coffee and cognac in Windhoek. Namibia's northern border of about 400 kilometers of river, swamps, bushland, rugged mountains, and desert was under the surveillance of the South West Africa Police (SWAPOL), but it had only 1,350 men. SADF was confined to bases and UNTAG had been not fully deployed.

The first report that a SWAPO unit crossed the Kunene river about 15 kilometers west of Ruacana reached the police there at 7.40 a.m. on April 1, and soon there were more reports of suspected crossings. The police forces, including aircraft, went immediately in action. There were casualties on both sides as skirmishes continued throughout the day. At 10 a.m. news from the borderlands reached the AG, who asked Ahtisaari to authorize SWAPOL to use force based on the principle of self-defense. Ahtisaari supposedly agreed.[6]

Botha reached Perez de Cuellar over the phone and told him that the police urgently needed reinforcements to repel SWAPO's violations of resolution 435. He also said that because UNTAG was not equipped to intercept the intruders and not even deployed, such a reinforcement is available only from SADF, now confined to the bases. The SG immediately requested SWAPO representatives to do "whatever they could to affect the situation positively."[7] At a press conference at Windhoek airport Botha declared that "unless the Secretary General makes his position clear on the flagrant violation of international agreements, the South African government will be left with no choice, but to require UNTAG to depart from Namibia, until SWAPO can be brought to its senses."[8] As the first day on Namibia's road to independence turned out to be yet another day of war, UNTAG's leadership was confronted with hard choices. The South African threats had to be taken seriously.

By the end of the day an agreement was reached between Pienaar and Ahtisaari to lift the restriction to the base of six SADF battalions and of one South African Air force unit. To satisfy the provision of resolution 435, which stipulated that law and order during the transition period was to be kept by the South African police, the released contingents were put under the SWAPOL's command.[9]

The decision exposed a failure by UNTAG in dealing with an emergency situation. Commonly, the delay in deployment of the UN troops is blamed for that failure. But that argument is not entirely convincing.

The UNTAG's Force Commander, General Prem Chand, with combat experience in the British and Indian armies, was among the most outstanding military leaders the UN ever had. He had led ONUC's forces in a successful operation against secessionist forces in Katanga in 1962, and as UNIFICYP Commander, prevented the takeover of the airport in Nicosia by the Turks in 1974. He ought to have been informed about the high probability of a SWAPO infiltration from Angola for at least two reasons. Firstly, the general had already traveled with about 20 senior military officers for 2 weeks in the northern borderlands. He visited SA military bases, spoke to the rank and file, and was given extensive briefings on the security situation. It is inconceivable that the South Africans would not pass to him the information about SWAPO's presence south of the 16th parallel.[10] Secondly, placing UNTAG's observers in Angola to monitor SWAPO's restriction to bases north of the 16th parallel was obviously among the general's initial tasks. The Angolan and SWAPO's utmost reluctance—if not opposition—to accept the monitoring arrangements was also an obvious warning signal. SWAPO's ambiguous position was also known in the UN Headquarters, as testified in a record of a meeting between Sam Nujoma, SWAPO's President, and Marrack Goulding, UN Undersecretary General for Peacekeeping.[11] But UNTAG's Commander did not act either before the likely emergency or after it materialized.

In the aftermath of April 1, Prem Chand was conspicuously absent from the limelight and apparently issued no orders to the force under his command, even if 921 UNTAG troops had already arrived.[12] Indeed, of 300 monitors and observers, 211 had already been deployed in Namibia and Angola prior to April 1, but largely absent in the most sensitive area of the Kunene river.

Dispatched to Namibia under the classical peacekeeping mandate, UNTAG was unable to force SWAPO fighters to return to Angola, but the SA would accept no less. Even a fully deployed UNTAG would not do the job. Faced with an imminent risk of a collapse of his mission, Ahtisaari had shown great political courage in taking decision that saved the peace process and prevented Namibia from sliding back into a protracted war. But the UN was embarrassed. In the first press release, which referred to the events of April 1 in Namibia, there was not even a mention of the authorization of the SADF troops to intercept the SWAPO insurgents.

In the South African version of events as many as 1,000 "SWAPO elements" had crossed from Angola into Namibia on April 1 and 2. Those captured claimed that they were ordered to cross the border to establish bases in Namibia and that the UN would take care of them in case of troubles. SWAPO in turn said that its forces observed the cease-fire but were attacked inside Namibia and only responded in self-defense. It also expressed "dismay and shock" that the UN had agreed to release the 101st battalion or the "killer squad" of the SADF, which it had asked

UNTAG to protect its people from, to again kill and maim Namibians. The UN reproduced the SWAPO statement without comments.[13]

The next few days brought more fighting and frantic diplomatic efforts to arrest the escalation. UNTAG call for restraint was not heeded and the hunt for SWAPO guerillas continued. By April 7 the number of their casualties had reached well over 200. There was no single South African account of attempts to negotiate surrender or withdrawal by the intercepted SWAPO fighters.[14] But since April 5, South African authorities had been broadcasting appeals to SWAPO forces to return to Angola and had offered them safe conduct to locations north of the 16th parallel.

The UN and Ahtisaari have been violently criticized. Apart from questioning the political decision and the capability of UN troops, another element of UNTAG's role in the crisis was also put in doubt. In terms of resolution 435, the UNTAG's civil police (CIVPOL) had the task of monitoring the SWAPOL operations, which now included the released SADAF battalions. UNTAG was obliged to monitor their movements but it declined to do so. Its representative Cedric Thornberry observed that "if we go beyond that and accompany military or police on their missions, it would certainly take us well beyond the mandate we have at this stage."[15] In fact, any UNTAG presence at the combat missions against SWAPO would only compromise the UN mission. Claims from some quarters that even a token UN presence on the SADF expeditions against SWAPO could restrict the fighting and decrease the number of casualties are highly implausible.[16] South African combat vehicles known as "Casspirs," notorious for carrying bodies of dead guerillas roped up for display, were hardly appropriate vehicles for UN monitors to follow.

On April 8 an extraordinary session of the JMMC began at a hunting lodge in Mount Etjo in central Namibia. The representatives of Angola, Cuba, and South Africa took part, with observers from the United States and Soviet Union but no SWAPO delegates. Ahtisaari and Pienaar attended the meeting on the second day. A declaration was adopted on a reciprocal recommitment to the peace process, supplemented by a detailed agreement on the withdrawal of SWAPO forces. SWAPO fighters were to be called by broadcasts to gather at UNTAG assembly points to be escorted out of Namibia. Eventually, only a few individuals, mostly sick or wounded, followed the call. The rest chose to make their own way to the border. A number of new skirmishes resulted, with most casualties on SWAPO's side.

The JMMC met again on April 20 and decided to facilitate the return of SWAPO forces to Angola by withdrawal of the SADF battalions to their bases on April 26. At another meeting, held from April 27 to 29 in Cape Town, the UN representative had been invited only to be informed that the Commission decided to release the SADF again for 2 weeks in order to verify SWAPO's withdrawal and to locate and lift arms caches. Despite the effectively reached full deployment of the military component of UNTAG, the UN swallowed this impertinence.[17]

In May, SWAPO was confined to its bases in Angola, north of the 16th parallel, and the SADF went been back to their bases. The UN mission in Namibia was back on track. But hundreds of lives, mostly those of SWAPO fighters have been lost, UN credibility had been damaged and hatreds and mistrust inflamed.

SOLDIERS' AND POLICEMEN'S CONTRIBUTION

With a delay of 6 weeks, UNTAG could begin its political mission. Its military forces, which consisted mainly of three infantry battalions from Finland, Kenya, and Malaysia and a logistic battalion from Poland, did not need to fire a shot during the operation. Both sides to the conflict complied strictly with the military provision of resolution 435 now and UNTAG was the first large peacekeeping operation which suffered no casualties from hostile actions. Eleven people died in traffic accidents, caused mainly by UNTAG members who forgot to drive on the left side of the road.[18] But maintaining a presence of about 4,500 international military made UNTAG quite an expensive symbol and an ironic outcome of fierce debates in the UN General Assembly regarding the deployment of a larger force. That now no one argued for a reduction of UNTAG was understandable, because such a move could be easily misread in the volatile situation in the country. However, misconceived opinions about the insufficient strength of UNTAG have a long life. A few years after the mission ended, some analysts claimed that "The force was insufficient even to monitor the actions of 1.5 million Namibians ... and with the enormous areas to cover, UNTAG was often unable to verify whether the South African forces were confined to bases."[19] In fact, monitoring actions of every Namibian was neither needed nor possible but monitoring of SADF was, despite the enormous size of the country, a relatively straightforward task. Observation posts at strategic junctions on the very few paved roads and at the only North–South railway line were sufficient to make the monitoring of any large movements effective. By June 24, as required, SADF was reduced to 1,500 and confined to bases in Grootfontein and Oshivelo. On November 21, after the certification of the election by Ahtisaari, the last South African soldiers left the Territory.

While the UN military waved the flag and monitored, CIVPOL, which increased its original strength to 1,500 personnel, should have had much more to do than observe, but was not authorized to do so. Maintaining law and order in the Territory was the responsibility of SWAPOL, reinforced by the remobilized special counterinsurgency police unit Koevoet (Crowbar), renowned for its brutality.

Intimidation of the population, including firing at unarmed crowds, especially in the mostly pro-SWAPO Ovamboland, was frequent but UNTAG could do nothing except reporting through the SRSG to the AG.[20] While the presence of CIVPOL had some restrictive influence on the behavior of the local police, its effectiveness depended on cooperation it was getting and that was very limited. Gradually, however, at least at public gatherings and political meetings, CIVPOL became the only visible police force and, to everyone's surprise, the electoral campaign and the balloting process passed without violent incidents. The only problem at most of the polling stations was to keep order among overly enthusiastic voters, who arrived early at the polling stations and all of whom wanted to be the first to cast a ballot.

THE ELECTIONS AND INDEPENDENCE

Never before had the UN devised a peace and independence plan supported by such a web of political agreements, institutional arrangements, and administrative buildup as in the case of Namibia.

At the international level UNTAG had the consistent steady support of the SC and the solid political backstopping of the Contact Group. At UN Headquarters, the SG established a task force for current operational support for the mission. A checklist of seventeen items, concerning various understandings reached between the Contact Group and the frontline states illustrated eloquently the dimensions and weight of the Group's involvement. The checklist spelled out obligations for all concerned regarding provisions such as guarantees for freedom of speech, of assembly, of movement, and of press, supplemented by obligations to repeal all discriminatory legislation, release political prisoners, and approval of the right of return for Namibians in exile.

UNTAG's political presence in Namibia took shape in a network of regional and district centers. The centers were supposed to take the independence plan and elections to all sectors of the population in order to open a dialogue between various factions and leaders. Since some of the faction members and leaders did not talk to each other ever, Ahtisaari's definition of UNTAG as a door-opening job was quite appropriate. The mission succeeded in general in that part of its task and a change of political climate was felt throughout most of the country.

The Electoral Proclamation of the AG became the subject of controversies and difficult discussions with UNTAG. Eventually, it was published only 1 month before the election. Out of about 40 political parties intending to take part in the elections only 10 met the conditions set up in the proclamation.[21] An astonishing 97 percent of registered voters cast ballots between November 7 and 11. The final results were published on November 14. No party has achieved the two-thirds majority required to draft Namibia's constitution alone. SWAPO had obtained 41 out of the Assembly's 72 seats. Its main opponent, the SA supported Democratic Turnhalle Alliance (DTA) received 21 seats. The rest went to five other parties. A few minutes after the declaration of the election results, Ahtisaari spoke in public from the steps of UNTAG's headquarters in Windhoek. He certified that the electoral process in Namibia had been free and fair and that it had been concluded to his satisfaction. "Namibia," he declared, "the youngest democracy, has given the whole world a shining lesson in democracy, exemplary as to commitment, restrain, and tolerance."[22] He also paid tribute for the role played in the elections by the voters, the political parties, the South African authorities, and UNTAG.

The lesson of Namibia went largely unnoticed in the world, however. In the middle of the Namibian elections, on November 9, the Wall fell down in Berlin and the process of the reunification of Germany accelerated dramatically. The German question and the melting down of the Soviet Block overshadowed everything else on the international scene.

But what was that lesson? In political terms, Namibia was a unique case, decolonization exercise of the last big dependent territory. Moreover, the independence plan was construed under extremely favorable circumstances toward the end of the cold war, with all major powers and parties to the conflict involved in pursuing a political solution. A similar set of circumstances is unlikely to reappear soon. Namibia's political lessons for conflict resolution by drawing and steadily supporting a detailed but realistic settlement plan are invaluable but largely ignored.

On the operational level the operation proved that the best-case scenario is not sufficient a base for planning of peacekeeping missions. Grave violations of cease-fires and other peace agreements are to be confronted by force if need be if the peace process is to be saved. Moreover, what the military force is ready to do is more important than its size. Finally, restriction of civil police mandate to monitoring of the local police force is not sufficient for prevention of abuses and consequent obstacles in conduct of the mission. The resumption of war on April 1 could have been avoided should UNTAG be ready to monitor the border with Angola and to intercept the infiltrators. Abuses of civil population by SWAPOL could have been prevented by giving the UNTAG's police an executive instead of a monitoring mandate.

The next chapter presents a case of a more ambitious but less successful peacekeeping operation in Cambodia.

The Failed Authority (Cambodia)

CAMBODIA was part of the French Indochina before the Second World War. After Japan's defeat in 1945, Paris endeavored in vain to rebuild its empire in this part of the world. But the drive for independence, supported by the international communist movement, prevailed over the *ancient regime*. The spectacular defeat of the French administered by Vietnamese guerillas in the battle of Dien Bien Phu marked the end of the French colonial era for Indochina. Three independent states emerged: Vietnam, Cambodia, and Laos, but their fate remained entangled in the currents of the superpowers' claims to dominance and regional rivalries. With most deadly results for Cambodia.

The civil war in Vietnam, between the South supported by the United States and the North supported by the Soviet Union and China (until the schism in the communist camp left the North with only the Soviet backstopping), spilled over into Cambodia during the 1970s. Officially neutral in the conflict, Cambodia was wracked by civil war and subject to American bombing. In 1975, fanatic communist guerillas, the Khmer Rouge, took over Phnom Penh and initiated the "year zero" policy of terror. The population was forcibly expelled from towns and settled in the countryside for harsh labor and political reeducation. Class enemies and other elements considered not eligible for reeducation were exterminated. According to conservative estimates, more than 1 million people were killed, including most of the members of the overthrown ruler of the country, Prince Sihanouk's family.

The regime of the Khmer Rouge under the leadership of the enigmatic Pol Pot was nevertheless granted international recognition and obtained a seat in the United Nations General Assembly. Khmer Rouge's genocidal rule finally ended through armed intervention by Vietnam, which in late 1978 installed a new government in Phnom Penh, with Hun Sen, a defector from the Khmer Rouge's ranks, at its helm. Genocide had been stopped, but the war continued. Defeated on battlefields, but supported by China, the Khmer Rouge retreated to the jungles bordering Thailand. In the 1980s, a bizarre tripartite anti-Vietnamese coalition emerged to fight the puppet Hun Sen's regime in Phnom Penh. The Khmer Rouge, or the Party of Democratic Kampuchea (PDK), was joined by the remnants of the United States backed Lon Nol regime under the name of the Khmer People's Liberation Front (KPNLF). The royalists, under the grandiloquent name of the United Front for an Independent, Neutral, Peaceful and Cooperative Cambodia (FUNCINPEC), under the leadership of Prince Sihanouk, then also joined forces with their enemies of yesterday. But Hun Sen's government was in power in most of the country, protected by its Vietnamese sponsors. Both sides sought the UN's support to resolve the military and political stalemate.

Ultimately, the UN was called upon to establish a transitional authority in Cambodia, which was in all but name the first UN protectorate. The only past precedent, the United Nations Temporary Executive Authority (UNTEA) in West New Guinea (now West Irian in Indonesia) concerned a case totally different in its scale and nature.[1] Cambodia presented a chance to assert a new role for the UN in the post-cold war world. This chapter shows how these chances were wasted by bowing to threats from a weakened and demoralized group of political extremists and to a coup d'etat performed by a government defeated in elections.

TOWARD A UN PROTECTORATE

In November 1979 the UN General Assembly called for withdrawal of foreign forces from Cambodia and for self-determination of its people, but little changed until the Paris conference in 1988. All four Cambodian factions, Vietnam, and seventeen other states participated and the Conference gave a momentum to breaking of the stalemate. The Vietnamese announced a unilateral and unverified withdrawal from Cambodia in September 1988, but the Hun Sen government continued in power in Phnom Penh.

The end of the cold war brought the Big Powers to cooperation in the former Indochina. In resolution 668 of September 20, 1990, the SC endorsed an elaborate settlement proposal for Cambodia's self-determination to be established by means of free and fair elections under UN supervision. A Supreme National Council (SNC) accepted the settlement as a framework for a peace agreement to be worked out later. In 1991, upon appeals by the UN SG, France, and Indonesia, a de facto cease-fire went into effect on a voluntary basis.

Between October 1991 and March 1992 a small advance—United Nations Advance Mission in Cambodia (UNAMIC)—deployed initially 116 and over 1,000 military personnel later, mainly to demine the country. The head of the mission was Ataul Karim (Bangladesh) and the commander of its military component

General Michel Loridon (France), who later became the Deputy Commander of the United Nations Transitional Authority in Cambodia (UNTAC).

At the second session of the Paris Conference in October 1991, Cambodia was represented no more by four competing factions, but by Prince Sihanouk, the chairman of the SNC. The Peace Plan which emerged consisted of a Final Act and two agreements: on a Political Settlement of the Cambodian Conflict, on Sovereignty, Independence, Territorial Integrity and Inviolability, Neutrality and National Unity of Cambodia, and a Declaration on the Rehabilitation and Reconstruction of Cambodia. The baroque titles of the diplomatic documents could not have been in starker contrast with the political realities. There was no potential in the tormented country for achieving all these noble goals without a massive and decisive international involvement on the ground. Therefore the decisions taken in Paris marked a benchmark for UN peacekeeping. Providing temporary political assistance in post-conflict phase was not an entirely new concept, but as James A. Schear noticed, nothing on the scale of UNTAC had ever been attempted by the organization before.[2]

The United Nations was charged with unprecedented responsibilities. Besides the traditional peacekeeping tasks, it was to exercise functions attributed to sovereign governments. These included organization and conduct of elections, ensuring respect for human rights and repatriation of refugees, launching an international program for rehabilitation and reconstruction, and supervision and control of existing administrative structures, including the police. The outgoing UN SG, Perez de Cuellar, was wary of the capacity of the organization to undertake such daunting tasks.[3]

But Ghali, Perez de Cuellar's successor, submitted to the SC the implementation plan for UNTAC and it established the mission by resolution 745 of February 28, 1992. The SNC was declared the unique legitimate body and source of authority in Cambodia, which was, however, to delegate to the United Nations all powers necessary to ensure the implementation of the Paris Agreements. UNTAC in turn would comply in discharging its duties with advice offered by the SNC, provided that this advice was reached by consensus and that it was consistent with the objectives of the Agreements. The UN was given the right to overrule the SNC, and the Agreements were quite specific in this regard. Should its chairman be unable to decide, his power would be transferred on the SRSG. In fact it was the latter who drafted the agenda of the SNC sessions and appointed members of UNTAC-chaired technical committees of the Council. UN was given full control over Cambodia.

In January 1992, Ghali appointed Yasushi Akashi from Japan as the SRSG in Cambodia. The uncrowned king of the tormented country arrived at Phnom Penh with UNTAG Force Commander General John Sanderson of Australia on March 15. The personnel of UNAMIC were absorbed by UNTAC, which consisted of seven components: Human Rights, Electoral, Military, Civil Administration, Civil Police, Repatriation, and Rehabilitation. Altogether, UNTAC at its height included 15,547 troops, 893 military observers, 3,500 civilian police, 1,149 international civilian staff, 465 UN volunteers, and 4,830 local staff. Members of the military contingents, military observers, and civilian police force came from 46 countries.

THE REASSURING MILITARY PRESENCE

Effective supervision of the cease-fire and subsequent cantonment, disarmament, and demobilization of all armed forces was a necessary initial step to success in a country torn apart by four armed factions. But cease-fire violations were the order of the day before and after UNTAC's deployment and the mission unfolded only reluctantly. It was clear from the outset that one of the signatories of the Paris Agreements had no intention to comply with UNTAC's plans. PDK, which now was the official designation of the Khmer Rouge fraction, provided neither information on troops to be cantoned nor allowed UNTAC's entry to the territories under its control. It was regrouping into larger units and putting hard-line commanders on the frontline.

The total number of Cambodian regular or semi-regular forces to be demobilized was about 200,000 personnel, apart from about 250,000 armed militias that operated in most of the countryside. From the very beginning, UNTAC allowed a reinterpretation of the military provision of the Paris Agreements. The number of regrouping and cantonment areas was strongly reduced and the militias have been released from the cantonment obligation altogether. The release was justified by the need to avoid crippling of the economy by depriving it of the part-time farming work of the militia members. Some 55,000 troops from parties to the Cambodian conflict, except from the Khmer Rogue, had entered the UNTAC's cantonment areas but 40,000 were released on "agricultural leave." Ultimately, the process was officially suspended.[4] It was a logical outcome and an unavoidable consequence of the appeasement policy toward the Khmer Rouge.

On May 30 a few Khmer Rouge soldiers who put a bamboo pole across the road prevented Akashi and the Force's Commander Sanderson from proceeding on a field trip. The UN rulers of Cambodia engaged in negotiations and after failing to persuade the soldiers to remove the pole, turned back.[5] At Akashi's request Ghali demanded from the PDK assurances of cooperation but received none. The Khmer Rouge could not have been mistaken in reading the message of that incident. On June 9, they informed Akashi in writing that they were not in a position to allow UNTAC to deploy in areas under their control. The falsely alleged continued presence of Vietnamese troops in Cambodia and the actual lack of supervision of the existing administration in Phnom Penh were given as reason. Ghali informed the Security Council about this noncooperation by the Khmer Rogue but insisted that the mission should continue as planned. On this and other occasions, the SG advocated "quiet diplomacy" for bringing the Khmer Rouge back into the peace process.

But neither several meetings of Akashi with Khmer Rouge's nominal leader Khieu Sampan, nor international conferences and bilateral efforts by the cochairmen of the Paris Conference, France and Indonesia, could move them to refrain from their opposition to UNTAC's authority. Violations of the cease-fire and regular artillery duels between Khmer Rouge and government forces increased with the onset of the dry season in November. Since December there were several incidents of shelling UNTAC's premises and temporary detention of its personnel.

UNTAC's appeasement policy toward the Khmer Rouge damaged its relations with the Phnom Penh government that began to obstruct UNTAC's supervision and control. It maintained, not without a reason, that UNTAC, which exercised no supervision in the Khmer Rouge controlled zones, was not impartial in attempting to control the administration of one party only. Akashi's and Sanderson's retreat from the bamboo pole held by the Khmer Rouge had a corroding spillover effect on the performance of UNTAC's civil component, thus.

Toward the end of 1992 and in the beginning of 1993, armed attacks on political party offices and staff members multiplied, as did assaults on the Vietnamese-speaking minority. UNTAC did not prevent ethnic cleansing from occurring but duly monitored it, counting expulsion of 21,659 people who crossed the border to Vietnam at its checkpoints. The violence continued almost to the time of the elections and UNTAC began to take casualties as well. In April 1993, shortly before the start of the elections, 7 UNTAC personnel were killed and 15 injured.

Both of the main rival Cambodian factions publicly campaigned against UNTAC for its inability to control the violence and to create a neutral climate for the elections. In January the frustrated Prince Sihanouk declared that in view of the persistent attacks on FUNCINPEC's staff he could no longer cooperate either with UNTAC or with the Hun Sen government. It took about 4 weeks of Akashi's diplomacy to bring the Prince back to UNTAC's fold. But it did not prevent him from stating his views bluntly on UNTAC going ahead "despite the fact that none of the conditions for the elections have been met. None. It is a hideous comedy."[6] To the Prince it looked as if UNTAC was dividing his country even further by allowing an election that would not include a *de facto state* within a state or the Khmer Rouge-controlled zones.

UNTAC's failure to perform the military functions foreseen by the Paris Agreements reduced it to what its commander called a reassuring presence around the voters' registration centers and later around polling stations. Random violence continued in spite of this presence; in May six more UNTAC military and civil police personnel were killed and many more wounded. The overall toll of UNTAC's fatalities was 82.

THE MIRACLE OF ELECTIONS

The elections took place from May 23 to May 28, 1993. The Khmer Rouge boycotted the elections but refrained from disrupting it. Apart from isolated incidents, voting took place undisturbed, notwithstanding the rainy season and the looming threats. About 15–20 percent of the territory of the country was excluded from the elections, but almost 90 percent of the registered voters turned out at the polling stations. In spite of the harassment of the royalist FUNCINPEC by the Hun Sen government, it emerged a clear victor of the elections, gaining 45.47 percent of all votes cast. Cambodian People's Party, or Hun Sen's post-communist party, received 38.23 percent and the Buddhist Liberal Democratic Party only 3.81 percent. Accordingly the share of the seats in the Constitutional Assembly was 58 for the royalists, 51 for the post-communists, 10 for the Buddhists, and 1 for a marginal party called Molinaka.[7]

The massive turn out of voters in a climate of uncertainty, threats, and violence was a dramatic expression of the majority of the Cambodians' determination to see the end of the war in their country. It was also a major success of the electoral component of UNTAC working in extremely difficult conditions. But the other UNTAC components proved not able to build on this success.

On May 29, a day after the election, Akashi declared its conduct free and fair and repeated it at the meeting of the SNC, chaired by Prince Sihanouk on June 10. But at the same meeting, Hun Sen announced that his party could not recognize the results and demanded investigation into the irregularities. The Khmer Rouge failed to disrupt the balloting process but the post-communists managed to sabotage its results. Hun Sen declared that until the irregularities, his government would stay in place. He also asserted that his deputy, Prince Norodom Chakrapong and the Minister of National Security, General Sing Song, had formed a secessionist movement and that a number of provinces had decided to secede, rejecting the result of the elections. There were anti-UNTAC demonstrations and attacks in the secessionist provinces of Kampong Cham, Prey Veng, and Svay Rieng. On June 12 and 13, UNTAC withdrew its nonessential civilian personnel.

At a press conference in Phnom Penh, Akashi described the unfolding effort for an overthrow of the election results as a negotiating ploy. But the SRSG contributed to the final deal himself. During the vote count Akashi maneuvered behind the scenes and lobbied FUNCINPEC to offer Hun Sen the olive branch to pacify him.[8] On June 14, the Constituent Assembly began its work, declaring Prince Sihanouk the head of state with full powers. But without UNTAC's support for upholding the results of the elections, the prince bowed to Hun Sen and proposed establishment of a joint interim administration with Prince Ranariddh from FUNCINPEC and Hun Sen serving as cochairmen.

The SC endorsed the results of the elections in Cambodia in resolution 840 of June 15. It also requested UNTAC to play its role during the transition period. But there was no role left over for the failed authority, save withdrawal. The UN mission in Cambodia with its 22,000 personnel ended on September 24, 1993, when Prince Sihanouk promulgated the new Constitution for the Kingdom of Cambodia and was elected king. The new king appointed Prince Norodom Ranariddh the first prime minister and Hun Sen the second prime minister. Akashi left Cambodia 2 days later.

IN THE BACKGROUND OF A DECLARED SUCCESS

The Security Council in resolution 880 of November 4, 1993, expressed its great satisfaction that the goal of the Paris Agreements, which it now chose to present as restoring to the Cambodian people and their democratically elected leaders, their primary responsibility for peace, stability, national reconciliation, and reconstruction, had been fulfilled. The exclusion of the population of the zones controlled by Khmer Rouge from the electoral process, the continuous division of the country, the violence and intimidation of political opposition, and the overthrowing of the results of voting by a government installed by a foreign power did not affect the Council's appraisal. In the international media the very fact of conducting the first democratic elections in Cambodia's history was seen as offsetting UNTAC's failure to disarm the combatants and establish civilian control over the Phnom Penh government. Also most of the scholars pronounced UNTAC's mission a success.[9]

The opinions which declare UNTAC's mission success on account of the elections confuse the means for the goals. The Paris Agreements had been concluded not to hold elections in Cambodia but to restore peace, independence, and territorial integrity of this country under the UN Transitional Authority. The elections had been but one of the means to achieve a goal which was not attained because the UN failed to assert its authority either on military or on civilian level.[10] UNTAC arrived at a critical junction when the Khmer Rouge denied it full and free access to the zones under their control, reneging on the Paris Agreements. As in so many cases before and after, faced with a belligerent adversary, the UN bowed to force.

UNTAC's Commander, General Sanderson, confirmed that on a number of occasions his force was called on by people both within and outside the UN to conduct operations against the Khmer Rouge. These would have been offensive operations, the general explained, while peacekeepers can only use their weapons in self-defense.[11] It was his deputy, General Michel Loridon, who maintained, that by entering Khmer Rouge's territory, UNTAC's contingents would do nothing else than go about their legitimate business. He supposedly proposed that the Khmer Rouge should be forced to comply with their prior commitments, even if it cost the lives of 200 soldiers, including himself.[12] Loridon himself presented a less dramatic scenario of the possible course of events. The general, who lost his job as a result of the controversy with his boss, claimed later that a tough UNTAC stance would not provoke a military backlash by the Khmer Rouge. In doing so he referred to reports surfaced in 1993 about an order by Pol Pot not to oppose UN units by force.[13]

Loridon was right in demanding that UNTAC should have at least tried to make the Khmer Rouge to honor its right to freedom of movement. Those who subscribe to the view that forcible deployment of UNTAC would have resulted in a full-fledged and futile war with the Khmer Rouge like to point out that neither the Lon Nol regime nor the Vietnamese army had been able to defeat them. This argument ignores the political and military losses suffered by Khmer Rouge since their expulsion from Phnom Penh more than a decade ago. It also demonizes a marginalized, defections-prone, and largely demoralized force.[14] Similar misleading historical arguments were to be employed later in ex-Yugoslavia, purporting the invincibility of the Serbs on account of the equally inaccurate record of Tito's partisans during World War II.

The persistent and failed diplomatic efforts by Akashi and his entourage to persuade the Khmer Rouge to honor the Paris Agreements only propped up the discredited leadership. It also left in its hands the lucrative chunks of the Cambodian economy by export of precious stones and timber from the zones under their control.[15]

Stymied at the political and military level, UNTAC was hampered by inexplicable delays in deployment of its staff, starting with the arrival of the head of the mission 2 months after his nomination. Moreover, his own directors of departments criticized his leadership. The political vacuum created by these delays and leadership problems left room for actions by disruptive local forces. The difficulties arising from recruitment delays were then exacerbated by poor qualifications of the personnel deployed. Up to 80 percent of the military police was reportedly unable to operate in either of the mission's languages, many could not drive, and a substantial number had not been trained as military policemen.[16]

Compared to the outcome of the UN missions in ex-Yugoslavia and Somalia, the operation in Cambodia enjoyed a measure of success. However, compared to its goals, it was a pathetic failure. Contrary to the minimalist mandates for UN Forces in ex-Yugoslavia and a grandiose but largely rhetorical nation-building mandate in Somalia, UNTAC was authorized for a takeover of governance of a country and equipped with detailed instructions on how to proceed. It also had the benefit of support and cooperation by a popular national leader, Prince Sihanouk. The first significant UN authority in its history failed as a result of a bewildering combination of political, administrative, and personal factors. The right of use of force in self-defense was exercised by the troops when under assault but was not in defense of the freedom of movement or of the mandate.

Administratively, the UN took upon itself a task to which it was ill prepared. Politically, it was also handicapped by the lack of contingency planning for a case of noncompliance of the parties to the Paris Agreements. These handicaps were reinforced by the determination of both leaders of the mission, Akashi and Sanderson, not to take risks in facing the violations of the Agreements by its most important parties, Hun Sen's government and Khmer Rouge and by poor quality of some of the troops and of the civilian personnel. Hun Sen, the former Khmer Rouge leader, who lost the elections in 1993, is in power in Phnom Penh, still.

The civilian and military components of UNTAC had chances to adopt more assertive stance both before and after the elections but did not use them. The failures could have been avoided by compelling all Cambodian parties to respect the Paris Agreements.

But the UN badly needed a success in peacekeeping and there was nothing better at hand in 1993 as Cambodia. Ghali followed the announcement of the success in that country with the appointment of Akashi as his new Special Representative in ex-Yugoslavia.

Appeasing the Khmer Rogue in Cambodia, the UN sponsored a more assertive, if not aggressive, approach to peacekeeping in Somalia. If he believed the tribal Somali leaders be an easier adversary to deal with, the Secretary General was proved wrong.

Defeated by Warlords (Somalia)

SOMALIA, like nearly all the sub-Saharan states of Africa, was an invention of European colonial powers that established it within the artificial borders of British Somaliland and the neighboring Italian colony of Somalia. It had never been before governed by a centralized authority and consisted of a loose congregation of fiercely independent clans and subclans whose loyalties and allegiances to each other and to external powers were shifting and uncertain. The independent state of Somalia was put on the map of Africa in 1960 as a result of abdication of the colonial governments and of mounting nationalist pressures. The creation, modeled on centralized, democratic nation-state structures adapted from the West, lasted only about 3 decades.

Independence left large numbers of Somalis beyond the arbitrary borders with Kenya, Ethiopia, and Djibouti (a former French colony). Internal tensions, nationalistic dreams about Greater Somalia and the superpowers' competition in the strategically important Horn of Africa, all contributed to the country's sliding from an infant democracy into a dictatorship and thence into total disintegration.[1] Military interventions by the United Nations and the United States during the final stages of this process did nothing to revert or even arrest it. Somalia's seat at the United Nations stood empty as the country returned to precolonial disunity and feuding of major clans, now under disguise of political parties.

This chapter shows how the misreading of Somali realities in New York and Washington, reinforced by confounding humanitarian needs and the humanitarian aid industry's interests turned a routine peacekeeping mission into a most ambitious nation-building operation and how it ended in a spectacular and humiliating failure.

FROM A WAR IN THE DESERT TO THE COLLAPSE OF A STATE

The Somali experiment in democracy ended abruptly in 1969 with the assassination of the country's elected President Abdirashid Ali Shermake. A military junta under the leadership of General Mahmoud Siad Barre took over and the Horn of Africa saw the establishment of an ostensibly Marxist dictatorship. Soviet aid, military personnel, supplies, and bases followed in due course. One of the new ruler's close lieutenants, General Mahmoud Farah Aidid, became Chief of Staff of the Somali army, but soon fell out of grace and went to prison. In 1977 Siad Barre decided to resolve the long-standing dispute with Ethiopia over the Ogaden Desert, populated by Somali nomads, and gave his army marching orders. Aidid was released from prison and distinguished himself in the campaign. Reasonably enough, Siad Barre counted on weakening of the Ethiopian military potential in consequence of the revolution, which overthrew the firmly pro-American Emperor Haile Selassie. But the military junta now in power in Addis Ababa found new protectors in Moscow and Havana. The Soviets abandoned Siad Barre whose army, after initial successes, was ultimately defeated in 1978 by the joint Ethiopian–Cuban forces. The dictator changed sides, expelled the Soviets, and offered military bases to the Americans. Somalia became the largest recipient of the U.S. aid in Sub-Saharan Africa. But it never recovered from the war adventure and defeat.

The war left the economy in shatters and burdened it with the tremendous problem of supporting displaced persons and refugees. More and more of the foreign aid had been requested in the form of food, and Somalia became an important market for disposing off other countries' agricultural surpluses, including those of the United States. Distribution of food, supplied by a host of international aid organizations and controlled by the government, became a tool for rewarding friends and punishing opponents of the increasingly oppressive regime. Selling food on the open markets helped purchase more arms to defend the regime against the growing opposition.

Siad Barre played and manipulated tribal politics to stay in power and in doing so he relied increasingly on members of his own clan, the Daaroods. Clan loyalties and affiliations also molded the political opposition. The strife, in which the powerful Hawye clan played a major part, culminated in 1988 in an open civil war that resulted in ousting the dictator from power in early 1991. By that time most of the humanitarian organizations had left the country, unable to function in conditions of chaos, anarchy, and common banditry. In a pattern known from other troubled places in the world, the fall of the repressive regime instead of bringing peace, triggered more strife and bloodshed. The liberators began fighting for spoils of the war and for the new loot. There was nothing else left to loot but the aid supplied by foreign humanitarian organizations. Fighting in Mogadishu was mostly over control of relief supplies.[2]

When Aidid, now a member of the United Somali Congress, arrived with his victorious forces to Mogadishu, he found another contender for power already installed. Ali Mahdi, businessman from a subclan of Hawye, was elected an interim president of Somalia at the reconciliation conference in Djibouti in July 1991. Aidid did not recognize the nomination and the city split into two hostile sectors. Heavily armed gangs, loyal to Aidid or Mahdi, or just to their own bosses, controlled parts of the city, the seaport, and the airport. Heavy fighting continued in Mogadishu since November 1991 but the countryside was split into areas of factional fighting and pockets of relative calm. Equally diverse was the food situation. People were starving in some places while in other places food was either sufficient or hoarded for speculation. But in the international mass media the image of the collapse of law and order in Mogadishu gained currency for the whole of the country.

FAMINE EMERGENCIES AND FALLSTARTED MISSION

The worsening Somali crisis in 1989–1991 with its mainly man-made famines and brutal civil war in a peripheral African country coincided with much more powerful earthquakes on the world's political stage, such as the fall of the Wall in Berlin, the end of the cold war, and the Gulf War. In the early 90s Somalia could not have been but a footnote in the international political news. But it was not so for the international humanitarian aid industry. It was losing a substantial market that worked relatively smoothly under the Siad Barre's regime, which both created and exaggerated food emergencies. Military intervention for protection of humanitarian aid came to be presented as the only and just solution to the Somali famine.[3] There were no calls for deployment of UN peacekeeping forces to prevent starvation in another country stricken by war and famine—Sudan, where 250,000 people were believed to have died in 1988 alone. Somalia, a smaller country easily accessible by sea and air, was a more feasible target for large supplies of aid.

The CNN syndrome took hold, images of starving children proliferated in the mass media, pressures grew on the politicians by the humanitarian organizations, and the country started to rise out of oblivion. Something had to be done, and the UN Security Council stepped in. On January 23, 1992, with resolution 733 and invoking Chapter VII of the United Nations Charter, it imposed a complete embargo on all deliveries of weapons and military equipment to Somalia; and asked all parties to commit to a cease-fire and to allow undisturbed continuation of humanitarian assistance. The modest beginning of UN involvement in Somalia coincided with the first month in office of the new UN Secretary General, Ghali. He invited Ali Mahdi and General Aidid to New York and the first of many broken cease-fire agreements resulted on February 13. A few weeks later, on March 28, an agreement on the deployment of unarmed United Nations observers to monitor the cease-fire, to provide for the security of United Nations personnel, and to safeguard humanitarian aid in and around Mogadishu had been signed.

One month later, on April 24, the SC established by resolution 751 the United Nations Operation in Somalia (UNOSOM) and asked the Secretary General to deploy immediately 50 military observers and a 500-man strong unit in consultation with the Somali parties. A few days later Ghali nominated an Algerian diplomat, Mohamed Sahnoun, his Special Representative in Somalia. It took 2 months for the Chief Military Observer, General Imtiaz Shaheen of Pakistan to reach Mogadishu with no less than three observers. The UN mission in the Congo under Dag Hammarskjold and deployment of the first military contingent from Tunisia in less than 48 hours belonged to prehistory.

The arrival of Shaheen coincided with landing in Mogadishu of an Antonov aircraft chartered by the World Food Program but bearing the UN markings. Aidid alleged that it carried cash and armaments from Nairobi for his opponent Ali Mahdi and ordered Shaheen and his observers out of the country. It was only thanks to the conciliatory talents and negotiating skills of the SRSG, Sahnoun, that the deployment could resume.

Meanwhile, the SG developed a new, strikingly ambitious vision of further UN involvement in Somalia. The UN, he ordered, should establish a presence in all regions and adopt a comprehensive approach dealing with all aspects of the Somali situation, namely the humanitarian relief and recovery, the secession of hostilities and security, the peace process, and the national reconciliation in a consolidated framework. The country was to be divided in four zones: the northwest (Berbera), the northeast (Bossasso), the central rangelands and Mogadishu (Mogadishu), and the south (Kismayo). In each zone the UN mission would carry out humanitarian activities, monitor the cease-fire, and maintain security while helping combatants to disarm.

In resolution 767 of July 27 the SC approved the plan, and in resolution 775 of August 28, it also approved Ghali's request for an increase in the strength of UNOSOM to 4,219 personnel: 750 for each zone, 500 for the Mogadishu airport, and 719 for logistic personnel. The first military contingent arrived at Mogadishu from Pakistan in September and was forced to hire gunmen for their own protection. The Pakistanis practically became hostages, helplessly confined to the barracks at the airport.[4] The mission never reached its authorized strength and only some 900 men more were deployed in smaller contingents from Australia, Belgium, Canada, New Zealand, and Norway. All remained in Mogadishu and there was no deployment elsewhere.

The authorization for deployment of UN troops in the northeast zone (Bossasso) ignored the realities on the ground completely. It was in this zone, the former British Somaliland, that in May 1991 the local authorities had declared independence from Somalia. Not recognized by the UN or anyone else, Somaliland rejected foreign military involvement and political interference. When a representative of UNOSOM suddenly appeared in mid-1993 with a new map of the division of the country, he was politely but quickly sent home.[5]

After the deployment of UNOSOM, conditions on the ground went from bad to worse. On October 28, 1992, Aidid declared that the international troops would be not tolerated on the streets of Mogadishu anymore. He also ordered the UNOSOM's coordinator for the humanitarian assistance out of the country. The Pakistanis at the airport came under fire from the Aidid's faction, while Ali

Mahdi's forces shelled ships carrying food. All factions and armed gangs went on a rampage, competing to get hold of the goods brought in as international aid, the main source of income in the Somali war economy. Robberies, armed assaults on convoys, stores, and UN personnel became the order of the day.[6] UNOSOM was an impotent failure.

There were, however, brighter spots in this bleak picture. In the second half of 1992 the famine was already in retreat and death rates were also declining. Maize prices began to steadily drop from 4,000 shillings per kg in July to 1,300 in October. A good harvest in the Lower Shebele Valley combined with massive food relief deliveries in May and June contributed to this development, but the mechanism of a new and more massive military intervention in Somalia had already set in motion.[7] These developments coincided with an unhelpful change of the SRSG. Sahnoun's low profile and his openness in contacts with all Somali factions, and with everyone else, made him from the outset a popular figure. After chairing a successful Coordination Meeting on Humanitarian Assistance to Somalia in Geneva in October 12–13, where he publicly criticized UN agencies' performance in the Somali crisis, the Special Representative was encouraged to resign from his post and he did so. His replacement, Ismat Kettani from Iraq, adopted a "colonial" style of contacts, not helpful in the Somali context.[8]

The U.S. administration emerged in the picture at about that time. On November 25, Lawrence Eagelburger, the then acting Secretary of State, intimated to Ghali that should the SC decide to authorize use of forces to ensure the delivery of the humanitarian aid in Somalia, his country would be ready to take the lead in the operation.[9] The offer could not have been made at a more opportune time. The violent disintegration of Yugoslavia, met by impotence of Europe and by President Bush's declaration that the United States did not have a dog in this fight, gave rise to doubts whether the new world order announced by the victor in the Gulf War had ever existed. Ghali echoed the American president in his own way in saying that ex-Yugoslavia was a war among rich people and, as such, attracted a disproportionate amount of interest. A formidable rescue operation in Somalia was going to prove the international community's commitment to the new world order and readiness to use military might for saving people from starvation. If UNEF I in Egypt in 1956 was a unique face saving operation, Operation Restore Hope was the biggest military mission ever undertaken in support of humanitarian aid.

OPERATION RESTORE HOPE

The Security Council accepted the cautiously worded U.S. offer to help in creating a secure environment for the delivery of humanitarian aid to Somalia, and on December 3, 1992, in resolution 794, acting under Chapter VII of the UN Charter, authorized the United States to use all necessary means to do so.[10] President Bush decided a day later to launch the Unified Task Force (UNITAF);

he only afterward tried Ghali to obtain confirmation what the secure environment meant. In a letter of December 8 to the U.S. President, the SG set out conditions for the UN to take over operation from UNITAF: Effective neutralization of heavy weapons, disarmament of irregular forces, and extending of UNITAF authority to all of Somalia. He called for nothing less but the establishment of an occupation regime in a failed state.

Not surprisingly, neither of Ghali's conditions was met. Bush obtained approval for the operation from U.S. legislative bodies for saving starving children, not for fighting a war in an obscure country:

> First, we will create a secure environment in the hardest-hit parts of Somalia so that food can move from ships overland to the people in the countryside now devastated by starvation. And second, once we have created that secure environment, we will withdraw our troops, handing the security mission back to a regular UN peacekeeping force. Our mission has a limited objective, to open the supply routes, to get the food moving, and to prepare the way for a UN peacekeeping force to keep it moving.[11]

To the international public these limitations were far from obvious; the soldiers storming the beaches of Mogadishu in full combat gear on December 9 suggested that America was ready to use its power not only in defense of the oilfields and sheikhs of Kuwait, but also to bring bread and peace to a tormented country. The Somalis seemed to believe it as well and the marines met thousands of people cheering them at the beaches.

UNITAF under the command of General Robert Johnson was expected to build up to 28,000 men, including 10,000 U.S. Navy at a carrier battle group at sea who never came ashore. Contingents from twenty other countries as diverse as Australia and Zimbabwe were to contribute 17,000 troops. Ultimately, UNITAF, which Ghali wanted to exercise authority in all of Somalia, deployed about 37,000 troops, but covered only about 40 percent of the country's territory. It took over major airports, seaports, key installations, and escorted convoys to food distribution centers. The Force did not engage in any comprehensive disarmament and its attitudes were ambiguous; it destroyed anything that appeared to threaten it, particularly the battlewagons known as "technicals," but it did not search for weapons. And if it came across any, it let them be. At times its conduct amounted to sabotage. When French legionnaires seized some arms, they were obliged by the Americans to give them back.[12] Otherwise, UNITAF also refrained from major confrontations with the Somali factions, unless attacked. Through the good offices of Robert Oakley, the head of the U.S. Liaison Office, whose style was similar to Sahnoun's, the force maintained working contacts with the main factions. The relation soured, however, over incidents outside of Mogadishu.

In February 1993, the Belgian UNITAF contingent in Kismayo stood by as forces of General Mohamed Sayed Hersi Morgan took on Aidid's ally, Colonel Omar Jess, who held the town. By some accounts the battle raged for 3 weeks, ending with Morgan's victory; by others Jess just gave up and fled. UNITAF's indifference delivered an important message: the international forces will not interfere to stop warfare. It was not taken well in Mogadishu where crowds of Aidid's supporters took to the streets in violent demonstrations, accusing UNITAF of complicity with Morgan. Some of the international troops were reported to open fire.[13] American efforts to persuade Somali factions to cooperate, including courting of Aidid by Oakley, came to nothing. It did not matter much because the Operation was going to end soon.

When it was terminated on May 3, 1993, the U.S. administration declared it a big success that saved hundreds of thousands of lives. People in the field did not necessarily agree. Some claimed that the marines arrived when the famine was already abating.[14] Moreover UNITAF had concentrated on securing bulk food supplies to food centers, to which most of those who were starving did not have access. During UNITAF's deployment disease was a greater killer than famine. But first and foremost, the underlying reason of the catastrophe in Somalia was a lack of law and order. And on this account there was a consensus within the aid community: UNITAF failed to create anything resembling a secure environment for sustained humanitarian relief operation.[15] The formidable international army under the command of world superpower left the forces of local warlords intact and the country in grip of factional fighting and widespread banditry. Food was distributed but hope was not restored.

THE UN SECRETARY GENERAL TAKES OVER

The failures of UNOSOM I and UNITAF to bring the Somali crisis any closer to resolution did not discourage Ghali from drafting a grandiose plan for a further buildup. The new mission established under Chapter VII of the UN Charter was now expected to complete the task begun by UNITAF by restoring peace, stability, and law and order. It was also authorized to assist the Somali people in reestablishment of institutional structures, in achievement of national reconciliation, in recreation of a Somali state based on democratic governance, and in rehabilitation of the country's economy and infrastructure. The mandate, covering the whole territory of Somalia, included military tasks as well. UNOSOM II was to monitor the cessation of hostilities, prevent resumption of violence, take appropriate action against any faction that continued to use violence, and maintain control of heavy weapons. The new UN Force was also to seize small arms from all unauthorized armed elements; secure all ports, airports, and lines of communications needed to deliver humanitarian assistance; and protect personnel, installations, and equipment of UN agencies and NGOs, including the use of the force as needed.

Contrary to other UN missions, the deployment of UNOSOM II in this massive nation-building exercise was to be at the discretion of the Secretary General, his Special Representative, and UNOSOM's II commander. Ghali appointed retired Admiral Jonathan Howe (United States) the new SRSG and General Cevic Bir

(Turkey) the Force Commander. UNITAF left behind some American forces acting outside UN control.

The Security Council unanimously approved Ghali's recommendations and established UNOSOM II by resolution 814 of March 26, 1993, with authorized strength of the Force of 28,000 of military personnel and 2,800 civilian staff. Thirty-four countries committed their contingents to the UN command.[16] The largest military operation for humanitarian relief has been replaced by the most ambitious nation-building expedition ever. Michael Maren alleged that the unrealistic mandate had been drafted at the office of the U.S. Chief of Staff, General Colin Powell.[17] Whether true or not, the mandate fitted the U.S. tactics presenting UNITAF's mission as groundwork to be completed by the UN. And the organization tried to do it.

In March, Lausanne Kouyate of Guinea, the Deputy SRSG, chaired an impressive assembly of the representatives of 15 Somali political factions in Addis Ababa.[18] At a western style conference sponsored by foreigners, leaders of major factions sat next to political exiles from Nairobi, who represented small and insignificant groups in Somalia. A set of documents provided a detailed, comprehensive, and well-defined blueprint for an immediate end of the civil war, the reconstruction of the Somali State, and the institutional build-up for civic participation in the government. It was accepted by the invited Somalis and several agreements were duly signed on March 27, 1993. The Somalis already knew the strange affection of UN officials for signed papers. They also knew that the UN was not inclined to act against signatories of such papers who chose to ignore whatever their text might have represented. But the ceremony in Addis Ababa followed the Security Council resolution 814 by 1 day only. Thus, everything looked fine, on paper at least.

WAGING AND LOOSING A WAR

The major Somali players did not have any intention to adhere to agreements sponsored by the organization that they had earlier opposed with impunity. As early as June 5, an incident in Mogadishu turned into a bloodbath for a UN Pakistani unit and spurred a UN retaliatory action that turned UNOSOM into a faction in an urban civil war. Under an agreement between the UN and the Somali factions, the heavy armor was to be stored at the Authorized Weapons Storage Sites. Pakistani soldiers who arrived for a routine checkup faced a hostile crowd concerned that the troops intended to shut a popular radio station nearby. The demonstration degenerated into a shoot-out, later labeled an ambush, in which 25 soldiers were killed. An additional 10 were missing and 54 wounded. The bodies were mutilated and publicly disgraced. There were many casualties among Somali civilians from Pakistani fire.[19]

The Security Council reacted swiftly. In resolution 837 of June 6 it requested the Secretary General to take all necessary measures against those responsible, including their arrest and detention for prosecution, trial, and punishment. The retaliation started on June 12, on the ground and from the air. The UN troops took over the radio station and allegedly destroyed several arms caches. Air attacks caused large-scale destruction and many civilian casualties. The Pakistanis were accused of having killed 20 civilians by firing into a demonstration on June 13. On June 17, Admiral Howe called for Aidid's surrender and also issued the first arrest warrant in the history of the UN. Wild West style posters for the "wanted" leader were put up in town, promising $25,000 reward for help in his capture. Aidid was never intercepted, but the posters became collectors' items later. Provoking a short-lived crisis between Rome and the UN Headquarters, the Italians, the former colonial masters of Mogadishu, who managed to conclude practicable arrangements with the Somali factions, openly opted out of what they considered UNOSOM's misconceived adventure.

Explaining the decision to capture and detain General Aidid, the U.S. representative to the UN, Madeleine Allbright wrote that "Failure to take action would have signaled to other clan leaders that the United Nations were not serious. For Somalia's sake and ours we must persevere."[20] Ghali was firm too, declaring that "The readiness and capability of the UN troops to apply force are the preconditions for the success of relief operations. Distribution of food in Somalia requires the disarmament of irregulars. We have to be in position to apply military force. The force for peace."[21] But it took only a few months of perseverance by a local warlord to make the representative of the world's sole superpower and the leader of the world organization to do precisely the opposite of what they had avowed.

Since June 1993, Mogadishu became an enemy town for the UNOSOM personnel, who could move only during the day in heavily armed convoys. Snipers and landmines took a toll on UN Forces in spite of all precautions. Italian, Malaysian, and American soldiers were among the victims. On July 12, 1 month after the UNOSOM troops went to war against Aidid's clan; the Americans went into action. Cobra helicopters fired ten missiles into a house where the elders of the Hawye clan were meeting. About 50 people, among them respected community members and opponents of Aidid's rule, were killed. Afterward, the angered crowds tore four foreign journalists to pieces in public. The situation deteriorated further and on September 25, Aidid's followers shot down an American Black Hawk helicopter killing the crew of three. One of the bodies was decapitated and the head put on display.

The Americans retaliated on October 3. United States Rangers, who had already been sent to beef up the Quick Reaction Force on the ground, launched an operation to intercept a number of Aidid's key lieutenants. They detained 24 suspects, but at a heavy cost. Two helicopters were lost and the Rangers came under fire while evacuating the prisoners. An intense battle raged for 17 hours instead of the 90 minutes allotted for the operation. Several hundreds of Somalis died, as did 18 U.S. soldiers, and 75 others were injured. The bodies of the U.S. soldiers were dragged through the streets and subjected to outrageous acts by the mobs, and the TV broadcast the tragic scenes.

The decision to use U.S. Special Forces against Aidid's suspected stronghold was taken at the Headquarters of the Central Command in Florida. Howe was not informed about the action and the UNOSOM Commander was only told about it shortly before it began. Unprepared for the action, the UN could send only a Nigerian contingent to support the Americans.[22]

The reaction of the U.S. administration to the debacle was twofold and contradictory. Announcing an immediate reinforcement of the mission, President Bill Clinton simultaneously announced the decision to withdraw all U.S. troops from Somalia no later than the end of March 1994. Shortly afterward, Belgium, France, Germany, Italy, and Sweden also declared the intention to withdraw. Aidid quickly realized what his response should be and, a few days after the message from across the Atlantic reached Mogadishu, declared a unilateral cessation of hostilities. He did not need to wait long for the results. Robert Oakley, the U.S. Special Envoy to Somalia, returned to Mogadishu and started meeting the man on whose head Admiral Howe had put a price of $25,000 only a few months ago.

Ghali also visited Mogadishu and was met by angry demonstrators. Afterward, he also issued a clarion call for retreat, dressed in beautifully phrased UN language. Three options were presented: (1) No change of the UNOSOM mandate with the understanding "that UNOSOM will not take the initiative to resort systematically to coercive methods to enforce disarmament"; (2) UNOSOM would not use coercive methods anywhere, but would rely on the cooperation of the Somali parties and use force only in self-defense. The deployment could be reduced to 16,000 men; (3) UNOSOM would only keep secure airports and ports with a force reduced to 5,000 men.

On November 16, the SC decided by resolution 885 to postpone the review of the UNOSOM II mandate, but ordered immediate reversal of its own recent decisions. Pending the results of ordered inquiries, UNOSOM was requested to suspend arrest actions, and by January 17 all detainees were released.[23] Albright voted for the resolution, thus helping to end the short-lived manhunt for Aidid, an action which 3 months before had been a proof of the credibility of the United Nations.

Outside of Mogadishu the country resembled a mosaic of violent confrontations interspersed with pockets of relative calm. Continuing violence around Kismayo contrasted with seminormal conditions in and around Baidoa, where the French contingent pursued effective disarmament of irregulars and achieved a measure of success in establishing local councils.[24] UNOSOM II did not cover the whole of the country and no UN Forces have been interposed between the rival clans from the central regions and Migiurtinia.[25]

The SG presented the situation on January 6, 1994, as follows. Progress, he reported, had been achieved in establishing district councils, but Aidid's faction refused to participate. Banditry continued to plague parts of the countryside and there were outbreaks of interclan fighting. Several nongovernmental organizations had been forced to suspend operations. In Mogadishu the security situation was deteriorating. UNOSOM was meanwhile promoting voluntary disarmament, but the factions were actively rearming in anticipation of renewed fighting. Despite that gloomy picture Ghali maintained to believe in UNOSOM's presence being essential for the peace-building process. He had therefore approached a large number of UN member states for more troop contributions, but did not get any offers.[26] This was hardly surprising, given the effects of that presence to date, including the promotion of voluntary disarmament.

On February 4, the Security Council approved resolution 897, revising the UNOSOM mandate and authorizing a gradual reduction of the Force to the level of 22,000 men. The objectives of the mission did not change but the means to achieve them did. The UN troops were not supposed anymore to enforce anything; now it was up to the Somalis to disarm in what was termed cooperative disarmament, to observe cease-fires, and to rebuild national institutions. UNOSOM was ready to assist, but no more. The new SRSG, James Victor Ghebo of Ghana, courted General Aidid, who remained the key to any resolution of the crisis. Another declaration on national reconciliation was signed on March 24, a year after the Addis Ababa conference, this time in Nairobi, Kenya. The results were the same— nothing changed on the ground.

In September, UNOSOM II redeployed troops to Mogadishu, Baidoa, and Kismayo, and in resolution 954 of November 4, 1994, the SC decided to terminate the mission in March 1995. Neither the Somali factions nor the humanitarian aid agencies pleaded the peacekeepers to stay. Under the protective cover of another U.S.-led operation labeled "United Shield," General Anthony Zini led the UN troops out of Somalia. The Americans came ashore in Mogadishu once more, but this time to protect a retreat of an international army defeated by local warlords and common gangsters. The last UNOSOM soldiers and their protectors left Mogadishu on March 3, 1995. But before the termination of the futile missions of UNOSOM I and II, 159 of their members lost their lives, excluding U.S. casualties.

As if in celebration of the end of the international intervention, the arch foes General Aidid and Ali Mahdi signed another peace agreement only to fall out again. Aidid was killed in a battle and succeeded by his son. There is a fledgling government of Somalia in exile in Kenya, but years after the combined U.S. and UN military intervention the country remains tortured by anarchy and violence.[27]

SOME LESSONS FROM THE FAILURE

The UN unequivocally failed in engaging Somalis in its grandiose nation-building design. Before the UNOSOM's humiliating retreat, the president of Eritrea, Isaias Afwereki, had put it bluntly:

> The Somali people must be placed at the center of all security, humanitarian, and political efforts. No outsider has the right to disregard the Somalis, in particular to decide who can or who cannot be part of future political arrangements. Hasty and misguided efforts to do so have had disastrous consequences.... The fact is that most UN officials involved in the Somali effort have compromised themselves and lost the confidence of the people.[28]

Political usurpation by imposing settlements not acceptable to all warring parties can only work when supported by overwhelming enforcement effort. Such was the case in Bosnia and Herzegovina and in Kosovo, which absorbed tens of thousands of international troops for years. There was no similar commitment for Somalia.

UNITAF's mission was the first major military intervention undertaken to protect delivery of aid and of those who distribute it, without engaging in protection of the aid's recipients. Humanitarianism was somehow reduced to feeding people while abstaining from protecting their lives. The principle was emulated later in Bosnia with equally negative effects. Ultimately, despite the initial support for the military intervention, some of the humanitarian organizations complained that the troops were an obstacle, not help.[29]

But it was along the fault line of enforcement that the showcase Somali operation collapsed into a disgraceful retreat. Disarmament of the factions was the first priority for the return to normal life and an end to suffering in Somalia. But UNOSOM I exposed its impotence at the outset of the mission. Hiring for its own protection local fighters whom it was supposed to control, it proved incapable of defending itself and its freedom of movement. A chance for effective disarmament by taking advantage of the initial display of awesome force by UNITAF was lost because of the American limited objectives. UNITAF and UNOSOM II applied force in reactive and retaliatory actions with no visible military strategy to discharge the mandate. Important tactical decisions taken in Florida, instead of Mogadishu, made a mockery of any operational planning by UNOSOM II, had there been any in evidence. There was also confusion within the mission. Its Chapter VII mandate did not prevent some of the participating contingents from insisting that theirs was a peacekeeping operation excluding enforcement.

After Somalia, "Crossing the Mogadishu Line," a phrase coined by the British general, Michael Rose, gained widespread currency for describing actions which jeopardize mission goals and lead straight to failure. But, since each conflict has its own dynamics, the phrase is prone to misuse and can be an easy substitute for a more realistic appraisal and an analytic nuance. Fred Cuny suggested other options for enforcement of the UN Somali mandate than fighting an urban guerilla war in Mogadishu, but his recommendations were ignored.[30] Discussing the Somali experience, Chester A. Crooker concluded, "When the United States decides it must act, it should act competently."[31] The same goes for the United Nations.

The first combined UN–U.S. mission was doomed to fail for lack of a coherent political and military strategy to reach its overambitious goals. Somalia had been an invaluable lesson for the United States and the UN in what is likely and unlikely to work in complex political–humanitarian emergencies that have become all too common. Drawing coherent policies and strategies, including military options and contingency plans, is no guarantee for success in these emergencies. But their lack in Somalia was a guarantee for failure.

The first opportunity to see how the results of the Somali lesson were absorbed by the UN and by the various governments, inaccurately referred to as the international community, presented itself soon. Eleven Belgians soldiers of UNAMIR in Rwanda had to die on April 11, 1994, in order to provoke the withdrawal of the Belgian contingent and the reduction of the Force to a symbolic size. It seemed that the henchmen from Kigali had better absorbed the lesson of Somalia than the international community represented by the UN. The next chapter describes the gruesome effects of that learning process.

Witnesses to Genocide (Rwanda)

IT IS IN JOSEPH CONRAD'S HEART OF DARKNESS, in the region of the Great Lakes, that two tiny, landlocked, densely populated, and extremely fertile African countries are tucked away. Devoid of the natural resources plentiful on the territory of their big neighbor, the Congo, excluded from major continental trade routes, poor in infrastructure, of difficult mountainous terrain, and of no strategic importance, Rwanda and Burundi remained largely unknown at the international stage. But in 1994, the tiny Rwanda, country of Thousand Hills, became, after the Holocaust and the Cambodian Killing Fields, the place of the third largest genocide in the XX Century.

This chapter shows the background and the record of UN military involvement in Rwanda prior, during, and after the genocide there. It looks into the daunting question of a virtual paralysis of the UN mission in the face of an evil unleashed with a stunning openness.[1] The little-known but intimate involvement in Rwanda of one of the Big Powers is also highlighted.

IN THE BACKGROUND OF THE UN INVOLVEMENT

Ruanda–Urundi, as the territory had been known within German East Africa at the end of the nineteenth century, was populated by three ethnic groups: the Hutu who made the majority of about 85 percent; the Tutsi who accounted for about 12 percent; and the Twas, the original inhabitants, pygmy hunters, who made up the remaining 3 percent. Tutsi were newcomers who took power and ruled the territory under an absolute king, Mwami. In the Big War of the White People in 1914–1918, the losing Germans applied a scorched-earth tactic and left behind a territory deliberately devastated. The new masters, the Belgians, ruled there from 1918 to 1962 under a trusteeship of the League of Nations, later confirmed by the United Nations. They did not change the ethnic arrangements and recognized Tutsi domination. But when traditional ways of life begun to fade away under the modernizing influence of colonialism, the ethnic divisions blurred. The trend was not to the liking of the Belgian administration. The new identity card issued defined the subjects as Hutu or Tutsi, and in case of doubt the issuing officials were equipped with a simple instruction—those with ten cows or more were classified as Tutsi, those with less, as Hutu.[2]

Belgian support for Tutsi was qualified by self-interest. When the White Man's order began to crumble in Africa in the late 1950s, Brussels took cautious steps toward granting independence and changed sides in the process. In the early 60s Tutsi chiefs had been summarily dismissed and replaced by Hutu. Suddenly elevated to the position of power, Hutu indulged in persecution of Tutsi, while Belgium turned a blind-eye. The first exodus from Rwanda brought about 100,000 Tutsi to the Congo, Burundi, Tanzania, and Uganda.

In 1961 a Hutu leader, Gregoire Kayibanda, proclaimed the Republic of Rwanda. Discrimination of Tutsi continued both under his regime and that of his successor, President Juvenal Habyiarimana. In the 80s, the number of refugees reached several hundred thousands. It was from their ranks that a guerilla army under the name of Rwandan Patriotic Front (RPF) came into being. The insurgents launched an offensive from Uganda on October 1, 1990.

The Rwandan regime was weak and its army was not in a better shape. Close to collapse after a few days of fighting, it was saved by a new and powerful ally. Acting upon a treaty on military cooperation, the French launched an intervention. The ostensible purpose of *Noroit* was to protect Europeans, but a clandestine element within it, called *Panda*, provided direct support to the Rwandan army. It was the French against whom the rebels stood no chance. A wave of Hutu persecutions followed and western diplomats reported fears of total extermination among the Tutsi.[3]

RPF launched the next offensive in February 1993. This time both Rwanda and Uganda asked the UN to deploy military observers along the border. In resolution 846 of June 22, 1993, the Security Council asked the parties to the conflict to seek a comprehensive peace agreement. A Canadian general, Romeo A. Dallaire was nominated Chief of the United Nations Observer Mission Uganda–Rwanda (UNOMUR), which in September reached its authorized strength of eighty-one men. As a result of negotiations in Arusha (Tanzania) the parties asked the UN to deploy an international force to assist in implementation of a peace agreement. It called for democratic elections, preceded by a broadly based transitional government, for the return of refugees, and for the creation of an integrated national army.

The SC by resolution 872 established the United Nations Assistance Mission in Rwanda (UNAMIR) on October 5, 1993. It authorized the deployment of

2,548 military personnel and 90 members of the police. Dallaire was nominated Force Commander and Jacques Roger Booh-Booh of Cameroon was appointed the SGSR. UNAMIR's mandate included contributing to the establishment and maintenance of a climate conductive to the secure installation and subsequent operation of the transitional government. The principal functions of the mission were to assist in the security of the capital of Kigali, to monitor the cease-fire agreements, and to establish an expanded demilitarized zone.[4] At the outset of the mission, UNAMIR designated a demilitarized zone and weapon-secure area in Kigali, where it deployed its Belgian and Bangladeshi contingents. More countries joined later and, in the crucial time of the mission it included also troops from Canada, Ghana, Romania, Russia, and Tunisia.

Despite the UN's arrival, early 1994 saw in Kigali an increase of violent demonstrations, roadblocks, assassinations of political leaders, and the killing of civilians. UNAMIR was understaffed and under-equipped. Battalions were without crew, weapons, and vehicles; the small armored personnel carrier fleet lacked spare parts and mechanics. There was neither an administrative nor a logistical system to employ the Force rapidly or to react to a crisis.[5] The only well-equipped members of UNAMIR were the 350 Belgian paratroopers who had their own armored personnel carriers, helicopters, and a transport aircraft. The Bangladeshis lacked even essential items and went hungry because they arrived without 60 days self-sustainment supplies.[6] Meanwhile, signs multiplied of more bloodbaths to come.

IGNORED WARNING SIGNS

Western diplomats had reported fears of a total extermination of the Tutsi after the failed rebel offensive in 1990.[7] Those who did not see the looming disaster themselves might have heeded the warnings of the Force's Commander, who had been told that the President could no longer control the extremists and that, as a result of intricate conspiracies, a Rwandan "Gang of Four" had emerged. It consisted of Agathe Kazinga, the President's wife and her three brothers, also known as the *Clan de Madame* or Akuzu. The Clan organized a network of determined followers in all key positions in the country, ready to act when the time was ripe.[8]

Dallaire reported this information in a cable of January 11, 1994, to General Maurice Baril in the UN Headquarters. Sent by the Prime Minister Designate, Faustin Twaguramungu, and identified later as Jean-Pierre, Dallaire's informant was a top-level trainer in the Interahamwe militia, the youth branch of the presidential political party. He disclosed a following plan: First, force the Belgian UN contingent to withdraw through targeted killing of its soldiers. Second, Interahamwe militia had trained 1,700 people and distributed them in groups of 40 throughout Kigali. All Tutsi had been registered and arrangements had been made to kill a thousand people every 20 minutes. Third, there was a major weapons cache in Kigali, ready for distribution. In return for a safe passage out of Rwanda, the informer was ready to disclose its location.

Dallaire informed the UN Headquarters that it was his intention to act within the next 36 hours. He requested guidance from the Secretariat as to how to proceed on the protection of the informant, but not on other actions he might take. There are conflicting accounts as to who read the cable in New York and when, but the Secretariat's reaction was quick and clear. It did not approve either the seizing of the cache of arms or the protection of the informant. The overriding concern of the Secretariat was the need to avoid actions that may lead to the use of force. Nothing was going to change that bedrock principle.

Dallaire was also told to pass the information received to President Habyiarimana and to the ambassadors of Belgium, France, and the United States.[9] Meetings took place with the president accompanied by leaders of an extremist political party. The only result was that a good 3 months before the beginning of the massacres, those preparing the genocide were forewarned.

Four years later, Annan, the Undersecretary General in charge of peacekeeping operations at that time, acknowledged Dallaire's cable, but stressed that it was only one component in a mass of information received, and noted that decisions were not taken on the strength of a single cable.[10] Perhaps. But the parliamentary inquiry in Brussels found 19 documents that mentioned either plans for destabilization or the likelihood of large-scale massacres in Rwanda. The inquiry established clearly that not only Belgians, but also French, Americans, and the United Nations had very specific information at least 3 months in advance. In short, there was compelling evidence that mass murder, if not genocide, was being prepared.[11] Yet Colin Keating, New Zealand's President of the SC at the time of the Rwandan crisis, was apparently not aware of Dallaire's information until 2 years later.[12] The sinister scenario of events disclosed to Dallaire by Jean-Pierre acquired the inevitability of a Greek tragedy.

FACING THE FINAL SOLUTION—THE HUTU VERSION

In resolution 909 of April 5 the SC encouraged the parties to the conflict to maintain their dialogue and extended UNAMIR's mandate till July 27, 1994.[13] On the next day the Presidents of Rwanda and Burundi were returning by air from a regional summit meeting in Dar es Salaam. On its approach to the Kigali airport the aircraft was shot down, killing everyone on board. Inexplicably, no one—not Rwanda, Burundi, the UN, or France, which donated the aircraft—initiated an official investigation.[14]

The death of Habyiarimana triggered the beginning of the Hutu version of the "final solution." Immediately after the crash the radio station *Mille Collines* called for the death of the leader to be avenged. Roadblocks went up, a curfew was introduced, and telephone lines cut. The carnage began in Kigali and spread like a bushfire to the rest of the country. According to the UN sources:

> ... civilian men, women, and children were shot down, blown up by rockets or grenades, hacked to death by machete or burned alive. Many were attacked in the churches where they sought refuge. Tens of thousands of bodies were hurled down into the rivers and carried down the stream. The genocide claimed between 500,000 and one million victims, mainly Tutsi, but also "moderate" Hutu, including the intellectuals supposed to sympathize with Tutsi. The killers included members of the Rwandan government forces, but in the main were drawn from the Presidential Guard and the youth militias, primarily Interahamwe, recruited and formed by the late President's party.[15]

Important actors are missing in this description, though. Without the ordinary Hutu, the man on the street, the neighbor, the killing on such a scale could not have occurred in such a short time. Mass killing involved a mass participation. The country's Hutus run amok. But the carnage seemed to have followed a carefully elaborated script. Degni-Segui, dean of Abidjan University, concluded that the massacres were a preplanned and systematically coordinated campaign of genocide. Habyiarimana's death was the excuse, not the cause of the killings.[16]

The UN considered the killing fields in Rwanda from the offices in the glass tower in Manhattan and from the close range in the field. The perspective shifted with geography, but the attitudes were similar, if not identical: nothing could have been done either to prevent the massacres or to stop them. The UN Secretariat could not require UNAMIR to intervene because the SC was not ready to change its mandate and provide reinforcements. UNAMIR's could not do anything, because in the words of its Commander, "Throughout most of this carnage, UNAMIR's hands essentially remained tied."[17]

Dallaire and Booh-Booh wanted a moderate Hutu leader, the Prime Minister Agathe Uwilingiyimana, to address the nation on the radio but she was dismissed by a group of extremists and murdered on the same day of April 7, as were the Belgian UN soldiers sent to protect her. Like Patrice Lumumba, she was murdered in presence of the UN troops in a country that had invited them to keep the peace. The murder of the courageous women along with the UN soldiers sent to protect her, as described by an inquiry ordered by Annan, is an eloquent contribution to the appraisal of the UNAMIR's mission.[18]

In the small morning hours of April 7, 1994, a group of ten Belgian paratroopers led by Lt. Lotin was dispatched from the airport to the Prime Minister's residence to increase the number of guards. At about 7.00 a.m. Lotin informed his commander by phone that he was surrounded by twenty armed soldiers of the Rwandese Government Forces (RGF) with guns and grenades, who wanted the Belgians to surrender. Colonel Devez told him not to do so and repeated it one and half hours later, asking Lotin to negotiate. Lotin replied he no longer could do so, because four of his men were already disarmed. Now the surrender was authorized, the Belgians were disarmed and taken to Camp Kigali. Calling Devez from there, Lotin said that he feared murder. Devez passed that information to his Sector Commander who asked the RGF (whose members had detained his men) and the UN Bangladeshi battalion to intervene. He could not know that at the same time the Bangladeshi government's representative was calling Annan to ask for the safety of his country's soldiers in Kigali to be assured.

The Force's Commander was also on the phone. At 9.20 a.m. Dallaire called New York and told Iqbal Riza, Assistant SG for Peacekeeping Operations, that UNAMIR might have to use force to save the PM. Riza confirmed that UNAMIR was not to fire until fired upon. He thus effectively confirmed the death sentence passed over Madame Agathe by the Kigali henchmen. She was shot dead less than an hour after Riza's ordered Dallaire not to intervene. Riza could not know that even if he had authorized the use of force it would be already too late, because the Belgians had surrendered already.

Following the first message from Lotin no one had moved a finger except to dial his superiors. Meanwhile, the paratroopers have been badly beaten in the presence of the UN military observers stationed in Camp Kigali; later, after the observers were kicked out of the Camp, the Belgians were brutally murdered—the UN inquiry stated.

Dallaire admitted that from a car he saw a couple of soldiers in Belgian uniforms on the ground in Camp Kigali, but did not know if they were injured or dead. The general ordered the car to stop, but the driver refused. He happened to be a major of RGF whose members had killed the Belgian soldiers Dallaire was looking at. The Force's Commander used a RGF vehicle and driver after being ordered out of his own UN vehicle. He did not learn about the death of his men until about 15 hours after their detention. Later he insisted that an armed operation to rescue the Belgians had not been feasible because of the high risk of casualties and a high potential for failure.

As the bloodbath begun on April 7, a number of other prominent Rwandan personalities were killed or kidnapped, while the UNAMIR troops assigned to protect them fled, looked away, or even socialized with the executioners.[19] Thousands of civilians seeking UN protection at the compound of the *Ecole Technique Officielle* were massacred after being abandoned by the UNAMIR troops stationed there. Captain Luc Lamaire from the Belgian contingent, who was in charge of that compound, testified that people begged to be shot by the Belgians rather than be hatched to death by machetes. Lamaire tried to disguise the departure of his unit under the pretext of a routine mission, but when the terrified people saw through that mischief and blocked the exit from the compound, shots were fired in the air. As soon the UN soldiers were outside the gate, the massacre started.[20]

The presence of the UN troops implied protection and made the potential victims highly visible to their persecutors. The pretence of protection came dangerously close to complicity in murder. On the margin of the killing orgies,

UNAMIR managed to save a few thousand people but while "The rivers were full of corpses when I arrived," according to Dallaire,[21] there were many more when he left. But no one was to blame; the UN peacekeeping policy of not firing unless fired upon had been upheld at every level of the operation.

The carnage went unabated for 2 weeks before the SC took up the subject of Rwanda again. However, some of the UN members acted swiftly on their own. The Belgian government called for reinforcements of the mission only to be told by Ghali that the SC had no stomach for intervention.[22] The Belgians decided to withdraw.

But as some Belgians were about to leave, others arrived. The kingdom was sending paratroopers to evacuate its nationals and other Europeans. They were followed by a second French military intervention in Rwanda, code-named *Amaryllis*, charged ostensibly with a similar task. The widow of the French ally, President Habyiarimana, left on the first French aircraft leaving Kigali. She was not alone. Apart from a few hundred French nationals and other Europeans, 394 Hutus were evacuated. But Tutsi employees of the French Embassy in Kigali were left behind to face certain death. As Lamaire testified, the French have been applauded by the Hutu militias and by the Rwandan government forces and gendarmes.[23] None of the newcomers had been authorized to intervene in the ongoing massacres. People clutching to the vehicles of the French and Belgian paratroopers were being intercepted by Hutu militias and massacred on the spot. Moreover, UNAMIR's function changed overnight from peacekeeping to assisting in evacuation of expatriates. Captain Lamaire and his unit, who abandoned refugees at the school to their death, were among the helpers.[24]

When the SC took up the Rwandan crisis again on April 21, hundreds of thousands of people had already been killed. General Baril, a military adviser in the Department of Peacekeeping Operations (DPKO) and a member the same French Canadian brigade as Dallaire, warned the members of the Council that the UN troops could not hold out much longer. The main problem for the UN in Kigali was lack of food for 16,000 fugitives seeking UN protection and for 2,000 UN soldiers bogged down in the surrounding chaos and violence. Ghali presented three options to the Council—total withdrawal, reinforcement, or a token force left behind. The last option was adopted on April 21 in resolution 912, which the President of Tanzania, Ali Hassan Mwinye, aptly designated as the most disastrous decision that body ever took.[25] Apart from the permanent Big Five— United States, China, France, Russia, and the United Kingdom—the following countries supported the resolution: Argentina, Brazil, Czechoslovakia, Djibutti, Nigeria, New Zealand, Oman, Pakistan, Spain, and Rwanda. A representative of the murderous gang that had seized power in Kigali participated in the Council deliberations in the full rights of a member. Thus, he was able to inform his masters that they could go about their business of slaughtering Tutsi without risking any outside intervention.

In addition to reducing the strength of UNAMIR from 2,548 to 270 men, the Council also decided to adjust UNAMIR's mandate. The Forces main task was now to act as an intermediary between the parties in an attempt to secure a cease-fire. Contribution to security in Kigali was no more on its agenda.

The disastrous resolution 912 closes the first chapter of UN involvement in Rwanda. But after the expatriates were evacuated, French troops were to come once more.

THE FRENCH CONNECTION'S FINALE

There was an air of an undeniable intimacy in the French involvement in Rwanda. The plane shot down over Kigali with the president of the country on board was a gift to him from an adviser of the French government on African affairs, who happened to be Jean-Christopher Mitterand, the son of the President of France. When the catastrophe triggered a bloody military coup d'état, some of the members of the Habyiarimana regime installed themselves in the French Embassy in Kigali and formed an interim government of Rwanda, recognized by France alone. And two and half months after the beginning of the massacres the French government offered to undertake a French-commanded multinational operation to assure the security and protection of displaced persons and civilians at risk. But at that juncture the displaced persons were mostly Hutu, including the perpetrators of the genocide, fleeing from the advancing RPF units. And most of the Tutsi were at no risk anymore. They were dead already.

The SC gratefully accepted the French offer and by resolution 929 of June 22 gave the expedition enforcement powers under Chapter VII of the Charter but kept it independent from UNAMIR. The French representative at the UN claimed that his troops could not have joined UNAMIR, because the latter was not any more perceived as neutral.[26] In fact, the opposite was true. UNAMIR was neutral ad nauseam, while the French were allies of the embattled extremist government. They descended on Rwanda the next day, and the *Operation Turquoise* began. It reached the strength of about 3,000 men, including some 500 troops from Chad, Senegal, Guinea–Bissau, Mauritania, Egypt, Niger, and Congo (Brazzaville) and lasted 2 months.

French politicians and the operation's Commander, General Jean-Claude Lafourcade, insisted that the principle of impartiality had been strictly followed. In fact, RPF opposed the French intervention, claiming that those who helped to put the massacres in motion should not be the ones to stop them. There were several skirmishes between RPF units and contingents of *Turquoise* at the outskirts of the humanitarian protection zone unilaterally declared by the French in the triangle Ciyangugu–Kibuye–Gikongoro in southwestern Rwanda.

Its establishment has saved some Tutsi, who had survived on the territory of the zone, but the main result of *Turquoise* was to arrest the advance of RPF forces. RGF and other elements involved in the genocide could therefore escape total defeat and retreat to Zaire with thousands of Hutu who feared revenge. On the remaining territory, the RPF took Kigali on July 4. Two weeks later, it established its control over the last stronghold of the interim government in Gisenyi. Shortly after, the RPF declared a unilateral cease-fire. By then the humanitarian catastrophe reached apocalyptic proportions; out of a total population of approximately 7 million, a million had been killed. Three million had been displaced within Rwanda and more than 2 million had fled to neighboring countries, with about three-quarters going to Zaire.

The Commander of *Turquoise* declared it a success achieved due to the liberty of action granted by the SC, which authorized it to "use all necessary means"; to a unified national command; and to an effective deterrent capacity of 700 vehicles, 13 helicopters, and 12 combat aircraft. General Lafourcade said that overwhelming force was never applied, but the mere threat of using aircraft was helpful in halting the RPF advance. Questioned as to whether the flight of those responsible for the massacres was facilitated under his operation, the general responded that arresting these individuals was not in the UN mandate. Addressing another query, he explained that it was false to think about the victims of genocide as killed by French arms supplied to the Rwandan government, because the militias were mostly equipped with non-French-made machetes, which were used in most of the killings.[27]

Strategically the main result of *Operation Turquoise* was to allow the civilian and military Hutu extremist leaders and their cohorts to flee to Zaire and to rebuild a power base among hundreds of thousands of refugees herded together in camps.

POST-GENOCIDE UN PRESENCE

Ghali used the term "genocide" in the Rwandan context for the first time on May 4, 1994. He also warned that if the UN did not act quickly, it might later be accused of passivity. The warning came from the same man who, 2 weeks ago, had proposed—and got approved—reductions in UNAMIR's mandate and strength. On May 17 with resolution 918, the SC, in an entirely empty gesture, imposed an arms embargo on Rwanda. It also authorized the expansion of UNAMIR to 5,500 troops and extended the mandate to enable the mission to contribute to the security and protection of refugees and civilians at risk, through means including the establishment and maintenance of secure humanitarian areas and the provision of security for relief operations to the degree possible.[28] The operative word was "to the degree possible." Contrary to the French operation, the extended UNAMIR did not enjoy the Chapter's VII authorization.

In Rwanda it was easier to reduce the strength of the UN Force than to beef it up again. When Ghali approached the 19 countries which had pledged a total of 31,000 troops for future peacekeeping operations under the UNSAS system, not even one agreed to contribute.[29] While *Turquoise* landed the day after the SC resolution authorizing the operation, UNAMIR took 5 months to reach the authorized strength of 5,500. It took about 10 months to deploy 89 police observers, out of which only 25 spoke French, the official language of Rwanda. Shaharyar

M. Khan of Pakistan became the new SRSG and General Guy Tousignant from Canada replaced his countryman, Dallaire, as the Force's Commander.

The peacekeepers' main tasks were to ensure stability and security in western Rwanda, to stabilize and monitor the situation throughout the country, to encourage the return of displaced persons, to provide support and security for the humanitarian organizations, and to promote, through mediation and good offices, national reconciliation in Rwanda.[30] But the Tutsi-led, victorious RPF was not much interested in the good services of the UN. Neither were the Hutu extremists lurking among the masses of the refugee in Zaire where from they mounted armed incursions into Rwanda. Both parties held UNAMIR in contempt. Its presence after the genocide had been marred by inability to facilitate the resolution of the enormous refugee crisis both inside and outside of the country and by the increasing hostility of the new regime.

Between February and May 1995 the security situation deteriorated and the new government restricted UNAMIR's freedom of movement, including the Kigali airport; its forces searched and seized UN vehicles and equipment and supported anti-UN demonstrations. The new masters of Rwanda simply wanted the mission to leave. The Rwandan ambassador to the UN explained that "the UN did nothing to prevent the massacres and they even did not assist people in danger, so it is not surprising that people do not like to see them enjoying themselves now."[31] But the SC wanted UNAMIR to stay and suggested its mandate to shift from peacekeeping to confidence building. Reduced in size, and restricted to nonmilitary functions, UNAMIR continued its uneasy presence for sometime yet, but the Rwandans insisted that while the UN assistance in rehabilitation and reconstruction was welcome, its military presence was not. The SC by resolution 1029 of December 12, 1995, decided to terminate UNAMIR's mission as of March 8, 1996. A few days later, the Canadian UN Force's Commander left the mission and an Indian general, Shiva Kumar, was nominated acting Commander.

Upon his departure the Indian declared to be proud of what UNAMIR had achieved. There was little that any force or a stronger mandate could have done to prevent the bloodletting, he added.[32] Satisfaction on the departure was also expressed from the other side, albeit for different reasons. Paul Kagame, the Vice-President of Rwanda and its Minister of Defense, a graduate from Fort Leavenworth, Kansas, when asked how he felt about the UNAMIR's departure responded: "It means a lot of good things. It means we have done away with the false hopes, the false sense of security the UN has given us since the genocide. They have been basking in the sunshine, burning fuel, doing nothing, and receiving credit for creating this peaceful environment. We do not accept that. We are happy they are gone."[33]

UN FORCE'S COMMANDER TESTIFIES BEFORE A TRIBUNAL

General Dallaire defended his mission on several public occasions and was successful in doing so. His reasoning that UNAMIR lacked both the mandate and means to do anything to stop the genocide has been generally accepted. On the material side there is no doubt; the Force was understaffed and underequipped, even if the superiority of a UN rifle to a Hutu machete should not be forgotten. But the question of mandate is not that clear. The mandate's diplomatic language had to be translated for the benefit of the military men into ROE. In his long and emotional testimony at the UN International Criminal Tribunal for Rwanda (ICTR), Dallaire made contradictory statements concerning his mandate and ROE.[34]

According to the UN inquiry, his draft of ROE, submitted to New York for approval on November 23, 1993, included in paragraph 17 a rule specifically allowing the mission to use force in response to crimes against humanity and other abuses. "There may also be ethnically or politically motivated criminal acts committed during this mandate which will morally and legally require UNAMIR to use all available means to halt them," he wrote in the draft. "Examples" he continued "are executions, attacks on displaced persons or refugees." Headquarters never responded formally to Dallaire's request for the ROE's approval, but Baril told the inquiry that he considered the draft a good one. He also said that Headquarters did not have a procedure in place for ROE's approval. Therefore, in absence of any reaction, the Force Commander must have considered the ROE implicitly approved and in effect. The inquiry considered such a conclusion reasonable. Moreover, as the general testified, the ROE was accepted by all UNAMIR's contingents with some minor amendments made by the Belgians. The same draft of the ROE was sent to New York again after the genocide began and the UN Headquarters did not object to paragraph 17 concerning the crimes against humanity.[35]

At a session of the ICTR, Nicholas Tiangaye, defense attorney for Jean-Paul Akayesu, suggested that if the United Nations was unable to end the massacres, government authorities could not have been expected to do so. "Why did UNAMIR not apply Article 17?" —he asked. Dallaire responded, "'I did not order offensive operations ... because I was not, fundamentally, neither equipped nor provided with enough supplies, neither was I fundamentally mandated and this was confirmed to me by my superiors." The general added that "... neither did I have the right to give them (his soldiers) the order to systematically attack those who were carrying out the killings or massacres."[36]

In effect, the general disregarded his own ROE. Admitting that, from the moral point of view, he had the right to give the order to attack those who were carrying out the massacres, Dallaire added, "if you look at my mandate of 5 October you would not see any reference ... to write what I wrote under paragraph 17 ..." Finally, Dallaire pointed out to the Tribunal that "... on the evening of 7 April, technically speaking, (because of the breakdown of the cease-fire) I no longer had a mandate and ... I could simply have ordered that people should pack up and leave."[37]

Thus, contrary to the solemn protestations by the UN, its troops in Rwanda were in fact authorized to use force in response to crimes against humanity. No one in the UN withdrew or contradicted his ROE, but the Force's Commander disregarded them himself. The general repeated before the Tribunal his claim that with a force of 5,000 men he might have been able to stop the genocide. Thus, a question poses itself—why if 5,000 men would be able effectively oppose the killers, a half of that number of soldiers at the disposal of UNAMIR could not confront them at all?[38] At other occasions the general claimed that as little as 1,500 additional men and a clear mandate would be sufficient for bringing the unleashed violence under control.[39]

But the crux of the matter is not in numbers. It is in strategy, tactics, and the resolve of men on the ground to take risks in defense of their mission and in protection of the lives of men, women, and children in mortal danger. It appeared that the members of UNAMIR were not prepared to do much. One of them remembered a street scene in Kigali seen from the balcony of UNAMIR's headquarters: ". . . he just held him by his shirt and started dragging him . . . and just raised the machete and hacked him in the head. After that he just rubbed his bloodstained machete on his buttocks and then searched his pockets . . . we all screamed at this. Not long after . . . there was a tipper truck (dump truck) . . . detailed to collect bodies from the street."[40]

Even the most underequipped military contingents dispose of means more persuasive than their vocal chords. In Rwanda they choose to use the latter only, hedging behind the artifices of peacekeeping doctrine and a muddy mandate. Referring to Dallaire's instructions from the UN headquarters preventing UNAMIR from using force under any circumstances, a French general, Christian Quesnot, former Chief of the Presidential Staff, observed that knowing when to disobey is for military men a matter of honor.[41] But the old-fashioned term went out of use in discussions of military matters ages ago and did not appear in the Rwandan context either.

WHAT HAPPENED TO THE UN IN RWANDA?

In a clear break with the long tradition of UN infallibility, Annan, released a report of the "Independent Inquiry into the Actions of the United Nations during the 1994 Genocide in Rwanda."[42] For the first time, an independent inquiry, led by the former Prime Minister of Sweden, Ingvar Carlsson, sought to establish the truth about the role of the United Nations in a failed peacekeeping mission. Serious mistakes and errors of the UN Secretariat which are part of that truth are mitigated in the report by the generalizations referring to the debacle in Rwanda as a failure by the United Nations system as a whole and a lack of political will by the international community. Neither the doctrine of peacekeeping nor the responsibilities of individuals is raised up. While examples of appalling failures are not lacking in the report, its appraisal of the role of the UN Force is ambiguous. The inquiry claims that a force numbering 2,500 should have been able to stop or at least limit massacres, but at the same time asserts that the peacekeepers who remained throughout the genocide, including the Force Commander, deserve recognition for their efforts. Like no other mission, Rwanda illustrated the tragic results of a narrow interpretation of peacekeeping doctrine and of the mission mandate prevailing over the principles of the UN Charter and over the basic human impulses. In no other mission had the false hopes of UN protection ended in so many deaths. UNAMIR's efforts in support of cease-fire between RGF and RPF after the genocide began were counterproductive since the latter was the only force willing, and probably capable, of stopping the massacres. Moreover, the failure to dismantle the Hutu killing machine, whose members evacuated from Rwanda under the cover of *Operation Turquoise*, brought further destabilization in the region of the Great Lakes in another civil war in Congo (former Zaire) that eventually involved five other African countries—Angola, Namibia, Rwanda, Uganda, and Zimbabwe. Ultimately, Rwanda provided a clear case for a nonintervention being less harmful than an ill conceived and poorly executed peacekeeping mission.

In face of monstrous crimes against humanity the UN failed unequivocally and deplorably. The all too common disadvantages of its mission, such as delayed deployment of troops and other capacity and logistic problems are not sufficient for an explanation of a failure of that scale. Neither is performance of the military men involved, even if the passive attitude they had adopted was evidently not the only option available. The reasons for that failure are to be sought in the doctrine of peacekeeping and in the attitudes of United Nations' Security Council and Secretariat. UNAMIR was established only 3 days after a debacle in Mogadishu, where the U.S. Rangers had lost eighteen men killed, seventy-five wounded, and two helicopters shot down. It was in the shadow of Somalia, that the United States initially opposed any mission to Rwanda and dropped its opposition only under the assumption that the mission would be small, inexpensive, and safe for a success. The UN needed such an outcome and conveniently believed that Rwanda was promising it. In doing so it ignored Rwanda's recent history of persistent ethnic hatreds, persecutions, and civil wars.[43] Ignoring the current experience from Cambodia, ex-Yugoslavia, and Somalia, where peace agreements and cease-fires were trampled upon, the UN took at face value the Arusha peace agreement between the Rwandan government and the RPF. Not for the first time, the UN appeared to believe in an overoptimistic scenario. When it began to unravel sooner that UNAMIR became fully operational on the ground, the Secretariat did nothing to alert the Council to the realities of the conflict and to a looming disaster.

Given the monstrosity of what happened in Rwanda, the admitted errors of omission can hardly be accepted for a sufficient explanation. Unfortunately, the Secretariat did not seem to encourage those who would like to have a closer look at the roots of its failure.[44] But Michael Barnett argues that an understandable temptation to accuse it of incompetence and cynicism, or both, should be resisted before looking at available alternatives. He feels that disclosure of full information about Rwanda in early 1994 involved a risk of the Security Council adjusting UNAMIR's mandate to a more robust one, without providing means to discharge it. Safe areas in Bosnia, established by the Council in May 1993 are a case in question.[45] A shift in UNAMIR's role without beefing it up considerably might have had involved, in the Secretariats view, risks of high casualties without any guarantee of a success of the operation. Thus, argues Barnett, in opposing an intervention in Rwanda the Secretariat was guided by situated responsibilities and grounded in ethical considerations. More UN casualties in another failure in Rwanda was a risk too high for the organization already overextended and damaged at other peacekeeping fronts. That risk should have been averted because UN responsibilities to the world are larger than Rwanda.[46] But if this was the main line of thinking at the UN glass tower in Manhattan, it proved that the shadows of Yugoslavia and Somalia reached too far. Contrary to the belligerents in these countries, the forces preparing and committing genocide in Rwanda were militarily weak and excelled only in terrorizing and extermination of civilians.

Whatever were the motives of the UN diplomats and of the men in the field, Rwanda exposed all of them to be hostages of their own, most restrictive interpretation of what the United Nations peacekeeping is about. In effect they betrayed Rwandan people and disgraced the organization. The Secretary General was responsible for not disclosing full information about the crisis in a way that might either persuade killers in Kigali to abandon their plans or shame the UN members into counteraction. The disgrace of Rwanda would not have taken place had the UN given its own mission an executive mandate, similar to the one granted to the *Operation Turquise*, to equip it accordingly, and had the men in the field followed their own rules of engagement.

The Predictable Disaster (ex-Yugoslavia)

THERE IS NOTHING INEVITABLE about a country's going to war unless it is attacked. Yugoslavia, best-known by the millions of tourists for the beauty of its landscape and for the independence of the local communists from the Eastern Bloc, had not been invaded by anyone. The enemy was within. The examples of the Soviet Union and Czechoslovakia showed that even the most radical changes of the constitutional order of multiethnic states were possible without restoring to the use of force. The inability of Yugoslav leaders to find a political solution to a constitutional crisis had been reinforced by a confused international response of uncoordinated diplomatic initiatives and by the pretence of a military intervention. The result was a resurrection of the horrors of World War II at the doorsteps of affluent Western European democracies. The multifaceted and complex wars, which lasted more than 4 years, ended with the humiliation of the United Nations peacekeepers, the destruction of a multiethnic Bosnia and Herzegovina, and the *de facto* confirmation of the results of the ethnic cleansing. After the decisive involvement of the United States on the diplomatic front, the largest UN peacekeeping operation ever had been replaced by a no less massive deployment of NATO troops. This chapter focuses on the performance of the UN international military contingents in reaching the proclaimed goals of the intervention: protection of the UN Protected Areas in Croatia, protection of humanitarian convoys, and deterrence of attacks on safe areas in Bosnia and Herzegovina. The history of the multiple wars in Yugoslavia and of the massive international diplomatic efforts to reach a political settlement will be discussed only when relevant to these UN peacekeeping objectives.

BREAKING UP A FEDERATION

Slovenia

The first war in Europe since the end of the Second World War started on June 27, 1991, when the Yugoslav People's Army (JNA) entered Slovenia and the Yugoslavs started to kill each other. The Yugoslav Federation consisted of six republics: Bosnia and Herzegovina, Croatia, Macedonia, Montenegro, Serbia, and Slovenia, which was more ethnically homogenous than the other. On June 25, 1991, Croatia and Slovenia had unilaterally declared independence, and the Slovene Territorial Defense Force took over control of the airport in Brnik (Lubljana), the port in Koper, and of the border crossings. From the disintegrating center of the federal power in Belgrade the JNA was called to restore law and order. The Commanders of the Fifth Army District in Zagreb informed the Slovenes that a force of 2,000 troops, accompanied by 400 policemen and 270 federal customs officers, would reestablish the federal authority by means of a limited policing action. They did not expect armed resistance and were not ready for it. Upon learning that the army was moving into Slovenia in the early hours, the Slovene President, Milan Kucan, called the Federal Prime Minister Ante Markovic, who apparently did not know anything, and advised him to talk to the Fifth Army directly.[1] Kucan did so only to be told to calm down and go back to sleep. He went to his office instead and convened a meeting of the Slovene leadership, which reached the conclusion to resist by force what they considered an aggression.

The Slovene territorial units surrounded the JNA barracks, cut off the water, electricity, and telephone lines, and erected roadblocks and barricades. In the afternoon, an unarmed JNA helicopter was shot down over the center of Ljubljana, killing both occupants.[2] They were the first victims of what would become the first of the bloody wars for independence from the Serb-dominated Yugoslavia. The war in Slovenia lasted only 10 days and left 44 members of the intervening army killed. Slovenian casualties were four men, making a ratio 1:10, an unusual outcome in favor of the victim of an aggression.[3]

In early July at a meeting on the island of Brioni, in the former residence of the Yugoslav dictator Tito, an agreement between Slovenia and Yugoslavia brokered by the European Union, paved the way for Slovenia's secession. If the Slovenes truly wanted independence, they had shown that war might be the shortest and surest way to get it. Their option for war had been rewarded and the result hailed as a success of the European diplomacy.[4]

JNA withdrew to Croatia, where it begun to serve more and more openly as a tool of aggressive Serb nationalism.

Croatia

Croatia's declaration of independence aroused deep anxiety among the sizable Serbian minority in the republic. In some of the regions, especially in Krajina, they constituted a majority. But the Constitution of December 1990 referred to Croatia as the national state of the Croatian people and the state of members of other nationalities and minorities, which are its citizens. Thus, Croatian independence was perceived by the Serbs living on its territory as radically changing their status from being a part of a constituent nation in Yugoslavia to being a minority in Croatia. The clash of interests was obvious. With national emotions on the rise, many of the Croatian Serbs were likely to think as Vladimir Grigorov, son of the President of Macedonia, did. "Why" he asked, "should I be a minority in your state when you can be a minority in mine?"[5]

The newly proclaimed republic was suspected of links to the fascist puppet state established by the Nazis under Ante Pavelic's regime, which was responsible for murder of hundreds of thousands people, mostly Serbs and Jews. The adoption of traditional Croatian symbols appropriated by that regime also lent credibility to the propaganda emanating from Belgrade about the Serb people being under a direct existential threat again.[6]

The attitudes of the Croatian authorities toward the Serb minority were ambivalent. Promised civil rights in the new Constitution, the Serbs experienced abrupt dismissals from important positions, especially in the police forces, and difficulties in obtaining citizenship.[7] Appeals from Zagreb for a peaceful resolution of the emerging conflicts fell on deaf ears and the Serb communities followed self-appointed leaders who chose confrontation with the new republic. Under a surface of spontaneity there was a meticulous plotting. In 1990 a clandestine group of the Serb officers of the Yugoslav army, among them a colonel named Ratko Mladic, drafted a plan called RAM for establishment of Greater Serbia by force, if need be. In early summer 1991, Mladic became Chief of Staff of the Knin Corps of JNA in Croatia. The Serbs declared the "Serb Republic of Krajina" with Knin its capital. Since summer of 1990 a rebellion against Croatia built up from local Serb uprisings to a full-scale war.[8]

In Yugoslavia's dirty wars for land and power the JNA escalated since August 1991 from support of the Serb paramilitaries to open assaults on major Croatian towns. It acted with a brutality of which the wanton destruction of Vukovar followed by the executions of its defenders and the senseless shelling of the historical port of Dubrovnik became symbols. As a result of the hostilities, by November 1992 there were some 600,000 refugees in Croatia and a lesser number in Serbia and Montenegro.

Militarily weak, the President of Croatia, Franjo Tjudman, desperately sought political support abroad and international recognition of his republic. He had found a powerful ally in the recently reunited Germany. In support of the Croatians, the German Foreign Minister, Hans-Dietrich Genscher, broke with the European Union that was against the selective recognition of Slovenia and Croatia, as was the UN Secretary General, Javier Perez de Cuellar.[9] The presidents of Bosnia and Herzegovina and Macedonia also warned that recognition would widen the conflict.

The opponents of selective recognition argued that it would trigger a chain reaction culminating in a war in Bosnia. Genscher, however, was convinced that recognition of Croatia was necessary to end the war in that country.[10] Berlin's insistence carried the rest of the EU, which recognized the two republics on January 15, 1992.

The war in Croatia ended soon after its recognition but the end of major hostilities coincided with the Serbs reaching their territorial goals. The war in Bosnia was only 3 months away and the fact of the recognition of its independence by the EU and United States on April 7, 1992, did nothing to prevent the Serbs from beginning and then continuing the slaughter in the unfortunate country for the next 3 years.

Bosnia and Herzegovina

The controversy over the impact of the selective recognition of Croatia and Slovenia on the outbreak of the war in Bosnia cannot now be resolved but hypothetically. Richard Holbrooke's assessment seems to be, however, closest to the realities of that time: "The German decision probably hastened the outbreak of war in Bosnia, but the conflict would have occurred anyway once it was clear that the West would not intervene. To blame Bonn alone for causing the war in Bosnia evades responsibility of many others."[11]

Alone among the six Yugoslav republics, Bosnia and Herzegovina did not have any absolute ethnic majority in its population. It was a mini Yugoslavia itself: 43.7 percent were Muslims, 31.3 percent Serbs, and 17.3 percent Croats; the remaining part was Jews, Roma, Turks, and "Yugoslavs."[12] The mosaic of nationalities existed all over the territory of the republic.[13] Bosnia, which never was an independent state before, was viable only under a consensus existing among the major ethnic groups, but such a consensus was missing from the outset of the Yugoslav crisis. Like in Croatia, the Serbs adamantly opposed to living under any other sovereignty than that of the Serb-dominated Yugoslavia or of an enlarged Serb republic. If the Muslims want to be independent from Belgrade, why the Serbs cannot be independent from the Muslims? After the Croatian experience it was predictable that recognition of independence of Bosnia would trigger another round of "Greater Serbia" ethnic cleansing.[14]

On October 15, 1991, the Bosnian Parliament in Sarajevo declared the independence of the republic with the support of the Muslim and Croat deputies. The Serbs, under the leadership of Radovan Karadzic, walked out before the vote took place. The die was cast. On March 1, 1992, on the request of the European Communities, a referendum on the independence was held. About two-thirds of the population of the republic, including 99 percent of its Muslim and Croat citizens, supported multiethnic, independent Bosnia and Herzegovina.[15] But the Serbs boycotted the referendum and embarked on carving out a territory where they could live on their own. Throughout March, the Serb paramilitaries took over much of the territory of the republic. Still, its President, Alija Izetbegovic insisted that there would be no war, because his side would not fight.[16] But he was forced to, soon.

On April 1, "Arkan's Tigers," a paramilitary unit, experienced in ethnic cleansing in Croatia and led by a Serb wanted by Interpol, descended from Serbia on the strategically important Bijeljina in northeastern Bosnia. Its weak and ill-organized defenders were no match for the attackers. Arkan's men instituted a reign of terror that lasted 2 days, hunting Muslim leaders and summarily executing them. Izetbegovic turned to the JNA for help and the army moved in on April 3, only to help Arkan's gangsters in spreading terror. Izetbegovic then called for mobilization of the territorial defense forces. The Serb responded by attacking the Police Academy in the capital.

Until then, many of Sarajevo's residents hoped that they would be spared a war. Their town had been for centuries a place of tolerance where its nationalities intermingled. On April 5, Sarajevo's citizens protested the madness engulfing Bosnia and Herzegovina. A small crowd swelled to a mass of thousands and marched through the town to show its disregard of barricades and ethnic divisions: Muslims, Serbs, and Croats, all together, waving Yugoslav flags and carrying portraits of Tito. But when the procession came under fire from Serb irregulars, people panicked and dispersed. A young woman, Sauda Diberovic, a medical student in Dubrovnik, was fatally shot in the chest and became the first war victim in Sarajevo.[17]

The Bosnians were not a match for the Serbs. The latter, like their compatriots in Croatia, declared their own republic, Republika Srpska. In a successful blitzkrieg, within 6 weeks they conquered 60 percent of the territory on which they constituted a minority.[18] They were well prepared and determined to deliberately use mass and individual terror for purging the Serb lands from Muslims and Croats. Shelling towns to soften defenses and unleashing paramilitary units to loot and burn houses, to torture and execute men, and to rape and kill women and children, quickly became a pattern. Muslim males were put in concentration camps.[19] There were hundreds of thousands of Muslim and Croat refugees, but there were also thousands of Serb refugees seeking safety among their own kin. Bosnian Croats, who initially supported the Bosnians, later turned the guns against them and created their own mini republic in the south of the country. Both Bosnian and Croatians also committed atrocities against the Serbs and against each other, but on a much smaller scale. That was confirmed by Tadeusz Mazowiecki, who also recognized that ethnic cleansing was not a result of the war unleashed by the Serbs but its goal.[20]

THE INTERNATIONAL RESPONSE

Myriad of abortive diplomatic initiatives related to the war in Yugoslavia could project an impression of a deep interest of the international community in bringing peace to its tortured peoples. But the stark truth is that the European Council of Ministers, who led the international policy on Yugoslavia at that time, not only decided not to intervene militarily to end the war, but publicly declared that they were not prepared to do so. Upheld after the attacks on Vukovar and

Dubrovnik, this policy meant only appeasing the Serbs. Those few who were in favor of intervention were overruled. One of them was a French General, Jean Cot, who later arrived to Zagreb as commander of a UN peacekeeping force. "Along with many others," he wrote, "I am convinced that the Serbs could have been stopped in October 1991 with three ships, three dozen planes and about three thousand men deployed in Dubrovnik and Vukovar to emphasize the unequivocal determination of the European Community."[21]

The United Nations' involvement in the Yugoslavian crisis began with the SC resolution 713 of September 25, 1991, to impose a general and complete embargo on all deliveries of weapons and military equipment to Yugoslavia. Projected as an expression of impartiality in the conflict, the decision benefited Serbs, who had the JNA, the fourth army in Europe, at their disposal. Croatians and Bosnians, who had to organize their defenses from scratch, as well as many independent observers, saw it as passive intervention in favor of the Serbs.[22] Supporters of the embargo argued that arming the Bosnians (and the Croatians) would diminish their readiness to accept peace, prolong war, and increase its casualties. Thus, the international community favored peace, but on terms decided by force.[23]

But the horrors of the war in Yugoslavia, reported daily by the media, caused widespread public outrage. Something had to be done and so the UN SC stepped in again. Peacekeepers were dispatched first to Croatia, and later also into the Bosnian inferno.

PROTECTED AREAS AND PINK ZONES IN CROATIA

The SC in resolution 743 of February 21, 1992, established the United Nations Protection Force (UNPROFOR). It was deployed in areas of Croatia under the Serb control, designated as UN Protected Areas (UNPA) and was later supplemented by "pink zones." Its mandate was in the main to ensure that these areas were demilitarized, through the withdrawal or disbandment of all armed forces in them, and that their residents were protected from any persecution or discrimination and that the civilian displaced persons can safely return home.[24] The UNPAs, divided in four sectors, were established in Western and Eastern Slavonia, and in Krajina. UNPROFOR, under the command of General Satish Nambiar of India, included international troops, military observers, and police and civilian components in the authorized total strength of 13,400 men. By the end of April it had about 8,000 military personnel deployed and its headquarters in Sarajevo. In June, UNPROFOR's functions were extended to pink zones in Croatia and in August border controls were added to its duties.[25]

None of the mandated tasks were fulfilled during the first year of UNPROFOR's deployment and its impotence became even more evident later. It failed to demilitarize the UNPAs and the pink zones and an atmosphere of intimidation and terror exercised by the local Serb forces and paramilitaries toward the remaining Croat population reigned. The UN, unable to control the situation, was itself under control. In Erdut, the headquarters of the Sector East, the UN Belgian contingent had learned who was the master. Led by Arkan, the Tigers, guilty of the Bijeljina and other atrocities, took over the water tower at UNPROFOR's compound for military exercises.[26] UNPROFOR's only achievement was the storage of Serb heavy weaponry under the UN and Serb joint control and a dual lock system.

On January 22, 1993, the Croatians launched a major offensive in the Sector South of UNPROFOR to which the Serbs responded with raiding several UN monitored arsenals and making off with tanks and other heavy armor. Croatian troops shelled UN soldiers near Zmunik and there were French casualties among them.[27] The Serbs turned their wrath for the Croatian assault against the Croats remaining in the UNPAs and pink zones. UNPROFOR, to save their lives, turned to evacuating them to Croatia, helping in the ethnical cleansing, which it was mandated to reverse and prevent. Tjudman claimed rightly that the UN presence contributed merely to maintaining status quo. He insisted that unless UNPROFOR's mandate is not amended to ensure implementation of the SC resolutions, the Force be withdrawn before the end of November. In October the SC in its resolution 871 extended the Force's mandate for 6 months under Chapter VII of the Charter and specifically authorized it to use force in self-defense. The gesture intended to placate the Croats but did not change anything on the ground.

After another half a year of a low-key warfare and hostilities between Croatia and the Serb Republic of Krajina and much of international shuttling to conclude cease-fires, the Croats started talking about getting rid of UNPROFOR again. In a bid for another extension of the mandate, Ghali asked the SC for strengthening the operation by 1,600 men and a helicopter squadron with 200 staff. Despite Croatian misgivings, UNPROFOR's mandate was extended until March 31, 1995, by the SC resolutions 908 and 947.

By now both parties to the conflict ignored UNPROFOR's presence. In November 1994 a battle involving Bosnian Serbs and Muslim rebels in their assault on the UN safe area in Bihac and on Velika Kladusa in Bosnia and Herzegovina raged few miles from the observation posts manned by Polish UNPRPOFOR soldiers. Blocked by the Serbs, the Poles remained in underground shelters. A few months earlier, Croatian refugees protesting UNPROFOR's impotence cut them off from the outside world for several weeks. Only supplies from the air by the UN helicopters allowed them to survive.[28]

In January 1995, Croatia announced that it would not agree to a further extension of the UN mandate. Frantic diplomatic efforts followed under the banner of support for the Force's presence as a vital guarantee of regional peace and security. How an impotent Force could provide that guarantee did not seem to bother the diplomats, but their efforts bore fruits. UNPROFOR was to stay, but under a new name. By resolution 981 the SC established the United Nations Confidence Restoration Operation (UNCRO) with a diluted version of the previous mandate.

On May 1 the Croatian Army launched military offensive in Western Slavonia. It took everyone by surprise and in few days the Serbs were routed while the

Croatians made several incursions into other Sectors. The victors imposed a total restriction of movement on UNCRO for 7 days. Tensions remained high and culminated on August 4, when the Croatian Army launched another massive attack in the sectors North and South of Krajina. It was a real blitzkrieg: Krajina's capital Knin fell on the next day. The fighting spread also to Sector East in Eastern Slavonia. Both sides assaulted the UN soldiers as they pleased, and 98 UN observation posts were overrun and destroyed by the Croatian Army. Its soldiers fired upon the posts, used peacekeepers as human shields, arrested the UN personnel, and confiscated UN equipment. Four peacekeepers were killed and 16 wounded. The UN reported killing and harassment of Serb civilians and burning and looting of their houses during and after the offensive, following which 200,000 people fled the province, mostly to the rump Federal Republic of Yugoslavia (Serbia and Montenegro).[29] The Croatians admitted ugly incidents but rejected UN claims as exaggerated and stressed that the Serbs left on their own in contrast to the Croats expelled earlier from the province by force. Carl Bilt, the UN mediator, threatened Tudjman of prosecuting him for war crimes. By contrast, no one threatened Milosevic for his conquest of Srebrenica, which had never a Serb majority before. The Croatian victory had important strategic implications on the Bosnian front. The tide was also turning against the Serbs in Bosnia and the myth of their invincibility was shattered.[30]

UNCRO was terminated on January 15, 1996. Eastern Slavonia returned to Croatia in 1998 after 2 years under the United Nations Temporary Administration for Eastern Slavonia, Baranja, and Western Sirmjum (UNTAES). The UN military presence in Croatia ended 3 years after Ghali informed the Security Council in May 1993 that it was not possible for UNPROFOR to fulfill its mandate.[31] But the Deputy Head of the UNPROFOR boldly insisted that, as the operation was a constant butt of attack and even ridicule in Croatia, it has been a victim of its own success, because it maintained a shaky cease-fire for 10 months.[32] Some researchers suggested that UNPROFOR's presence, which stabilized an unfair *status quo*, gave Croatia time to build up an army to regain its territories.[33]

HUMANITARIAN MISSION IN BOSNIA AND HERZEGOVINA

Initially, UNPROFOR's headquarters had been located in Sarajevo, the capital of Bosnia. The Force's Chief of Staff, General Lewis MacKenzie of Canada, who later became the first UN Sarajevo sector commander, was getting the news about the outbreak of a war in his duty station straight from the BBC World News TV Channel. On the same screen he saw crowds storming his hotel in a hunt for snipers, who were shooting at people from the roof.[34] As the city and the country descended into a war, UNPROFOR had no mandate for Bosnia. It tried to assist in cease-fire negotiations that were conducted by the representatives of the European Communities. The Security Council resolutions merely, and in vain, called for cessation of outside interference in Bosnia by the Yugoslav and Croatian armies and for disarmament of irregular forces.

The horrors of Sarajevo were widely reported and the CNN syndrome set in. Something had to be done, but the policy of nonintervention adopted for Croatia was upheld for Bosnia. Humanitarian aid becomes a substitute for an intervention to stop the war. To deliver aid to Sarajevo, the UN needed a cease-fire and access to its airport, captured by the Serb rebels in a heavy battle. In the midst of negotiations with Serbs, on June 18, UNPROFOR installed at the airport an 80-man strong advance party. UN soldiers were present along with the Serbs who continued shelling of the closest Bosnian localities of Dobrinja and Butimir. As a result, MacKenzie received on June 27 a letter signed by 2,000 inhabitants of Dobrinja who informed the UN peacekeeper that they would demand his punishment as an accomplice of the Serbs and a war criminal.[35]

Ultimately, the UN flag was hoisted at the airport on June 29, the next day after a surprise visit to Sarajevo by the President of France, Mitterand. But the deal was flawed in favor of the Serbs who were authorized to check everything imported and to have a cut on all supplies. Therefore, UNPROFOR's relations with the Bosnian government were marred from the outset. In fact, the UN controlled the airport under a leasing contract, which the Serbs called off and on at will and whim, till the end of the war.[36] Sarajevo's Mayor, Muhamed Krevesljakovic, went in July 1993 on hunger strike because of dwindling UN aid. On April 25, 1994, the members of the Contact Group[37] could not have left Sarajevo because of the shelling of the airport; closures in July and December were also reported. By early June 1995, Serb gunmen shelled the airport continuously; humanitarian aid could not have reached Sarajevo for more than 2 months.[38]

UNPROFOR tolerated the Serb breaches of the airport agreement under protest but continued to carry out its own obligations. The UN troops patrolled the runways and turned away people who sought to leave Sarajevo. Many died when the lights used by UN soldiers exposed them on the runway, providing easy targets for the nearby Serb snipers. UN officials explained that, short of provoking the ire of the Serbs and compromising the airlift, UNPROFOR had to stick to its part of the agreement.[39]

The largest and longest lasting airlift ever undertaken celebrated in March 1995 its 1,000 days, delivery of more than 150,000 tons of humanitarian aid in more than 12,000 sorties.[40] The pilots and the UN technical staff keeping the airport working under a constant threat of life were the real heroes of the lifeline operation for the Bosnia's beleaguered capital. Another historical event comes to mind: the American airlift to West Berlin during the cold war. But there is a sad difference; in Berlin, the airlift preserved and buttressed freedom in its Western part, while, in the words of George Soros, Sarajevo was a concentration camp and the UN was part of the system that maintained it.[41]

Half a year after the outbreak of the fighting in Bosnia, the SC in resolution 776 of September 14, 1992, extended the UNPROFOR's mandate and strength.

General Philippe Morillon of France became the UN Force Commander in Bosnia and his manpower increased to 6,000 from about 1,400. His task was to support efforts of the UN High Commissioner for Refugees (UNHCR) and, in particular, to provide protection for delivery of humanitarian relief throughout the country by all necessary means, including the use of force.[42]

Morillon quickly declared that he had no use for such an authorization. "There is no intention to force our way through any blockade," he said at a press conference, and added, "Our first priority here will be to try to deblock not only Sarajevo but all towns and cities which are besieged." He added that "The suffering cannot last any longer" and finally stressed that there was no military solution except 100,000 deaths and absolute catastrophe.[43] Patricia Purves, a UNPROFOR speaker, was even more explicit. Talking to the journalists a few months after the authorization of the troops to use "all necessary means" to get the humanitarian aid in Bosnia going she said, "Our mandate is quite clear, without any doubts. We should bring medicaments, food, and other aid to the oppressed people—*when we are allowed* (italics added). And no more."[44]

UNPROFOR's abdication from the use of force in crossing innumerable roadblocks and barricades had been justified by fears of reprisals. You get one convoy through, but it is the last one; you are at war and the whole humanitarian operation is jeopardized—claimed UN people—typically equating any coercive action with war. Many local military leaders accepted a linkage. The convoys could proceed if the obstructing party gets its share of the goods in transit. Initially it worked on a case-by-case basis, but later became institutionalized.[45]

Despite the UN readiness to negotiate, many convoys were attacked, held up for weeks, or forced to return. The Secretary General admitted that in the first year of UNPROFOR's mission in Bosnia, the operation was persistently thwarted by obstruction, mines, hostile fire, and refusal of the parties on the ground, particularly, but not exclusively, the Bosnian Serb party, to cooperate. Nonetheless, between November 1992 and January 1993 alone the aid escorted by the UN soldiers reached about 800,000 people in 110 locations.[46] The UN effort was supplemented by airdrops made mainly by the U.S., German, and French aircraft from the U.S. base in Frankfurt am Main.

As the war progressed, instances of depriving certain localities from any aid for a longer time were multiplying. Apart from Sarajevo, Bihac, Gorazde, Srebrenica, Maglaj, and Mostar, where the Croats were fighting Muslims, were among the worst trouble spots. UNPROFOR itself was not free from obstructions and in December 1994 had to suspend most of its activities in Sarajevo because of lack of fuel. In June 1995, UNHCR was able to deliver only 20 percent of the targeted supplies to the safe areas and 8 percent to Sarajevo.[47] Beginning July, a UN spokesman described the situation in Bihac as the worst crisis of the Bosnian war; 30,000 people were at risk of starvation because of blockades of convoys.[48] At the same time people were already dying from starvation in Srebrenica, as Reuters and AFP reported on July 7.

UNPROFOR claimed success as a supporting arm of the relief effort. Thornberry even described it as an immense success.[49] Shashi Tharoor, the official in charge of the ex-Yugoslavia desk in the UN headquarter, saw it differently. In a confidential memo he claimed that UNPROFOR was in many areas unable to supply itself, unable to protect the delivery of humanitarian aid, unable to deter attacks, unable to fight for itself, and unable to withdraw.[50] In the end, however, the humanitarian aid saved lives, and it was the only bright spot in the bleak picture of the international intervention in ex-Yugoslavia. And yet, the aid was to a large extent hostage to selections made by the warring parties and part of it fuelled and prolonged the war.

SREBRENICA AND OTHER SAFE AREAS

Srebrenica had been one of the few places in Eastern Bosnia retaken from the Serbs by the forces loyal to the government in Sarajevo. It was a thorn in the body of the surrounding "Serbian Republic." The commander of the Bosnian militia in Srebrenica, Naser Oric, a former bodyguard of Slobodan Milosevic, often attacked Serbian villages. On January 7, 1993, he again attacked north of the town; his forces killed civilians, looted the abundant food ready for the festivities of the Orthodox Christmas Eve, and burned the houses.[51]

In March 1993 the Serbs intensified their attacks on Muslim enclaves in eastern Bosnia, including Srebrenica. UNHCR reported that thousands were seeking refuge in that town, notwithstanding the conditions that caused 30 to 40 deaths daily from military assaults, starvation, exposure to cold, and lack of medical treatment.[52] General Morillon decided to intervene himself. On March 11 he departed for Srebrenica in a convoy of an armored personnel carrier manned by five Canadians, a jeep carrying two Americans to guide from the ground the parachuting of aid, three representatives of the *Medicins sans frontiéres*, a representative of the UNHCR, four UN observers, and a truck carrying ten tons of medicaments. Upon reaching the town, Morillon assured Oric that everything possible would be done to secure a cease-fire and humanitarian aid. But when he wanted to leave, a living wall of hundreds of women and children rose around the UN vehicles and prevented his departure. People wanted that, before leaving, the highest UN officer in Bosnia give them security assurances. And the general obliged. He went up to a balcony and proclaimed that they were under the protection of the United Nations that would never abandon them. But the Bosnians did not want him to leave, still. Morillon tried to sneak out in a disguise on foot under the cover of the night but changed his mind and returned. Eventually, upon promising to go to Belgrade to arrange for an end of the Serb attacks, he was allowed to leave.[53]

But after the general left, shelling of Srebrenica continued. When the first aid convoy reached the town and offloaded, the trucks were stormed by hundreds of desperate women and children determined to leave for safety. They piled on top of each other and on the way to Tuzla six persons died from suffocation. Nicknamed by the press Hero of Srebrenica, Morillon, highly upset by the failure to deliver on his promises, undertook a second expedition. Three of his vehicles were turned back from the town of Sokolac and the general struggled further with the other two. At Zvornik he was surrounded by hundreds of women and children, this time Serb. More aggressive, they jumped upon the UN vehicles, ripped off whatever they could and sprayed them with paint. The crowd shouted "Morillon Hitler" and the latter name was scribbled on the general's vehicle. Humiliated and shocked, the UN Commander turned back to the Bosnian-held Tuzla. One month after his balcony declaration, on April 12, the Serbs launched an intensive artillery assault on Srebrenica, killing fifty-six people in less than an hour, including several children at a schoolyard. A 6-year-old child had been decapitated. The Bosnian defenders were at their last legs and ready to talk surrender.

Morillon's actions exposed UNPROFOR's impotence and alarmed his superiors. The general and the mission's civilian head, Thornberry, were dispatched to negotiate the demilitarization of Srebrenica in exchange for a cease-fire. Demilitarization was a substitute for surrender that would be hardly palatable to the international public. The UN envoys met the Bosnian Serbs Army Commander, Ratko Mladic, and his Bosnian counterpart Sefer Halilovic at the Sarajevo airport on April 16. The agreement signed as a result amounted to the Bosnian surrender but for emptying the enclave of its Muslim population. An UNPROFOR's Canadian unit was to be deployed in Srebrenica to collect arms from the Bosnians under the supervision of the Serb liaison officers.[54] The town became a refugee camp, the most horrendous in the experience of the UNHCR representative Jose Maria Mendiluce.[55]

The SC covered the airport agreement with a new resolution. Acting under Chapter VII of the Charter it demanded in resolution 819 of April 16, 1993, that all parties treat Srebrenica as a safe area, which should be free from any armed attack or any other hostile action. It also requested an increase of UN troops' presence, evacuation of ill and wounded, and unimpeded delivery of humanitarian assistance, and condemned the forced evacuation of civilians. Five days later the UNPROFOR's Commander in Zagreb reported that 170 troops, civilian police, and observers were deployed in the town that had been successfully demilitarized. The diplomats liked the new formula and in resolution 824 of May 6 declared safe areas also in Sarajevo, Tuzla, Zepa, Gorazde, and Bihac. In doing so, the Council followed recommendations by Mazowiecki presented at the session of the UNHCR in Geneva in November 1992.[56] In an effort to give the new concept more credibility, the Council in resolution 836 of June 4 authorized the troops to deter the attacks against safe areas and, acting in self-defense, to take necessary measures including use of force in reply to bombardments, armed incursion, and deliberate obstruction of UN troops freedom of movement or of protected humanitarian convoys. It also authorized, under its authority, NATO's use of air power in support of UNPROFOR.[57] It was a milestone in the UN operation in

Bosnia, in the history of peacekeeping, and in the history of NATO. But the UN Secretariat and its representatives in the field cut the milestone to size.

In May 1994 Ghali proposed a refinement of the safe-area concept which boiled down to depriving it from any notion that it may include a defense of the area and its population. Semantic games have been employed: "ensuring security of the population" of resolution 836 became "enhancing security." Half a year later the Secretary General put the point over an "i" by submitting to the SC that he did not believe that UNPROFOR should be given the mandate to enforce the compliance with the safe areas regime.[58] From the Council there was no reaction. But, after the fall in July 1995 of Srebrenica and Zepa into the hands of the murderous Serbs, in resolution 1010 the Council expressed deep concern for the plight of the civilian population.[59] But thousands have been murdered. Fate of two small safe areas, Gorazde and Srebrenica, illustrate that abandoning these areas was not the only option available.

In March 1994, the Bosnian Serbs launched an offensive against Gorazde, employing infantry, tanks, and artillery. There were civilian casualties and the UN observers were endangered. While the situation deteriorated in April, the UNPROFOR's Commander in Bosnia, British General Michael Rose, called for NATO's intervention. The Alliance's aircraft went on the first bombing mission in what had been called a close air support as opposed to air strikes, meant to inflict more damage. On April 10, two NATO aircraft dropped three bombs, and on the following day two F/A 18A Hornets destroyed a Bosnian Serb tank and attacked other targets. As a result, during the following week, the Serbs detained 130 UN troops and observers (what in an official UNPROFOR's publication was termed elegantly "UN personnel facing confinement to accommodation . . ."). On April 16, NATO lost his first aircraft: a British Sea Harrier shot down on a reconnaissance mission. Shelling continued and a UN convoy to Gorazde was not permitted to proceed. Acting upon Rose's recommendation, the SC in resolution 913 issued on April 22 an ultimatum to the Serbs to withdraw heavy arms from the military exclusion zone of 20 kilometers around Gorazde and troops from 3 kilometers from the center of the town, or face air strikes. Akashi, the SRSG in ex-Yugoslavia and UNPROFOR's Commander, General Bertrand de Lapressle of France, went to Belgrade to discuss the situation with Milosevic and the Bosnian Serbs. The latter budged and a cease-fire agreement was signed on April 23. Ghali said that the international community had gone "to the brink of war to attain peace."[60] In fact, Gorazde had been saved by an effective mix of negotiation, arm-twisting, and military action undertaken or initiated by the UNPROFOR's Commander in Bosnia.[61]

But the risky course taken in Gorazde was not to be followed. The story of Srebrenica's fall, now reproduced, comes from a groundbreaking report by the UN Secretary General, Annan, who succeeded Ghali, and who for the first time published an analysis of a UN failed mission.[62] After the demilitarization agreement in 1993 the enclave was spared major military action by either side, but the Serbs never ceased tightening the noose around it. The exact borders of the area were unclear and UNPROFOR could not help, because it misplaced a map, which had been agreed upon by the belligerents in May 1993. Since February 1995, movement of international convoys, the rotation and resupplying of the UN troops were further restricted.

The relative military calm ended on June 1, 1995, when Serbs raided the area, killed a number of civilians, and ordered UNPROFOR troops to move their observation post (OP) Echo off a strategic road. It happened in the midst of the hostage crisis in Bosnia and 2 days after Ghali presented the SC his recommendations on restricting UNPROFOR's role in safe areas.[63] The message could not be lost on anyone willing to listen.

When the Dutch did not follow the demand, the Serbs attacked with gunfire, mortars, and antitank weapons. The Dutchbat Commander requested close air support but his request, withheld at lower levels of the operation, did not reach UN headquarters in Zagreb. OP Echo surrendered to the Serbs, but the Dutch established two new positions, Sierra and Uniform.

A showdown was imminent. The Serbs used for the siege 1,000 to 2,000 well equipped and well supplied soldiers from the "Drina" Corps; additional units could be brought in, whenever needed. They disposed off tanks, tracked armored vehicles, artillery, and mortars. The Bosnians had 3,000 to 4,000 ill equipped and ill trained men, who had no heavy weapons except few light mortars and antitank missiles, which they did not know how to handle.

Between them, a handful of Blue Helmets dispatched by one of the respected democracies of Western Europe. Out of about 600 hundred Dutch soldiers, approximately 300 were infantry and the others served in support capacities. They established twelve observation posts but due to shortage of manpower there were blind spots in coverage of the perimeter of the enclave. After the fall of the OP Echo, the Dutch Commander wrote that the Dutchbat was not able to execute any action nor could it respond to the deteriorating situation . . . being hostage of the BSA for more than 3 months, something had to be done. But nothing was done and 3 weeks later he repeated his plea. Since the end of April the Serbs had not allowed a single soldier to leave the enclave or enter it—he reported. Those who were on leave could not return and he had lost about 150 men in this way. Supplies of fresh food were blocked, the restrictions on delivery of spare parts, engineering equipment, and fuel continued. UNPROFOR resorted to borrowing fuel from UNHCR and to patrolling on foot. Neither of these two reports, transmitted to Sarajevo, reached the UN headquarters in Zagreb, renamed UN Peace Force (UNPF) in March 1995.[64] UNPROFOR's headquarters in Sarajevo, disposed at that time about 30,000 troops in all of Bosnia.

The Serbs launched their final assault on July 6. The Bosnians approached the Dutch Commander to give them back the weapons they had surrendered in 1993.[65] Their request was refused, because, incredible as it may sound in retrospect, a superior UN officer in Sarajevo told the Dutchman that it was UNPROFORS's responsibility to defend the enclave and not theirs. As the Serbs started to directly fire at the UN OP Foxtrot, the Dutch Commander requested close air support in self-defense.[66] The UNPROFORS's Chief of Staff in Sarajevo, General Cees Nicolai of the Netherlands, discouraged the request, because it did not meet restrictive criteria of the UNPF Commander, General Bernard Janvier of France.

On July 7 the situation was relatively quiet but on July 8 the Serb relaunched their attacks and began hitting the OP Foxtrot again. Its antitank missile was incapacitated. The Dutch Commander considered the OP's position indefensible and ordered withdrawal. The Serbs allowed the crew to leave without their weapons. One of the UN soldiers was killed by the Bosnians furious about the Blue Helmets' surrender.

On July 9, the UN military observers in UNPROFOR's Sector North East reported that the enclave, including its UN contingent was left at the mercy of the Serbs. By the evening OP Mike, Uniform, Sierra, and Delta were in Serbs hands, their crews disarmed, held hostages, and told that they could go home in the Netherlands. The Serbs advanced within 1 kilometer south of the Srebrenica town. In agreement with the SRSG, General Janvier decided, at 18.00 hours, that the Dutch should establish blocking position on the southern access roads to the city. He expected them to open fire when under attack and to ask for a close air support.[67] This decision was faxed—as a warning—to the Serb General Tolimir. Its wording implied that air power would be used only in defense of the UN troops, but not in defense of Bosnians. Consequently, the Serbs endeavored to bypass the Blue Helmets.[68]

Early morning of July 10, a detachment of six APCs and about 50 soldiers begun to establish the blocking positions. They were instructed to fire warning shots when attacked and to engage the Serbs in combat if attack did not stop. At 13.00 hours, three positions were in place; the fighting continued around them, but they were not fired upon. At about 18.30 hours the Serbs were seen advancing toward the ridgeline where the Dutch attempted to establish the fourth position. Another request for close air support was made and not followed. The Dutch fired warning flares and warning shots. The Serbs did not return fire but fell back over the ridgeline in southwestern direction. The Company Commander ordered all crews of the blocking position to withdraw nearer to town so that the Serbs would not outflank them in the night.

Annan's report on Srebrenica's last day does not provide for clarity in the question of use of the air power. Janvier claimed that he did not authorize it on that day because it was already dark and the Dutch could better stop the Serbs on the ground. The Dutch Commander in turn did not consider close air support useful any more and asked for air strikes at 6.00 hours the following morning. He convened a midnight meeting with the Bosnian leadership to inform them that at 6.00 hours on July 11 or 5–6 hours later, NATO would conduct massive air strikes on the Serb positions if they do not withdraw.

On July 11, at about 4.00 hours, the Dutch spoke with UNPROFOR's Sector North-East and were told that 40 targets had been identified and that NATO planes would be over them at 6.50. When the strikes did not materialize, the Dutch telephoned again only to learn that there was no request either for air strikes or for close air support on record and that none was forthcoming. At the same time the NATO aircraft were in the air awaiting orders for action. A new request was made at 7.45 but did not reach Zagreb before 11.00. At 12.10 the UN crew of OP November withdrew under fire. The Serbs shelled the town and fired on OP Hotel, and on the Dutch Company compound. Akashi approved the request for close air support at 12.17. A Serb flag was hoisted over a bakery at the southern end of the town at 14.07 hours. Srebrenica had fallen. Until that point, at least three, but possibly five, requests for air support by the Dutch had been turned down. The Dutch had not fired a single shot directly at the advancing Serbs.

At 14.30, eighteen NATO aircraft appeared over the town and at 14.40 two planes dropped two bombs on what were thought to be Serb vehicles. Other aircraft were unable to locate targets. The first and last action of a joint United Nations and NATO close air support for Srebrenica was over. The town suffered the most brutal and complete ethnic cleansing, including massacres in cold blood of thousands of men taken prisoners. Mass executions begun 3 days after Janvier ordered the already defeated UN troops to block the advance of the Serb attacks and two and a half years after the Hero of Srebrenica, General Philippe Morillon's balcony speech, promising all inhabitants the protection of the world organization. The Serbs overran another safe area of Zepa shortly afterward.

INQUIRIES IN FUTILITY

Nowhere in ex-Yugoslavia were the UN peacekeeping goals achieved except, partly, in delivery of the humanitarian aid. The conflicts flared up after deployment of UNPROFOR and were resolved or contained by forces independent from the UN. In the report on the fall of Srebrenica, Annan said that (in ex-Yugoslavia)

> With benefit of hindsight, one can see that many of the errors the UN made flowed from a single and no doubt well-intentioned effort: we tried to keep peace and apply the rules of peacekeeping when there was no peace to keep. Knowing that any other course of action would jeopardize the lives of the troops, we tried to create—or imagine—an environment in which the tenets of peacekeeping—agreement between the parties, deployment by consent, and impartiality—could be upheld.... We tried to eschew the use of force except in self-defense, which brought us into conflict with the defenders of safe areas, whose safety depended on our use of force.[69]

The UN efforts to avoid use of force did not save the lives of 212 UN-PROFOR's troops or the mission. A fragile peace maintained by 57,000 NATO peacekeepers to Bosnia, Kosovo, and Macedonia, 8,800 of who were Americans, had been achieved outside of the UN peacekeeping.[70]

But Annan's assessment addressed a problem wider than Srebrenica left open—the question why the futility of the UN policy was not recognized in due time. Neither the French nor the Dutch parliamentary inquiries on the role of their respective governments in the fall of Srebrenica were of much help in this respect.[71] The Dutch inquiry was preceded by an investigation by the Netherland's Institute for War Documentation (NIOD). After the publication of its findings[72] in 2002 the Dutch government recognized its political responsibility and resigned. No actions of French authorities are now in the follow up of the French inquiry which admitted that France shared responsibility for the fall of the enclave.

As to the role of the Dutch contingent stationed in the enclave the Dutch and French inquiries differ in conclusions and, in a crucial detail concerning a directive of Janvier of May 29, 1995, they also disagree as to the facts. The directive issued to UN commanders of various areas stressed that the execution of the mandate is secondary to the security of the UN personnel. Janvier maintained that his directive concerned positions around Sarajevo and specifically denied that it related to Srebrenica.[73] The Dutch disagree because eastern enclaves were indeed mentioned in his directive.[74] Janvier maintained further that his order to erect blocking positions was an order for battle, which was not followed. He added that should he have had 400 French in Srebrenica, they would have fought and repelled the Serbs.[75] It is an unfair assessment by the commander who left the Dutchbat at the mercy of the Serbs for months and denied them the air support when they were under attack. Moreover, Janvier's conclusions contradicted UN claims that a 7,500 strong force was needed to defend each of the safe areas. But the French Inquiry indirectly endorsed Janvier's views by declaring, not very accurately, that the French effectively defended the safe areas of Sarajevo and Bihac till the end of the war. The Serbs never tried to take over Sarajevo by ground forces. They kept it under siege and shelling to push the Bosnian government toward a surrender and Bihac was mainly saved by developments at other fronts.

It is symptomatic that the largest UN peacekeeping operation launched in ex-Yugoslavia in the largest armed conflagration in Europe after the Second World War, deployed under the most restrictive mandate and even more restrictive ROE. The troops resorted to the right of defense when under attack incidentally only, and rarely attempted to defend their mandate, even when it was established under Chapter VII. The substitution of restoration of peace by humanitarian intervention put the UN troops in power of the aggressors. Despite the efforts and sacrifices of the men in the field the resulting humiliation was an unavoidable outcome.[76] Most of the bloodshed in Yugoslavia could have been avoided should the UN identify the aggressor (or aggressors) and effectively apply sanctions provided in its Charter.

Politicians and journalists use to explain the UN failures in Yugoslavia by lack of political will in the anonymous international community. But the UN response to that crisis emerged in seventy-six resolutions adopted by the Security Council up to June 16, 1995. Thirty-four of the most important had been sponsored by France, joined by the UK, twenty-eight by the United States, and twenty by the Russian Federation. It was not the mythical international community but the representatives of Paris, London, Washington, and Moscow, assisted by the rotating diplomats of lesser powers like Spain or Italy or of tiny countries like Cape Verde, who acting upon instructions of their governments and with support from the UN Secretariat, failed in preventing the slaughter in ex-Yugoslavia. In the process they made the peacekeepers scapegoats and disgraced the organization.[77] Gestures and substance are the usual mix of all politics, but the Council seemed impervious to the relationship between its decisions and reality. Ex-Yugoslavia was not the only case in question.

The Prospects

THE DETERMINATION to "save the succeeding generations from the scourge of war," proclaimed in the United Nations Charter, did not prevent 150 conflicts, including more than 125 in the developing countries, which cost some 22 million lives.[1] Nevertheless for its efforts in promoting peace the organization was awarded the Nobel Peace Prize in 1988 and, notwithstanding Srebrenica and Rwanda, obtained the prize in 2001 again. Since 1948, UN launched 60 peacekeeping operations at an estimated cost of $41.04 billion and 2,242 fatalities.

From all major operations only in the Congo, half a century ago ONUC and recently MONUC, undertook offensive actions in defense of their mandates. UN engaged in combat also in Somalia (UNOSM II) but in retaliatory and punitive actions. Everywhere else the UN contingents kept peace to the extent they were allowed to do so by the belligerents. Otherwise they witnessed and reported, or left. In a recurring pattern some of the UN contingents (or observers) were overrun by invading armies, suffered losses, and were forced to cooperate with the invaders later. It happened in the Israeli attack on Gaza in 1963, in the Egyptian attack over the Suez Canal in 1973, in the Israeli invasion of Lebanon in 1982, and in the Croatian attack on Krajina in 1995. It also happened in Cyprus during the Turkish invasion of the island in 1974. The Blue Helmets can be hardly expected to combat armies of the UN member countries. But the fact that no invader ever suffered sanctions for overrunning the UN positions tells volumes about the credibility of the organization. The UN did not develop mechanisms for effective response to challenges and threats to international peace and in the arsenal of tools for conflict resolution peacekeeping proved to be not a very useful tool.

Part of the problem is in the tentative if not illusory character of the commonly applied model of peace process in the prevailing intrastate conflicts. Internationally sponsored negotiations are supposed to move the warlords or rebels to disarm, their fighters to go home back to work or integrate into a national army, free and fair election to follow, and the peacekeepers to go home. Such a virtual scenario, based on western standards, ignores the adversary's inclination to act in bad faith and of the warlords' and other extremists' commitment to war at all costs.[2] It also ignores the likelihood of the representatives of the often-obscure belligerents and corrupt governments enjoying repetitious, endless, and free of charge "negotiations" in luxury international hotels—with no bearing on the killing fields back home.

The last decade had all these shortcomings acknowledged. A flurry of official and unofficial research and debates continued, reports of high-level panels followed those of eminent persons, new doctrines emerged, and a vast body of important academic contributions shed light on all aspects of peacekeeping in conjunction with conflict resolution theory. Future operations were to be robust and effective to be ever undertaken. Protection of populations endangered by ethnic cleansing and genocide began to emerge as a new right, superseding sovereign rights of governments either unable to stop or being guilty of it.

Meanwhile the international security environment steadily deteriorated. A decade ago Somalia was the only failed state in Africa, now Sierra Leone, Liberia, the Democratic Republic of Congo, and Ivory Coast joined the club. Others are tilting on the brink, as also Afghanistan and Iraq are as a result of post-9/11 developments.

Ultimately, some of the actors in the peacekeeping theatre seemed to welcome a reform of the present system or its substantial adjustments at least. But—as developments in Sudan demonstrated—the stereotypes and constraints of the past proved to be stronger from inclinations to change.

SUDAN—A DEMONSTRATION PROJECT

It is a big project with multiple actors: the government of Sudan and its sponsored militias, the rebel movements in Southern Sudan and in Darfur, the UN Security Council and Secretariat, the African Mission in Sudan (AMIS), and the UN Mission in Sudan (UNMIS).

Interests and cultures of the Arab and the Black African citizens of the largest African country clash on two main fronts: in Southern Sudan and in its western province of Darfur. To make things worse, cross-border attacks on the neighboring Chad from Darfur gave the conflict international dimensions. The South, plagued by civil wars for decades, saw the end of the last one in 2005. After about 2 million deaths and 4 million southerners displaced, a Comprehensive Peace Agreement (CPA), sponsored by the United States, the UK, and the UN was signed in Kenya between the Arab-dominated government and the Sudanese People's Liberation Movement. As a rebel leader became the vice president of the country, peace took a shaky hold on the territory after 21 years.

Yet, the Agreement concluded in Kenya was comprehensive in name only. It did not even mention the ongoing civil war in Darfur. In 3 years it claimed 70,000 to 400,000 lives and resulted in 2 million displaced into camps as a result of deliberate campaigns of atrocities and rape by government forces and their allies. The U.S. administration called it genocide in 2004.[3]

But the SC in each of its eight resolutions adopted on Sudan in 2004 and 2005 addressed both emergencies.[4] It was continuously condemning the ongoing violence and human right abuses committed in Darfur and repeatedly called upon all parties to observe the cease-fire agreement signed in N'djamena (Chad) on April 8, 2004. The Council also demanded disarmament and punishment of the leaders of the allied with the government Janjaweed Arab militia, notorious for vicious crimes and rapes. In resolution 1556 of July 30, 2004, acting under Chapter VII of the UN Charter, the Council "... *expressed its intention*" (italics of the original document) to consider measures as provided for in Article 41 of the Charter in the event of noncompliance by the government of Sudan with that demand (that article provides for measures other than use of armed force). A year and a half later, the intention continues, as does the killing. According to the foreign secretary of Britain, Jack Straw "... there is no cease-fire in Darfur. The government of Sudan and the rebel movements break it every day.... Innocent people are still being killed. Women and girls are being raped. Children are dying."[5] The secretary warned individuals directly responsible of dire consequences, including actions by the International Criminal Court. But waving a stick from a safe distance, the secretary offered an instant carrot in providing one more million of British pounds to finance the ongoing peace process in the Nigerian capital Abuja.

The professed intention not to use armed forces in Darfur did not disturb the Council in dispatching them into Southern Sudan. It established in March 2005 United Nations Mission in Sudan (UNMIS) of an authorized strength of 10,000 military personnel and appropriate civilian and police components. The mission's head, the SRSG, Jan Prank of the Netherlands, covers all of Sudan from his office in Khartoum. But the military wing of UNMIS solely covers Southern Sudan. The mission is not established under Chapter VII and its mandate is to support the CPA by "monitoring," "providing guidance," and "assisting" the parties to the agreement. The same resolution which dispatched an international army into a post-conflict environment, called for an increase in the number of human rights monitors in Darfur, where the killings were going on.[6]

UNMIS military component under the command of General Jasbir Singh Lidder of India reached only 6,300 uniformed personnel by the end of January 2006 or 63 percent of its authorized strength in 10 months, but presented the most colorful kaleidoscope deployed in UN peacekeeping missions ever. Sixty-one governments, from Australia to Zimbabwe, contributed military personnel (some of them provided police officers as well) and six, including Samoa and the United States, dispatched police personnel only.[7] On average the sixty-seven nations contributed ninety uniformed persons each. Building up of a functioning logistics in such an army is probably not among the easiest tasks of General Lidder.

But now, Darfur enjoys an international military presence, too. African Mission in Sudan (AMIS) deploys there, on a territory equal to France, 2,000 military observers and 5,000 troops, mainly from Nigeria, Rwanda, and Senegal. The idea behind the mission dispatched by the African Union (AU) was to let the African problems be solved by Africans. But the mission's mandate is ". . . to protect civilians encountered who are under imminent threat and in immediate vicinity, within the limits of mission capability, it being understood that civilian protection is the (Sudan) government responsibility." Thus, the armed missionaries are allowed to protect people when they stumble over them but not from the persecuting government forces, because the latter are themselves in charge of the protection. Thus, it should not come as surprise to hear a local AMIS commander, Colonel Raji Rajna of Nigeria, calling "laughable" expectations of people of Darfur who thought that the soldiers would deploy in camps and villages to ward off attackers. Neither is it surprising that the Janjaweed, expected to be disarmed in 2004, in January 2006 raided and depopulated the 55,000 population of the city of Mershing. The AMIS commanders obey the government curfew imposed on Darfur population, giving Janjaweed free rein at night. Some of Sudanese aircraft, including attack helicopters are painted white, to make them indistinguishable from AU aircraft.[8] Why shouldn't the government mock the peacekeepers, who mocked themselves in their mandate, in the first place?

In a few days after the publication of Straw's stern warning, the Sudanese forces supported by militia attacked villages of Likalik and Al Amin. Also AU peacekeepers were attacked, injured, and their vehicles stolen. When a transition from the AU to a UN-supervised mission entered in discussions about Sudan, the Security Council did not fail to commend AMIS for its successful deployment.[9]

The UN Secretary General Annan and United States President George W. Bush discussed Darfur on February 13, 2006. Neither of the two leaders ever uttered the word "genocide," and the Secretary General declared: ". . . I'm very happy that we have agreed to work together . . . to ensure that we do have an effective security presence on the ground to protect the IDPs (Internally Displaced Persons) and ensure that humanitarian workers have access to those in need."[10] The mandate for UNPROFOR in Bosnia to protect deliveries of humanitarian aid comes to mind: feed people before they might be killed. Reporting to the SC about Darfur, Prank said that "All we did was picking up the pieces and muddling through, doing too little, too late."[11] It seems not very likely that much is going to change.

NATO is reluctant to accept any bigger role in Darfur either, which is not surprising after the difficulties it experienced in getting troops for Afghanistan. But even the safe option of enforcing a no-flight zone over Darfur meets opposition. "Which NATO country would be willing to shoot down a Sudanese plane?" asked an anonymous diplomat.[12]

In his 1999 report about the fall of Srebrenica, Annan identified four main fallacies of the UN peacekeeping: "the gulf between mandates and means; the inadequacy of symbolic deterrence in the face of a systematic campaign of violence; the pervasive ambivalence within the UN regarding the role of force in pursuit of peace and an institutional ideology of impartiality even when confronted with attempted genocide."[13] That is a pretty accurate description of the attitude of the organization toward the ongoing crisis in Darfur.

Someone said about Bosnia that it was a triumph of a lack of will. A decade later it triumphs again. If there was ever a time to declare the king naked, it came about in Darfur. But putting the blame at the door of the UN alone would be cheap and unfair. The system that makes the Secretary General extend a begging bowl for contributions to each complex emergency is inefficient by definition. Moreover what can he expect from the membership that could not yet agree at its General Assembly session that Sudan was guilty of human rights violations in November 2005?[14]

UNITED NATIONS CONFLICT PREVENTION POTENTIAL

Saving succeeding generations from the scourge of war, promised by the UN Charter, proved to be an elusive if not utopian goal. While generations were not saved, some countries were helped out of the conflicts, though, but the organization's potential for promotion of peace in the previolent phase of conflicts remains largely untapped. There are three important instruments, an effective application of which could enhance the UN capacity and credibility in conflict prevention: sanctions, military observer missions, and preventive deployment of military contingents.

A return to that underlying purpose of the UN is possible within the existing provisions of the Charter, before a need for a military involvement ever arises. Article 41 of Chapter VII gives the SC wide powers in applying sanctions to effect compliance with its decisions. For a number of reasons sanctions is an unpopular instrument, but no one can deny its impact on the end of the apartheid regime in South Africa (and indirectly on the success of the peaceful settlement in Namibia) or on disempowering Iraq after the first Gulf War. Intelligent sanctions against violators of peace ought become an instrument more widely applied. But among the UN members themselves there are too many regimes that violate the Charter with impunity and their opposition is to be effectively confronted by the democratic majority in the organization.

For the preventive potential of the military observers' missions to be realized, they need to enjoy full freedom of movement and the means to make a good use of it. This is a necessary but not sufficient condition, however. To deter the potential violators of peace, the information on negative developments in the area of the mission's operation has to be followed up in appropriate actions by the

SC against the offending party. Otherwise it merely certifies the organization's impotence.

Deployment of international contingents could provide a most effective and least expensive tool in preventing major armed conflagrations, but it is also the most difficult to launch. A potential threat to international peace is an argument less persuasive for deployment of troops then blood spilled over in a violent confrontation. Therefore, perhaps, the UN tried a preventive operation only once.

For a few years the presence of the UN Preventive Deployment Force (UNPREDEP), established in 1995 in Macedonia, was the only light in the dark picture of the UN involvement in the former Yugoslavia. But in 2001 a low-scale civil war, instigated by Albanian infiltrators from a territory under the UN protectorate, Kosovo, left a considerable part of the Republic in the rebels' hands and about 150,000 people displaced in presence both of the UN's preventive force and of NATO's peacekeeping force.[15] Ultimately leaders of NATO and of the European Union negotiated a political settlement and an uneasy peace reigns in Macedonia. Next preventive missions have to learn from the Macedonian failure in intercepting armed infiltration.

The Iraq crisis exposed perhaps a historical opportunity for another kind of preventive deployment of UN troops. The UN did too little and the United States did too much for averting the alleged danger of mass destruction weapons in Iraq. The tedious and obstructed work of the arms inspectors could have been supported by the Blue Helmets troops that would also supervise vital military sites. Ultimately—as an alternative to a preemptive war—their presence could amount to a narrowly defined, preventive international occupation or protectorate, without removing the trappings of sovereignty from Baghdad. Shortly before the American invasion, a usually well-informed magazine in Germany published details of a project along these lines, supposedly worked out by the Germans and the French for presentation to the Security Council.[16] There were quick denials from official quarters. But even if an image of a Blue Helmets' patrol under the Great Leader's statue towering over a square in Baghdad is less enthralling than looking into a gaping mouth of the deposed tyrant on the TV screens all over the world, it would be less expensive for everyone.

Despite the Macedonian fiasco and the Iraqi likely missed opportunity, the preventive deployment of international troops at the preconflict phase might offer a most promising avenue to be explored, in high international risk cases in particular.

MILITARY CONTINGENTS OR OBSERVERS?

Peace support operations deployed during the violent phase of the conflicts or in post-conflict environment are part and parcel of peace process designed and carried out by diplomatic means. Therefore it is within that process that the operational objectives of the military components of these operations are to be defined in accordance with the mission's mandate and conditions prevailing on the ground. These objectives fall into three categories: bringing the parties to the conflict to a negotiating table by force if need be, stabilizing post-conflict presence including confronting spoilers of peace by force, and monitoring of the implementation of peace agreements.

There is a need for a reconceptualization of what the peace support operations are to achieve as opposed to what they should do. Whenever the mandate and conditions on the ground warrant a commitment of the parties to the peace process, an assistance from the UN by deployment of military observers missions is sufficient.

These missions have a long but not a very bright tradition in which UNTSO and UNMOGIP are sad examples of futility. But it must not be so, provided that parties to the conflict are not intransigent and the international diplomacy is more effective. An unexpected success in resolution of a conflict between Libya and Chad is a case in question. A low-scale, 20-years-long border war over the Azouzou Strip ended when both countries referred the dispute to the International Court of Justice (ICJ). Libya complied with a ruling in favor of Chad in 1994, and in the same year, the UN Azouzou Strip Observer Group (UNASOG) confirmed the withdrawal of its administration and forces from the contested territory.[17]

Should the Security Council and the Secretariat provide for basic respect of the UN military observers' missions by the parties to the conflicts, these have a potential of relieving armed contingents deployed without any executive powers in monitoring operations. What's the use of deployment since July 2000 of about 3,000 troops in the UN Mission in Ethiopia and Eritrea (UNMEE) at the yearly cost of $186 million when, among other restrictions, it is not allowed by the Eritreans to fly helicopters over their territory?[18]

In all other cases armed contingents with executive mandates are needed, ready to confront by force parties opposing or violating the truce or cease-fire demanded or agreed upon in a peace process. Military troops deployed in the post-conflict stage need to be supported by a strong police component, capable of preventing recurrence of local-level hostilities and of riot control. The current practice of peacekeeping tends to wasteful deployment of military contingents charged in fact with no more but monitoring tasks. Chances are slim for success of the international contingents until the profound confusion about what their armed presence is going to achieve is not finally clarified.

Firstly, it ought to be made clear and be understood that what is to be achieved by international armed contingents is not defined by "peacekeeping" or by any other general term, but by the mission's mandate and rules of engagement. A middle rank officer of UNAMIR in Rwanda saw nothing peculiar in the alleged deployment by his unit of an antitank weapon "only in an observer capacity." Furthermore, he absurdly claimed that his ROE required to seek an authorization by the UN Secretary General for the weapon to be fired, because it served in a peacekeeping mission.[19] Labels should never substitute for mandates and common sense.

The very term "peacekeeping," associated with the confusion of past UN military operations, ought be best dropped from political discourse. "Peace support operations," in use by NATO already, might be a useful replacement. It is neutral and potentially inclusive of all kinds of international military deployments, short of war.

Secondly, the division of the international military interventions into Chapter VI and VII of the UN Charter operations should be eliminated. It mainly serves in justifying an abdication in advance of use of force in defense of the mandates established under the former Chapter, without inducing such a defense of Chapter VII mandates, however. Operations that involve military contingents ought to be authorized under Chapter VII solely. As Article 40 of the Chapter provides for provisional measures other then sanctions provided in Article 41 or military actions provided in Article 42, the proposed rule merely removes obstacles in applying force as the last resort. By no means should it be interpreted as an intention to organize the future operations around the spectrum of enforcement exclusively. Only military observer missions should be authorized under Chapter VI of the Charter.

Thirdly, the Security Council and everyone else involved might be well advised to recover the true meaning of the standard phrase in authorizing the use of "all necessary means" in Chapter VII operations from oblique and confusing interpretations by advocates of profound ambiguities. It is insupportable to interpret that phrase both as a license to start a war against Iraq in 1991 and as insufficient for any action other than surrender in Srebrenica in 1995.

ON THE LOOKOUT FOR TROOPS

Rewriting the rules for peace support operations may be easy if there is a political will to do so. It is, however, not sufficient to fill in the boots needed in the field. The test case of Sudan shows that the enthusiasm visible for a monitoring mission in Southern Sudan by the warriors from sixty-one countries, including Burkina Fasso, Croatia, Kyrgystan, Moldova, and Zimbabwe, is somehow missing for the envisaged in the same country mission to Darfur. The latter, if ever undertaken, is likely to become too dangerous.

The reluctance of the governments, of developed countries in particular, to commit troops in complex emergencies in distant countries coincides most likely with the sentiments of their electorate. Expressing outrage at atrocities among the tribes of the Congo or Sudan by the public of affluent democracies is one thing, but dispatching your brother or son to risk his life down there is another. Looking into alternatives might be more promising then wringing hands over the facts of life.

Talking about national strategic interests the candidate for the U.S. presidency, George W. Bush, declared: We should not . . . send our troops to stop ethnic cleansing and genocide in nations outside our strategic interests. I don't like genocide and I don't like ethnic cleansing, but the President must set clear parameters as to where troops ought be used and when they ought be used." At another occasion the candidate disclosed that "I'm going to clearly say to our friends ... you can put the troops on the ground to be peacekeepers, America will be peacemaker."[20] President Bush did not deviate from his electoral promises. The problem is that combating genocide and ethnic cleansing lies outside national strategic interests of other potential troop contributors as well. Potential peacekeepers are many but they don't do fighting, genocide or not. They may be ready to appear when it is over.

No one can be blamed for putting national strategic interests first. But unless these are redefined with a view to closing or at least decreasing the international security gap and disorder by contributing troops for risky international missions, it is likely to grow. The only alternative to the present muddling through is to tap new sources of manpower. Such sources do exist, but remain untapped because of political constraints.

Firstly it is volunteers who would be recruited directly by the UN to serve under the Blue Flag and be permanently at the disposal of the Security Council. The United Nations, standing rapid deployment brigade of about 5,000 of volunteers is a concept already present in political and academic writing, but absent from the official discourse. Brian Urquhart, who during the cold war was against the UN standing force, advances the concept since early 1990s.[21] Such a new military instrument has clear and instant advantages over the unwieldy and unreliable UNSAS system of contributing troops on call. It would, finally, give the UN the missing capacity to react to emergencies in time and allow to conduct operations without the disadvantages inherent in coalition forces. Stephen P. Kinloch stresses that a different type of military force, drawing on the energy and resources of motivated individuals, directly recruited by the UN is indispensable for the efficient defense of universal values, which may require shedding of life.[22] A standing rapid deployment brigade would resolve a host of problems but not all of them, and it is also likely to create new ones, but no major change is risk-free.

Secondly, there are corporate warriors. The growing worldwide security vacuum gave rise to an unexpected attempt to fill it up. After about 200 years of absence on the world's scene, soldiers for hire reappeared and private military firms have got also a foothold at the peacekeeping theatre. Their deployment in the 90s by the governments of mineral-rich Angola and Sierra Leone in combating rebel forces proved these services viable but also triggered opposition and the contracts were eventually terminated.[23] These individual setbacks did not lead to a dampening of the growth of the private military industry which is a globalized phenomenon now and its clients include both governments and other parties.[24] It is an industry in flux and its potential impact on the international security landscape is yet to be appreciated. There are important obstacles for private armies to be granted a legitimate role in controlling intrastate armed conflicts, but subcontracting private military services, in other than combat capacities, is already an established trend in the American and other forces. That practice allows the contracting armies to better concentrate on fighting capabilities.[25] Why should the American GIs protect Serbian school buses in Kosovo when hired bodyguards can do it as well or better?

A hypothetical case of hiring a private army to stop the genocide in Rwanda in 1994 illustrates both the scale of the problem and a moral dilemma. Internal estimates of Executive Outcomes claim that it was capable of stopping the genocide by creation of security islands in an operation involving 1,500 personnel and own air and fire support at a total cost of $150 million or $600,000 per day, five times less than the respective expenses of the futile UNAMIR.[26] It is not clear whether the firm advanced that offer to any official party, but it is rather obvious that if presented to the UN, it would be rejected as legally and politically unacceptable.

Still, it is a shocking realization that a chance for saving hundreds of thousands of lives might have been lost in an exercise of political correctness. It is also difficult to avoid a disturbing question: why instead of initiating a similar emergency rescue plan the UN decided to withdraw all but a handful of the peacekeepers present on the ground? Whether the UN will consider employment of private military firms in combat capacity in the future or not, it certainly could learn from them how to put its own forces to a better use if it ever rewrites its present script for peacekeeping.

DIVISION OF LABOR

The existing peace support missions authorized by the SC are either directed and supported by the DPKO of the UN or deployed under the command of multinational coalitions, military alliances, or regional organizations.

The UN can now either stick to its present philosophy of consensual peace-keeping or redefine position and accept the new rules. The latter is most unlikely because of the lack of troops for other missions, because of the deeply ingrained pacifist tendencies in the UN Secretariat, and also due to its missing capacity for military leadership. The recent High-level Panel on Threats, Challenges and Change recommended deletion of the Article 47 of the UN Charter concerning the Military Staff Committee.[27] The trend is to steer the organization away from any direct responsibilities of a military nature.

The logical consequence should be restriction of the UN direct involvement in peace support operation to the military observers groups. Such a shift would amount to the Secretary General taking off the Sheriff's star and disarming the organization. It can only gain from abandoning the false promise of peacekeeping by noncombatant troops, maintained at tremendous costs and to no avail. Building up its capabilities in mediating in conflicts and humanitarian relief operations has a greater potential for the support of peace than feeble sable rattling. The money wasted on failed interventions could be released for a better use.

The execution of the peace support operations deploying military forces would then fall to the multinational forces commissioned by ad hoc coalitions of the willing under one lead nation, by military alliances, or by regional organizations.[28] These suffer from a lesser international legitimacy and the old power politics and spheres of influence may be back with them, but as an alternative to genocides and armed anarchy left unattended should be welcome. However, by all indications, the scope and conduct of these operations is susceptive to constraints similar to those of the UN-led missions. Furthermore, from the point of view of the troop contributing governments, the authorized operations have an important disadvantage—they are to be financed by themselves, not by the UN as the Blue Helmets are.

The prospects for an increase in effectiveness of the operations in support of peace by subcontracting them to NATO and other international organizations are not bright. Most of the NATO soldiers have not seen combat on the ground yet and in Afghanistan they staff provincial reconstruction teams. But as Michael Howard says "Tomahawk missiles may rule in the air but it is Kalashnikov submachine guns, which reign on the ground."[29] Other international bodies are as reluctant to accept new deployments as to put the lives of their soldiers at risk in peace enforcement.

As long there is no readiness of potential troop contributors to engage in high-risk operations outside of the sphere of their national (or corporate) interests, the international actions in support of peace will remain an illusory substitute for real interventions. But as the demand for such a substitute on the international political markets is not diminishing, it may have a future yet, but it would not differ much from the past.

Major violent conflagrations will be either attended by one of the three powers capable of swift and efficient military intervention, United States, UK, and France, or left to go their own course, while the other two SC permanent members, Russia and China, will be busy containing centrifugal forces in their empires. But the limited means of the three western powers are overextended already.

The present political climate in the international security environment is determined largely, if not exclusively, by policies and actions of the U.S. administration. The Iraqi crisis greatly strengthened those in that administration who are inclined to decrease rather then enhance a direct role of the UN in settlement of military conflicts and other emergencies. In such a climate projects like a UN rapid reaction brigade or a UN preventive occupation sound unrealistic if not utopian. But it is a relative qualification that depends on what value is attributed to the prevention of the world disorder from growing and the failed, terrorist-prone, state from spreading. If such a goal assumes a high priority, and no better alternatives are found, a reinvented peace support potential of the UN might turn from an unrealistic proposition to a pragmatic solution.

Military interventions in the intrastate conflicts that now dominate the world's international security landscape do not provide for a quick fix of a malaise caused by centrifugal political forces provoking collapse not only of government structures, but also of traditional social ties. But until a better governance and other cures can be applied, an efficient military deterrent can be the only lifeline for hundreds of thousands. It can also provide the necessary space for political solutions.

Everyone is in the process of learning how to address the new and growing challenges to international security. But the results of that process are disappointing. As in any learning, it is important to see through the rhetoric and the doctrinal constraints lingering from another era.This book wishes to be of some help in this respect.

Appendix: Extracts from Chapters VI and VII of the UN Charter

CHAPTER VI. PACIFIC SETTLEMENT OF DISPUTES

Article 33

1. The parties to any dispute, the continuance of which is likely to endanger the maintenance of international peace and security, shall, first of all, seek a solution by negotiation, enquiry, mediation, conciliation, arbitration, judicial settlement, resort to regional agencies or arrangements, or other peaceful means of their own choice.
2. The Security Council shall, when it deems necessary, call upon the parties to settle their dispute by such means.

Article 34

The Security Council may investigate any dispute, or any situation, which might lead to international friction or give rise to a dispute, in order to determine whether the continuance of the dispute or situation is likely to endanger the maintenance of international peace and security.

Article 36

1. The Security Council may, at any stage of a dispute of the nature referred to in Article 33 or of a situation of like nature, recommend appropriate procedures or methods of adjustment.

2. The Security Council should take into consideration any procedures for the settlement of the dispute, which have already been adopted by the parties.
3. In making recommendations under this Article the Security Council should also take into consideration that legal disputes should as a general rule be referred by the parties to the International Court of Justice in accordance with the provisions of the Statute of the Court.

Article 37

1. Should the parties to a dispute of the nature referred to in Article 33 fail to settle it by the means indicated in that Article, they shall refer it to the Security Council.
2. If the Security Council deems that the continuance of the dispute is in fact likely to endanger the maintenance of international peace and security, it shall decide whether to take action under Article 36 or to recommend such terms of settlement, as it may consider appropriate.

Article 38

Without prejudice to the provisions of Articles 33 to 37, the Security Council may, if all the parties to any dispute so request, make recommendations to the parties with a view to a pacific settlement of the dispute.

CHAPTER VII. ACTION WITH RESPECT TO THREATS TO THE PEACE, BREACHES OF THE PEACE, AND ACTS OF AGGRESSION

Article 39

The Security Council shall determine the existence of any threat to the peace, breach of the peace, or act of aggression and shall make recommendations, or decide what measures shall be taken in accordance with Articles 41 and 42, to maintain or restore international peace and security.

Article 40

In order to prevent an aggravation of the situation, the Security Council may, before making the recommendations or deciding upon the measures provided for in Article 39, call upon the parties concerned to comply with such provisional measures as it deems necessary or desirable. Such provisional measures shall be without prejudice to the rights, claims, or position of the parties concerned. The

Security Council shall duly take account of failure to comply with such provisional measures.

Article 41

The Security Council may decide what measures not involving the use of armed force are to be employed to give effect to its decisions, and it may call upon the Members of the United Nations to apply such measures. These may include complete or partial interruption of economic relations and of rail, sea, air, postal, telegraphic, radio, and other means of communication, and the severance of diplomatic relations.

Article 42

Should the Security Council consider that measures provided for in Article 41 would be inadequate or have proved to be inadequate, it may take such action by air, sea, or land forces as may be necessary to maintain or restore international peace and security. Such action may include demonstrations, blockade, and other operations by air, sea, or land forces of Members of the United Nations.

Article 43

1. All Members of the United Nations, in order to contribute to the maintenance of international peace and security, undertake to make available to the Security Council, on its call and in accordance with a special agreement or agreements, armed forces, assistance, and facilities, including rights of passage, necessary for the purpose of maintaining international peace and security.
2. Such agreement or agreements shall govern the numbers and types of forces, their degree of readiness and general location, and the nature of the facilities and assistance to be provided.
3. The agreement or agreements shall be negotiated as soon as possible on the initiative of the Security Council. They shall be concluded between the Security Council and Members or between the Security Council and groups of Members and shall be subject to ratification by the signatory states in accordance with their respective constitutional processes.

Article 44

When the Security Council has decided to use force it shall, before calling upon a Member not represented on it to provide armed forces in fulfillment of the obligations assumed under Article 43, invite that Member, if the Member so desires, to participate in the decisions of the Security Council concerning the employment of contingents of that Member's armed forces.

Article 45

In order to enable the United Nations to take urgent military measures, Members shall hold immediately available national air-force contingents for combined international enforcement action. The strength and degree of readiness of these contingents and plans for their combined action shall be determined within the limits laid down in the special agreement or agreements referred to in Article 43, by the Security Council with the assistance of the Military Staff Committee.

Article 46

The Security Council shall make plans for the application of armed force with the assistance of the Military Staff Committee.

Article 47

1. There shall be established a Military Staff Committee to advise and assist the Security Council on all questions relating to the Security Council's military requirements for the maintenance of international peace and security, the employment and command of forces placed at its disposal, the regulation of armaments, and possible disarmament.
2. The Military Staff Committee shall consist of the Chiefs of Staff of the permanent members of the Security Council or their representatives. Any Member of the United Nations not permanently represented on the Committee shall be invited by the Committee to be associated with it when the efficient discharge of the Committee's responsibilities requires the participation of that Member in its work.
3. The Military Staff Committee shall be responsible under the Security Council for the strategic direction of any armed forces placed at the disposal of the Security Council. Questions relating to the command of such forces shall be worked out subsequently. The Military Staff Committee, with the authorization of the Security Council and after consultation with appropriate regional agencies, may establish regional sub-committees.

Notes

Introduction

1. *The Blue Helmets*, 3rd edn. (New York: United Nations, Department of Information, 1996), p. 9.

2. "Life and Death of a Hero," *The New York Review of Books*, December 1999.

3. Andrzej Sitkowski, "Reflections on the Peacekeeping Doctrine," *International Peacekeeping, The Yearbook of International Peace Operations*, Michael Bothe and Boris Kondoch (eds.), Kluwer Law International, 7: 2001, 181–196. See also Michel Loridon, *Opérations des Nations Unies, Leçons de terrain* (Paris: Fondation Pour Les Etudes De Défense, 1995), p. 109.

4. Edward N. Luttwak, "Give War a Chance," *Foreign Affairs*, July/August 1999, pp. 36–44.

5. *The Blue Helmets*, pp. 37–39.

6. Brian Urquhart, *Hammarskjold* (New York: Harper Colophone Books, 1984), p. 194.

7. Shashi Tharoor, *Balkan War Report*, London, September 1994, p. 24 and 26; Tharoor interviewed by H. Kreisler in the cycle "Conversations with History" of the Institute of International Studies, UC Berkeley, February 8, 1999.

8. James J. Sadkovich, *The U.S. Media and Yugoslavia, 1991–1995* (Westport, CT: Praeger, 1998), p. XVI and pp. 241–242. Another example of a typical misinformation: the narrator in the "American Defense Monitor" broadcast, produced by Rear Admiral Gene LaRoque on November 14, 1993, claimed that in Bosnia the UN peacekeepers were lacking the mandate and the means to use force against those who blocked the convoys with humanitarian aid. But the Security Council in resolution 836 adopted almost half a year earlier authorized in paragraph 9 the use of force precisely for that purpose.

9. Michael Barnett, *Eyewitness to a Genocide, The United Nations and Rwanda* (London: Cornell University Press, 2003), pp. 1–21.

10. UN document A/50/60-S/1995, also published as the "Agenda for Peace," para. 35.

11. *The Blue Helmets*, p. 60.

12. S.M. Hill and S.P. Malik, *Peacekeeping and the United Nations* (Brookfield, WI: Dartmouth, 1996), p. 175.

13. UN documents A/ 54/549 and A/55/305-S/2000/809.

14. For theoretical considerations on peace enforcement as subdivision of peace support operations see John Gerard Ruggie, "The UN and the Collective Use of Force: Whither or whether?" in Michael Pugh's (ed.) *The UN, Peace and Force* (London: Frank Cass, 2001), pp. 1–20. For doubts about advisability of such a solution see Jerzy Ciechanski, "Enforcement Measures under Chapter VII of the UN Charter: UN Practice after the Cold War," in *The UN, Peace and Force*, pp. 82–104 and Mats Berdal "Lessons Not Learned: The Use of Force in Peace Operations in the 1990s," in *International Peacekeeping*, 7(4): Winter 2000, pp. 55–74.

15. Sir Michael Rose, *Fighting For Peace* (London: Warner Books, 1999), p. 354.

16. William J. Durch (ed.), *The Evolution of UN Peacekeeping* (New York: St. Martin's Press, 1993), p. 1.

17. *The Blue Helmets*, p. 5.

18. Only twice in its history the UN applied fully the provisions of Chapter VII to confront recognized aggressors with military might. In both cases, in Korea in 1950 and in the Gulf in 1991, the war effort was undertaken by a U.S.-led coalition authorized by the Security Council, and only in the first one under the UN flag.

19. John Gerard Ruggie, "The UN and the Collective Use of Force," in *The UN, Peace and Force* (London: 2001), p. 5; *The Blue Helmets*, pp. 525–526.

20. The increasing costs of the UN peacekeeping adversely affect the size of voluntary contributions by the member states to the development and humanitarian funds of the organization. Since 1992 the total cuts in funding available to the UN Development Program alone have reached about 30 percent. See Phyllis Bennis, *Calling the Shots* (New York: Olive Branch Press, 2000), pp. 69–71.

21. AFP, Reuters, "NATO says Afghanistan needs more peacekeepers," *International Herald Tribune*, October 7, 2003. Even in Kabul, ISAF did not dislodge factional militias more than 2 years after their requested withdrawal. UN document S/2003/1074.

22. Bert Hoengers, a Dutch legislator quoted by Judy Dempsey in "Dutch leave NATO hanging on Afghan force," *International Herald Tribune*, December 23, 2005.

23. Richard Bernstein, "U.S. is losing the sympathy of the world," *The New York Times*, September 11, 2003.

24. Reuters, UN and Congo forces kill dozens of rebels, *International Herald Tribune*, December 27, 2005, UN Press Release ORG/1457, January 5, 2006.

25. Brian Urquhart, *A Life in Peace and War* (New York: Harper & Row, 1987), pp. 178–179.

26. Ralf Beste, Olaf Ihlan, Siegesmund von Ilsemann, Romain Leick, Georg Masculo, Gabor Steingart, "Das Projekt Mirage," *Der Spiegel*, Hamburg, No. 7, 2003.

27. Shashi Tharoor (ed.), Jim Whitman and David Pockock, *After Rwanda* (New York: St. Martin's Press, 1996), p. 25.

28. A.B. Fetherston, "Peacekeeping, Conflict Resolution and Peacebuilding: A Consideration of Theoretical Frameworks," *International Peacekeeping*, 7: 190–218, 2000.

29. Security Council resolution 161.

30. Report of the Secretary General pursuant to the General Assembly resolution 54/35 on the fall of Srebrenica; UN document A/54/549, November 15, 1999; Report of the Independent Inquiry into the Actions of the United Nations During the 1994 Genocide in Rwanda, released by the UN in New York on November 15, 1999, http://www.un.org/news/ossg/rwanda, accessed on February 7, 2000.

31. As of January 31, 2006; http://www.un.org./Depts/dpko/bnote.htm, accessed on February 15, 2006.

Chapter 1

1. Thierry Tardy, *Peace Operations after 11 September 2001* (London: Frank Cass, 2004), pp. 1–9.

2. Brian Urquhart, *Hammarskjold* (New York: Harper Colophone Books, 1984), p. 194.

3. Mary Kaldor, *New and Old Wars* (Stanford: Stanford University Press, 1999), pp. 127–128.

4. UN document A/50/60-S/1995/1, January 3, 1995, para. 35.

5. UN document A/47/277-S/24111, June 17, 1992, para. 42–45.

6. UN document S/PRST/1994/22, May 3, 1994, p. 2.

7. UN document A/50/60-S/1995/1, January 3, 1995, para. 19. Also published as the UN Publication, ISBN 92-1-100-555-8, p. 10.

8. UN document A/54/549, November 15, 1999, para. 483, 493, 497, and 498.

9. UN document A/55/305-S/2000/809, August 21, 2000, Executive Summary and para. 48–64, 88, and 273.

10. UN document A/59/565, December 2, 2004, para. 210–220.

11. Ramesh Thakur and Albrecht Schnabel (eds.), *United Nations Peacekeeping Operations: Ad hoc Missions, Permanent Engagements* (Tokyo: United Nations University Press, 2001), pp. 3–25. The suggested stratification of peacekeeping operations is more elaborate than most. Yasushi Akashi identifies only three generations of peacekeeping operations. Ibid., pp. 149–154.

12. Peter Viggo Jakobsen, The Emerging Consensus on Grey Area Peace Operations Doctrine, *International Peacekeeping*, Autumn 2000, 36–56; John Gerard Ruggie, The UN and the Collective Use of Force, in *The UN, Peace And Force*, Michael Pugh (ed.) (London: Frank Cass, 1997), pp. 1–20; Lt Col Wilkinson, *Sharpening the Weapons of Peace: The Development of a Common Military Doctrine for Peace Support Operations*, International Security Information Service-Europe (ISIS) Briefing Paper No.18, April 1998; Philip Wilkinson, Sharpening the Weapons of Peace: Peace Support Operations and Complex Emergencies, *International Peacekeeping*, Spring 2000, 63–79.

13. Jerzy Ciechanski in Pugh, Enforcement Measures under Chapter VII of the UN Charter: UN Practice after the Cold War; Pugh, *The UN*, pp. 82–104.

14. Mats Berdal, Lessons Not Learned: The Use of Force in Peace Operations in the 1990s, *International Peacekeeping*, Winter 2000, 55–74.

15. Donald C. Daniel and Michael Pugh hope for a new dialogue on the impact of the crusade against terrorism on peace operations. At the same time they do agree that 9/11 has not improved the likelihood of avoiding past errors in these operations. Tardy, *Peace Operations*, pp. 179–189.

16. John Mackinley, Opposing Insurgents during and beyond Peace Operations; Tardy, *Peace Operations*, pp. 159–178.

17. Rod Thornton, The Role of Peace Support Operations Doctrine in the British Army, *International Peacekeeping*, Summer 2000, 45.

18. Brian Urquhart, The UN Oil-for-Food Program: Who Is Guilty? *New York Review of Books*, 2, 2006.

Chapter 2

1. Townsend Hoopes and Douglas Brinkley, *FDR and the Creation of the U.N.* (New Haven, CT: Yale University Press, 1997), pp. 112–118.

2. The original number of six nonpermanent members of the Council was increased in 1966 following an amendment of the Charter.

3. Gunnar Myrdal, "Realities and Illusions in Regard to Inter-Governmental Organizations," *L.T.Hobhouse Memorial Trust Lecture No.24* (London: Oxford University Press, 1955), p. 15.

4. UN document S/PRST/1994/22, May 3, 1994.

5. Brian Urquhart, *A Life in Peace and War* (London: Weidenfeld and Nicholson, 1987), p. 348.

6. *The Blue Helmets* (New York: UN Department of Information, 1996), p. 294.

7. UN document A/59/565, December 2, 2004, para. 244–260.

8. Warren Hoge, At the UN: Squabbling on Council runs anew, *International Herald Tribune*, November 14, 2005.

9. Madeleine K. Allbright, *International Herald Tribune*, June 19–20, 1993.

10. Interview by Matthias Nass, "Ja, Wir Fuehlen Uns Gedemuetigt," *Die Zeit*, No. 40, Hamburg, 1995; Butros Butros Ghali, "Nein, die UNO Ist Nicht Gescheitert," *Die Zeit*, Hamburg, No. 7, 1996.

11. Brian Urquhat, *Hammarskjold* (New York: Harper Colophon Book, 1972), p. 230.

12. *The Blue Helmets*, p. 156.

13. Kurt Waldheim, *In the Eye of Storm* (London: Weidenfeld & Nicholson, 1986), p. 86.

14. Javier Peréz de Cuellar, *Pilgrimage for Peace* (New York: St. Martin's Press, 1997), p. 43 and 495.

15. Butros Butros Ghali, *Der Spiegel*, No. 29, 1993.

16. Ghali's interview in *Die Zeit*, No. 40, 1995.

17. *The Blue Helmets*, p. 5.

18. Jim Hoagland, "More Muscle for the Peacekeepers," *The Washington Post*, August 4, 2000.

19. Felicity Barringer, "UN weighs peace force for Congo," *International Herald Tribune*, May 14, 2003; "Slaughter in the Congo," editorial, *IHT*, June 3, 2003. René Lemarchand, "The crisis in eastern Congo," *IHT*, July 4, 2003.

20. Jean-Philippe Remy, "Huit soldats de l'ONU tues en mission secrete contre les rebelles ougandais," *Le Monde*, January 25, 2006.

21. UN document A/59/565, December 2, 2004. Out of sixteen members of the panel only one was a military man: General Satish Nambiar, who commandeered the UNPROFOR operation in ex-Yugoslavia in 1992–1993.

22. Ibid., para. 203.

23. Ibid, para. 214.

24. Ibid., para. 104.

25. UN document A/5O/60-S/1995, January 3, 1995, para.19, 36, 77–80.

26. Shashi Tharoor, *Balkan War Report*, London, September 1994, p. 24 and 26.

27. *Verbatim report of the public hearing by the Dutch parliamentary enquiry committee Srebrenica on Friday 6 December 2002* (The Hague, Tweede Kamer, vergadejaar 2002–2003, 28 506, nr. 5), p. 683.

28. Tharoor interviewed by Harry Kreisler in *Conversations with History*, Institute of International Studies, UC Berkeley, February 8, 1999.

29. David Rieff, *Slaughterhouse* (New York: Simon & Schuster, 1995), p. 189 and 191. "By providing the humanitarian fig leaf . . . and pretending that their interests were not the parochial ones of a moral and intellectually bankrupt organization, . . . UNPROFOR and the Department of Peacekeeping Operations became accomplices to genocide. They were, as they said, only following their mandate. That had a nice ring to it. Could they hear the echoes of a similar sentence, uttered half a century earlier, in which the only change was that the word "orders" had been substituted for the word "mandate?"

30. *Gazeta Wyborcza*, Warsaw, July 28 and August 3, 1995.

31. He is the UN Undersecretary General for Information.

32. Michael Barnett, *Eyewitness to a Genocide* (London: Cornell University Press, 2002), pp. 4–20.

33. David Rieff, *Slaughterhouse* (New York: Simon & Schuster, 1996), pp. 169–189.

34. Pierre Le Peillet, *Les Berets Bleus de l'ONU* (Paris: Editions France Empire, 1988), p. 685.

35. Craig R. Whitney, Paris Calls UN Accomplice, *International Herald Tribune,* July 15–16, 1995.

36. Jim Hoagland, "Chirac Disturbs and Makes Clear," *International Herald Tribune*, July 20, 1995.

37. Published in the report *"The Clinton Administration's Policy on Reforming Multilateral Peace Operations"* of May 5, 1994.

38. Madeleine Allbright, Anthony Lake, Lt. General Clark, *Executive Summary of the Statement before the House Appropriations Subcommittee on Foreign Operations*, Export Financing and Related Programs, May 5, 1994, released by White House and published by the Bureau of Public Affairs 5(20), May 16, 1994.

39. Jean-Bernard Raimond, *Rapport d'Information*, No. 1950, pp. 7–74.

40. Rod Thornton, "The Role of Peace Support Operations Doctrine in the British Army," *International Peacekeeping*, London, Summer 2000, 41–62.

41. Peter Viggo Jakobsen, "The Emerging Consensus on Grey Area Peace Operations Doctrine," *International Peacekeeping*, London, Autumn 2000, 36–56.

42. H. Peter Langille, "Conflict Prevention: Options for Rapid Deployment and UN Standing Forces," *International Peacekeeping*, London, Spring 2000, 219–253.

43. Michael Rose, *Fighting for Peace* (London: Warner Books, 1998), pp. 354–355.

44. William Pfaff, "A thankless but necessary effort," *International Herald Tribune*, January 31, 2003.

45. Jean-Marie Guéhenno, "A fragile peace on a bloodied continent," *International Herald Tribune*, January 30, 2004.

46. UN document S/2003/1074, November 11, 2003.

47. The US military authorities introduced PRT concept; Background Briefing on Afghanistan Relief and Reconstruction, U.S. Department of Defense, *News Transcript,*

February 27, 2003. http://www.defenselink.mil/news, accessed on April 17, 2003; Jim Garamone, "Coalition Pursues Dual Mission in Afghanistan," Ibid., December 19, 2003; "ISAF mission to Afghanistan expanded," Federal Press Office, October 16, 2003; http://www.german-embassy.org.uk, accessed on April 17, 2003; Elaine Sciolino, "NATO role expanding," *International Herald Tribune*, February 21–22, 2004.

48. Reymer Kluver, "Verhuellte Blicke aus dem Obstgarten," *Sueddeutsche Zeitung*, February 2, 2004; "Kabul: Battle over drug trade leaves 7 dead, 8 injured," *IHT*, February 9, 2004.

49. Jaap de Hoop Scheffer, "A bruised alliance marches on," *IHT*, January 30, 2004; Sciolino, *IHT*.

50. Judy Dempsey, "Dutch pressed over Afghanistan," *IHT*, January 30, 2006.

51. Winrich Kuehne, "Peace Operations and Governance: Lessons Learned and Perspectives," in Thierry Tardy (ed.), *Peace Operations After 11 September 2001* (London: Frank Cass, 2004), pp. 101–124.

52. Paul Krugman, "Why Bush hasn't captured bin Laden," *IHT,* March 17, 2004.

53. Jeffrey Smith, "Failed NATO raid Humiliates the West," *IHT*, June 28, 2001.

54. Dpa/afp, "Deutschland lehnt groesseren Kongo-Einsatz ab," *Allgauer Zeitung*, January 30, 2006.

55. UN document A/6672, July 12, 1967.

56. Theo Sommer, *Die Zeit*, No. 52, 1993.

57. Hans Harald Brautigam, *Die Zeit*, No. 26, 1994.

58. Ibid.

59. Rose, *Fighting for Peace*, p. 212.

60. Reuters, AP; "UN Intends to Open All Bosnia Roads Without a Fight," *International Herald Tribune*, September 23, 1992.

61. Sean Maguire, "Sarajevo Diary," *London Review of Books*, January 28, 1993.

62. Général Morillon, *Croir et Oser* (Paris: Grasset, 1993), pp. 141–147.

63. Philippe Morillon in Brigitte Stern's (ed.), *UN Peace-keeping operations, A Guide to French Policies* (Tokyo: United Nations University Press, 1998), pp. 86–87.

64. *The Blue Helmets*, p. 557; *The UN and the Situation in the Former Yugoslavia*, Reference Paper, Revision 4 (New York, UN Department of Public Information, 1995), pp. 50–51.

65. Commission les affairs étrangères, *Rapport d'information* no 1950 (Paris, Assemblée Nationale, 1994), Auditions, pp. 112–124.

66. The British Coldstream Guards destroyed several trenches from which the Serb snipers attacked them and since then the area had been remarkably quiet. A Swedish Colonel, Hendrikson, got his first convoy through by putting a pistol to the head of a Serb standing in the way, and, Rose says, all parties respected the Swedes. But, as the Commander of the French sector in Sarajevo told Rose, he could count on a more robust approach only by the French, other NATO nationals, and the Scandinavians. Rose, *Fighting for Peace*, p. 25, 31, 39, 50, and 133. When ambushed by the Serbs near Tuzla in April 1994, two Danish tank platoons retaliated, killing nine of the attackers without losses to themselves. The UN officials hinted at overreaction; Rod Nordland "The Mouse Ate the Cat," *Newsweek*, May 16, 1994.

67. Rose, *Fighting*, p. 157 and pp. 364–370.

68. Lt Gen O. Kandborg, *Final Report of the Nordic/UN Peacekeeping Senior Management Seminar* (Copenhagen: Royal Danish Defence College, 1997), p. 34.

69. Rose, *Fighting*, p. 354.

70. Phillip Corvin, *Dubious Mandate* (Durham: Duke University Press, 1999), p. 206.

71. Betrand de La Pressle, "La FORPRONU . . ." and Jean Cot "Le soldat et l'ONU," *Operations des Nations Unies* (Paris, Fondation Pour Les Etudes De Defense, 1995), pp. 295, 369–371. La Pressle considered the combination of Blue Helmets and NATO's air power patently absurd.

72. Bruce D. Berkovitz, "Rules of Engagement for UN Peacekeeping Forces in Bosnia," *Orbis*, Fall 1994, pp. 635–646.

73. Cot's predecessor, the Swedish General Wahlgren maintained that if someone tries to enter (a safe area) with force, force would be used against him in self-defense. *International Herald Tribune*, April 23, 1993.

74. Brendan Simms, *Unfinest Hour* (London: Penguin Books, 2001), pp. 207–208.

Chapter 3

1. Martin Gilbert, *Jerusalem in the Twentieth Century* (London: Chatto & Vinclus, 1996), pp. 54–56.

2. Trygve Lie, *In the Cause of Peace* (New York: The Macmillan Company, 1954), p. 160.

3. Brian Urquhart remembered that the five permanent members of the Security Council have never been able to get to the point of enforcing their decisions. He also recalled that the UN Secretariat did not think that the situation in Palestine warranted an enforcement. See Edward Mortimer, *Roosevelt's Children* (London: Hamish Hamilton, 1987), pp. 108–109.

4. Lie, *In the Cause*, pp. 160–162. The UN Special Committee was composed of the representatives of eleven countries: Australia, Canada, Czechoslovakia, Guatemala, India, Iran, The Netherlands, Peru, Sweden, Uruguay, and Yugoslavia. Lie put fifty-seven staff members at the disposal of the Committee. It followed a similar, prewar British undertaking. In 1936 a Royal Commission chaired by Lord Peele recommended partition of the territory into independent Jewish and Arab states. Jerusalem, linked by a corridor to the sea, would be excluded from both of them. Arab violent opposition did not allow for any follow-up of the proposal. In 1943 a British Cabinet Committee, meeting in secret, again proposed a partition of Palestine between Arab and Jews with Jerusalem as a separate state under British supervision. The plan was shelved until the end of the war and never taken up.

5. Lie, *In the Cause*, pp. 162–163; Gilbert, *Jerusalem*, pp. 176–177.

6. Eugene L. Rowan and Avi Shlaim (eds.), *The War for Palestine* (Cambridge: Cambridge University Press, 2001), p. 196.

7. See Norman G. Finkelstein, *Image and Reality of the Israeli-Palestinian Conflict* (London: Verso, 1995), pp. 51–87; Martin Gilbert, *Israel* (New York: William Morrow and Company, Inc., 1998), pp. 175–178; Ilan Pappé, *The Making of the Arab-Israeli Conflict 1947–1951* (London: I.B. Tauris Publishers, 2001), pp. 77–101.

8. Lee, *In the Cause*, p. 163.

9. Ibid., p. 164

10. For a comprehensive account of the diplomatic battle which ensued after the question of Palestine was entrusted to the UN in February 1947 see Ilan Pappé, *The Making*, pp. 16–46.

11. UN document S/676, January 30, 1948, para. IV. 6.

12. Lie, *In the Cause*, pp. 165–167.

13. Ibid., pp. 169–172.

14. Brian Urquhart, *A Life in Peace and War* (London: Weidenfeld and Nicholson, 1987), p. 113.

15. Pablo Azcazarte, *Mission in Palestine* (Washington D.C.: The Middle East Institute, 1966), pp. 41–42

16. Walter Isaacson and Evan Thomas, *The Wise Men* (New York: Simon and Schuster, 1986), pp. 451–453. James V. Forestall submitted that "There are four hundred thousand Jews and forty million Arabs. Forty million Arabs are going to push four hundred thousand Jews into the sea. And that's all there is to it. Oil—that is the side we ought to be on."

17. Lie, *In the Cause*, p. 173.

18. Ibid., p. 169.

19. Ibid., p. 175.

20. Stern Gang, a splinter group of the Zionist movement, known under the name of Lehi, was combating British even during the WW II and did not shy from exploring an option of alliance with Nazi Germany against Britain. It justified the murder of Bernadotte as a preemptive strike in the coming military confrontation with an international army. Joseph Heller, *The Stern Gang* (London: Frank Cass, 1995), pp. 86–87, 257–258.

21. Count Folke Bernadotte, *To Jerusalem* (London: Hodder and Stoughton, 1951), p. 193.

22. Lie, *In the Cause*, pp. 195–196. Out of estimated 850,000 Arabs who left Palestine after the war 450,000 settled in Jordan, 130,000 in Lebanon, 85,000 in Syria, and 130,000 in Egypt. See also Henry Siegman, "Israel: The Threat from Within," *The New York Review of Books*, February 2004, for estimates of the consequences of Israel's war for independence.

23. I was not able to locate statistics on Arab casualties during the war. The conduct and the results of the war indicate to a great possibility of Arab losses being of higher order then the Jewish ones.

24. Quoted in Pierre Le Peillet, *Les berets bleus de l'ONU* (Paris: Editions France Empire, 1986), p. 39. Le Peillet does not provide source for that quotation, but similar views are reproduced in Glubb's own book, John Bagot Glubb, *Soldier for the Arabs* (London: Hodder and Stoughton, 1957), p. 62. He mentioned possibility of holding Jerusalem and Haifa out of the fighting by means of supervision by UN or some other powers and a peaceful exchange of population as realistic opportunities that were not seized upon.

25. Lie, *In the Cause*, p. 194.

26. The Jewish agency opposed the UN Trusteeship for Palestine proposed by the United States arguing that it was not a suitable form for an international regime in Jerusalem—see UN document A/544 of May 5, 1948. Rabbi Israel Domb in a cable of February 7, 1950 asked the President of the UN Trusteeship Council "to take into consideration wishes of the Jewish Orthodox population Neture Karta in Jerusalem to live under the international protection of the United Nations and not under the sovereignty of the State of Israel"—see UN document Supplement No.9 (A/1286), Enclosures, item 10. The Permanent Representative of Israel to the United Nation, A.S. Eban in a letter of May 26, 1950, to the President of the Trusteeship Council proposed introduction of the authority of the UN in the Holy Places—see ibid., Enclosure to Annex III.

27. *The Blue Helmets* (New York: UN Department of Information, 1996), p. 21; E.H. Hutchison, *Violent Truce* (New York: The Devin-Adair Company, 1956), pp. 20–22.

28. Le Peillet, *Les berets*, pp. 42–43.

29. Carl von Horn, *Soldiering for Peace* (New York: David McKay Company Inc, 1967), p. 62.The demarcation lines in Jerusalem were marked on the map with a thick wax pencil, representing anything from 6 meters to 40 meters on the ground and creating a no-man's-land including a number of inhabited houses. According to the Norwegian General Odd Bull in *War and Peace in the Middle East* (London: Leo Cooper, 1973), pp. 57 and 61, hastily drawn demarcation lines did more to encourage infiltration than to check it.

30. *The Blue Helmets*, p. 23.

31. Hutchinson, *Violent*, pp. 86–89, 151–153. See also Bull, *War and Peace*, pp. 63–70.

32. UNTSO's Chief of Staff in 1963–1970, the Norwegian General Odd Bull, recalled that during the war of attrition he was prevented from crossing the Suez Canal by boat to carry out inspection on both banks; when he was on the East Bank and wanted to get to the other side, he had to go back to Jerusalem, fly to Cairo, and then drive to the West Bank. From June 6, 1969, to July 12, 1970, UN Observation Posts were fired upon 345 times, 284 times by the Egyptians and 61 times by the Israelis. Amazingly, Bull's proposal to pull back the posts from the Canal was not accepted by the UN, because neither the Egyptians, nor the Israelis supported it. Ralph Bunche later called the observers unknown Middle East heroes and praised them for making the war along the Canal the best reported in history. He did not comment on their effectiveness. Bull, *War and Peace*, pp. 161–170.

33. Mona Ghali, *The Evolution of UN Peacekeeping*, William Durch, ed. (New York: St. Martin's Press, 1993), pp. 98–99.

34. Urquhart, *Life in Peace*, pp. 130–133.

35. Ibid., p. 133.

36. *The Blue Helmets*, pp. 37–38.

37. Urquhart, *Life in Peace*, p. 134.

38. Urquhart, *Hammarskjold* (New York: Harper Colophon Books, 1984), p. 179.

39. *The Blue Helmets*, p. 53.

40. E.L.M. Burns, *Between Arab and Israeli* (Beirut: The Institute For Palestine Studies, 1969), pp. 188–190, 271–273.

41. Odd Bull, *War and Peace*, pp. 99–105. The Chief of Staff of UNTSO recalls multiplying incursions and act of sabotage against Israel in 1966, but says that it was extremely difficult to determine where the perpetrators of these acts came from. See also Gilbert, *Israel*, pp. 361–364, who records between April 8 and November 12, 1966, six incursions attributed to Syria and two to Jordan. Israeli reprisals from the air led sometimes to local wars, as it happened in August over the Lake of Galilee with aircraft and tanks from both sides participating. Except for an Israeli retaliatory action in a village in Jordan (called Es Samu by Bull and Samua by Gilbert), where twenty Jordanians and one Israeli were killed, the number of casualties on the Arab side was not available.

42. Indar Jit Rikhye, *The Sinai Blunder* (London: Frank Cass, 1980), p. 16.

43. Ibid., p. 22.

44. Ibid., pp. 28, 36–41.

45. Ramses Nassif, *U Thant in New York* (London: C. Hurst & Company, 1988), p. 74.

46. Urquhart, *Life in Peace*, p. 212.

47. Majority of U Thant's own UNEF Advisory Committee, the representatives of Brazil, Canada, Denmark, and Norway, were against withdrawal. Those in favor were India,

Pakistan, and Yugoslavia, all Nasser's friends from the group of nonaligned countries. Rikhye, *The Sinai*, p. 67.

48. *The Blue Helmets*, p. 55.

49. Kurt Waldheim, *The Challenge of Peace* (London: Weidenfeld and Nicholson, 1980), p. 62.

50. Mona Ghali in *The Evolution of UN*, . . . p. 133; Mai Yamani, *International Herald Tribune*, American invasion plan stirs fierce Saudi debate, January 9, 2004.

51. Gilbert, *Jerusalem*, pp. 322–324.

52. Le Peillet, *Les berets*, p. 286.

53. Urquhart, *A Life in Peace*, p. 288.

54. Gilbert, *Israel*, pp. 433, 454, 457.

55. Waldheim, *In the Eye*, pp. 73–74.

56. *The Blue Helmets*, p. 80.

57. An array of domestic and external conflicts and confrontations in Lebanon provided for one of the most complex backgrounds for deployment of a UN peacekeeping force. A helpful reading on that subject is Itamar Raabinovich, *The War for Lebanon 1970–1985* (London: Cornell University Press, 1985).

58. *The Blue Helmets*, p. 115.

59. Urquhart, *A Life in Peace*, p. 288.

60. Le Peillet, *Les berets*, pp. 415–417.

61. *The Blue Helmets*, p. 83.

62. Ibid., p. 88.

63. Urquhart, *A Life in Peace*, p. 290.

64. *The Blue Helmets*, pp. 90, 93–94.

65. Urquhart, *Life in Peace*, p. 302.

66. Emmanuel A. Erskine, *Mission With UNIFIL* (New York, St. Martin's Press, 1989), pp. 62–70.

67. Marianne Heiberg, *Observations on UN peacekeeping in Lebanon* (Oslo, NUPI, Norwegian Institute of International Affairs, Note 305, 1984), p. 34.

68. *The Blue Helmets*, p. 100.

69. Ibid., p. 101.

70. Ibid.

71. Bassam Abu-Shari and Uzi Mahnaimi, *Tried by Fire* (London: Warner Books, 1995, pp. 175–178, 185–187.

72. Urquhart, *A Life in Peace*, pp. 345–347.

73. Gilbert, *Israel*, pp. 509–511.

74. Kjell Skjealsback and Martin Hjelmverik Ness, *The Predicament of UNIFIL* (Oslo, NUPI, Norwegian Institute of International Affairs, Report No 345, 1985), pp. 6–19. Ness is a former commander of the UNIFIL's Norwegian battalion.

75. Marianne Heiberg, *Peacekeeping in Southern Lebanon* (Oslo, NUPI, Report No. 453, 1991), pp. 10–12.

76. *The Blue Helmets*, p. 87.

77. Dmitry Litvinovich, Hizbollah ready to destroy Israel, *PRAVDA.RU* (English Ed.), Moscow, September 4, 2002; Adam Schatz, "In Search of Hezbollah," *The New York Review of Books*, April 29 and May 13, 2004.

78. *Newsweek*, May 20, 1996.

79. *Gazeta Wyborcza*, Warsaw, April 20–21, 1996.

80. http://www.un.org./depts/dpko/fatalities.

81. Reuters, *International Herald Tribune*, August 1, 2001.

82. A.J. Sherman, *The Mandate Days* (New York: Thames & Hudson, 1998), p. 222, 240.

Chapter 4

1. William J. Durch, *The Evolution of UN Peacekeeping* (New York: St. Martin's Press, 1993), p. 318; Brian Urquhart, *Hammarskjold* (New York: Harper Colophon Books, 1984), pp. 393–396.

2. Brian Urquhart, *A Life in Peace and War* (London: Weidenfeld and Nicholson, 1987), pp. 146–147.

3. Ibid., p. 159.

4. Thomas Franck in *Nation against Nation*, quoted in Rosemary Righter's, *Utopia Lost* (New York: A Twentieth Century Fund Press, 1995), p. 79.

5. Urquhart, *A Life*, p. 147.

6. *The Blue Helmets* (New York: UN Department of Information, 1996), p. 177.

7. Ibid., p. 178.

8. Carl von Horn, *Soldiering for Peace* (New York: David McKay Company, 1967), pp. 158–159.

9. Urquhart, *Hammarskjold*, pp. 442.

10. Urquhart, *A Life*, p. 169.

11. Ibid., p. 172.

12. Urquhart, *Hammarskjold*, p. 435, 438.

13. von Horn, *Soldiering*, p. 248.

14. von Horn reported other problems with some of these troops. Ibid., p. 213, 237.

15. Urquhart, *Hammarskjold*, p. 478.

16. Ludo de Witte in his book *The Assassination of Lumumba* (London: Verso, 2001), pp. 130–133, accuses the United Nations guilty of a deliberate neglect that led to the murder of Lumumba.

17. *The Blue Helmets*, p. 184.

18. Ibid., p. 186.

19. Urquhart, *A Life*, p. 174.

20. Urquhart, *Hammarskjold*, pp. 561–562.

21. William. J. Durch (ed.), *The Evolution of UN Peacekeeping* (New York: St. Martin's Press, 1993), p. 343; Urquhart, *Hammarskjold*, p. 556; *The Blue Helmets*, p. 191.

22. *The Blue Helmets*, p. 192.

23. Urquhart, *Hammarskjold*, pp. 561–562.

24. Urquhart, *A Life*, p. 185.

25. Dragoljub Nauman, quoted in Righter, *Utopia*, p. 79.

26. *The Ndola Disaster* (Stockholm: Swedish Ministry of Foreign Affairs, unpublished manuscript, undated).

27. For another account see "The Ndola Crash and the Death of Dag Hammarskjold," *The Journal of Modern African Studies*, 31(4) (1993), pp. 661–671.

28. *Notes For Media Briefing* by Archbishop Desmond Tutu, Chairperson of the Truth and Reconciliation Commission, Cape Town, August 19, 1998.

29. Inquires addressed to the South African authorities were left unanswered.

Chapter 5

1. Javier Pérez de Cuéllar, *Pilgrimage For Peace* (New York, St. Martin's Press, 1997), p. 293; *The Blue Helmets* (New York: UN Department of Information, 1996), pp. 204–205.

2. *The Blue Helmets*, pp. 205–207; Peter H. Katjavivi, *A History of Resistance in Namibia* (London: UNESCO Press, 1989), pp. 114–126.

3. de Cuéllar, *Pilgrimage*, p. 294; Marrack Goulding, *Peacemonger* (Baltimore, MD: The Johns Hopkins University Press, 2003), p. 141.

4. *The Blue Helmets*, pp. 208–209.

5. Peter Stiff, *Nine Days Of War* (Alberton, Republic of South Africa: Lemur Books, 1989), pp. 69–74.

6. Ibid., pp. 78–97.

7. *The Blue Helmets*, p. 216.

8. Stiff, *Nine Days*, p. 102.

9. Ibid., p. 103.

10. Ibid., pp. 55–56.

11. Goulding, *Peacemonger*, pp. 150–151.

12. Virginia Page Fortuna, *Evolution of the Peacekeeping* (New York: St. Martin's Press, 1993), p. 369 and *The Blue Helmets*, p. 214.

13. UN Press Release DH/382 (Information Service of the UN Office in Geneva, April 3, 1989); Willem Steenkamp, *The South Africa's Border War* (Gibraltar: Ashanti Publishing Ltd., 1989), p. 183.

14. Stiff, *Nine Days*, for daily accounts of the SADF engagement with SWAPO fighters, pp. 78–220.

15. Ibid., p. 168.

16. Kevin Jacobs, *UN Secretariat News*, New York, December 1989.

17. *The Blue Helmets*, p. 218.

18. http://www.un.org./Depts/dpko/fatalities. The UN statistic includes one UNTAG fatality from hostile acts in Namibia, which concerned a local night guardsmen machine-gunned while on duty in UNTAG's office in Outjo.

19. Stephen M. Hill and Shahin P. Malik, *Peacekeeping and the United Nations* (Brookfield, WI: 1996), p. 81.

20. Fortuna, *Evolution of UN*, p. 370.

21. The Administrator General and the Special Representative of the UN Secretary General in Namibia agreed on the following three conditions for the parties' legibility for elections: payment of a deposit of 10,000 Rands (about $ 2,500), evidence of membership fees paid by at least 2,000 persons, and the names of candidates qualified to take all seats in the Constituent Assembly.

22. *The Blue Helmets*, pp. 226–227. The elections have been free, but not quite fair. SA later admitted giving over $35 million to DTA and other political parties opposing SWAPO. See Fortuna, p. 370.

Chapter 6

1. UNTEA mission was deployed from October 1962 to April 1963 as a result of an agreement between Indonesia and The Netherlands. The UN administered the territory in an interim period.

2. James A. Shear, "Riding the Tiger: The UN and Cambodia," in William J. Durch's (ed.), *UN Peacekeeping, American Policy, and the Uncivil Wars of the 1990s* (New York: St. Martin's Press, 1996), p. 136.

3. Javier Perez de Cuellar, *The Pilgrimage for Peace* (New York: St. Martin's Press, 1997), pp. 453–454; Marrack Goulding, *Peacemonger* (Baltimore, MD: The Johns Hopkins University Press, 2003), pp. 254–255.

4. *The Blue Helmets* (New York: United Nations, 1996), pp. 456–457, p. 459, 464.

5. Stephen M. Hill and Shahin P. Malik, *Peacekeeping and the UN* (Brookfield, WI: Dartmouth Publishing Company, 1996), p. 175.

6. Tom Riddle quoting from the *Eastern Economic Review* in *Cambodian Interlude* (Bangkok: White Orchid Press, 1997), p. 96.

7. *The Blue Helmets*, pp. 470–471.

8. James A. Schear, "Riding the Tiger: The UN and Cambodia," p. 171.

9. Schear provides a useful list of examples of positive and critical appraisals of the UN Cambodian mission. Ibid., p. 178.

10. William Braning, *International Herald Tribune*, June 11, 1993 and Rosemary Righter, *Utopia Lost* (New York: The XX Century Foundation Press, 1995), p. 353. Extravagance, fraud, indiscipline, and disorganization marked every stage, particularly of the civilian mission. Failure in creating a functioning civil administration left Cambodia vulnerable to corruption and administrative chaos after the UN departure.

11. John M. Sanderson in Jim Whitman's and David Pockock's (ed.), *After Rwanda* (London: Macmillan Press Ltd, 1996), pp. 184–187. The General did not make use of his own Rules of Engagement (ROE) by which he was authorized to use force to resist attempts to prevent UN personnel from carrying out their duties (see Schear, "Riding the Tiger," p. 145). But he was right in expecting more casualties in actions against the Khmer Rouge, for which the troop contributing countries were not prepared.

12. Hill and Malik, *Peacekeeping*, p. 175.

13. Michel Loridon, *Operations des Nations Unies* (Paris: Fondation pour les Etudes de Défense, 1995), pp. 107–110.

14. Confusion reigned among the Khmer Rouges as to their own stance towards elections. Some defectors reported having orders to disrupt the elections; others claimed that these orders were cancelled. See Schear, Note 133 to "Riding the Tiger," p. 190.

15. William Shawcross, *Deliver Us From Evil* (London: Bloomsbury, 2000), p. 63; *Die Zeit*, Hamburg, No. 30, 1993.

16. Goulding, *Peacemonger*, p. 257; Raoul M. Jenner, *Operation des Nations Unies*, pp. 79–81.

Chapter 7

1. For history of Somalia see Ahmed I. Sematar (ed.), *The Somali Challenge: From Catastrophe to Renewal* (Boulder, Colo: Lynne Rienner Publishers, 1994).

2. William J. Durch, Introduction to Anarchy: Intervention in Somalia, in *UN Peacekeeping, American Policy, and the Uncivil Wars of the 1990s* (New York: St. Martin's Press, 1996), pp. 317–318.

3. Alex de Waal, *Famine Crimes, Politics and the Disaster Relief Industry in Africa* (Bloomington & Indianapolis, Indiana University Press, 1997), pp. 163–178. de Waal does

not deny the existence of a famine but contests the estimates of the volume of necessary aid.

4. Hiring security guards was common in Somalia but the UN inflated the prices. It paid for the protection of the Mogadishu airport alone $150,000 monthly while the International Committee of Red Cross was paying for protection country-wide $14,000. At least part of the money was fuelling the factional fighting which the UN was supposed to control. Durch, *UN Peacekeeping*, p. 318.

5. Gerard Prunier, "Somaliland, le pays qui n'existe pas," *Le Monde Diplomatique*, October, 1997.

6. *The Blue Helmets* (New York: UN Department of Information, 1996), p. 293.

7. de Waal, *Famine Crimes*, p. 167.

8. Marrack Goulding, *Peacemonger* (Baltimore: MD: The Johns Hopkins University Press, 2003), p. 277. Durch, *UN Peacekeeping*, pp. 316–317.

9. *The Blue Helmets*, p. 293.

10. In difference to the UN-led mission, an authorized operation has a lead nation, which provides the majority of forces, the core staff, and the commander.

11. Durch, *UN Peacekeeping*, p. 320.

12. *The Economist*, December 19, 1992.

13. Durch, *UN Peacekeeping*, p. 324; de Waal, *Famine Crimes*, p. 186.

14. de Waal, p. 185; Joshua Hammer, "Life on a Knife's Edge," *Newsweek*, September 8, 2003.

15. Stephen M. Hill and Shahin P. Malik, *Peacekeeping and the United Nations* (Brookfield, WI: Dartmouth Publishing Company, 1996), p. 138.

16. *The Blue Helmets*, pp. 296–297.

17. Michael Maren, *The Road To Hell* (New York: The Free Press, 1997), p. 221.

18. *The Blue Helmets*, p. 299.

19. Ibid., pp. 299–301.

20. Interview in the *UN Special*, Geneva, October 1993.

21. Interview "Gewalt für Frieden," *Der Spiegel*, No.29, 1993.

22. Hill and Malik, *Peacekeeping*, p. 139.

23. *The Blue Helmets*, p. 305.

24. Maurice Quadri, *Operations des Nations Unies, Lecons de Terrain* (Paris: Fondation Pour Les Etudes De Defense, 1995), pp. 153–154.

25. Gianpierro Rossi, Ibid., pp. 153–154.

26. *The Blue Helmets*, p. 307.

27. Abdulquawi A. Yusuf, "Preying on failed state," *International Herald Tribune*, January 21, 2004; Mark Lacey, "Militants in Somalia vow to set up a religious state,"*IHT*, June 6, 2006.

28. Isaias Afwereki, *IHT*, October 12, 1993.

29. Flora Lewis quotes the *Medicins sans Frontieres* in the *International Herald Tribune*, June 18, 1993.

30. Frederick C. Cuny, *Operational Concept Plan 2, November 21, 1992*, reproduced by Frontline/online on the website http://pbs.bikent.edu.tr/wgbh/pages/frontline/shows/cuny/laptop/Somalia.htm; his report was submitted to the National Security Council at the request of the Carnegie Endowment for International Peace and to the Center for Naval Analysis.

31. Chester A. Crooker, "The Road From Mogadishu," *Newsweek*, November 1, 1994.

Chapter 8

1. For historical background of the events of 1994 see Mahmood Mamdani, *When Victims Become Killers* (Princeton: Princeton University Press, 2001).

2. John Reeder, *Africa, Biography of the Continent* (New York: Knopf, 1998), pp. 617–621.

3. "Rapport de la Mission d'information parlamentaire sur la role de la France au Rwanda de 1990–1994," *Le Monde* (Supplement), December 17, 1998, II.

4. *The Blue Helmets* (New York: UN Department of Information, 1996), p. 343.

5. Romeo A. Dallaire, "The Relationship between UN Peacekeepers and NGOs in Rwanda," in Jim Whitman and David Pockock (ed.), *After Rwanda* (London: Macmillan Press Ltd., 1996), p. 208.

6. Per-Olof Hallquist, *UNMAS 1997 Final Report* (Copenhagen Royal Danish Defence College, 1998), pp. 37–38. Hollquist, Chief Administrative Officer of UNAMIR was deployed in Kigali on October 15, 1993, with no instruction, no money, and not even a copy of the mandate of the mission. Food deliveries did not begin before April 1994, about a week before UNAMIR started to evacuate.

7. "Rapport de la Commission d'enquete parlamentaire concernant les evenements du Rwanda" (of the Senate of Belgium), *Le Monde-Horizons*, April 1, 1998.

8. Mao's (the Chairman of the Communist Party of China) second wife, Chiang Ching, with three other high-ranking communists formed during the Cultural Revolution of the 60s and 70s a group known later under the name "Gang of Four."

9. Linda Malvern, "The UN and Rwanda," *London Review of Books*, December 12, 1996. Her information was later confirmed by an independent UN inquiry.

10. "Kofi Annan s'explique sure le genocide rwandaise," *Le Monde*, March 19, 1998.

11. Bronwyn Adcock interviewing Alain Destexhe in "The UN & Rwanda: Abandoned to Genocide," *Australia's Radio National Weekly Investigative Documentary*, February 21, 1999; http;//www.abc.net.au/m/talks/bbing/stories/s19237.htm.

12. Malvern, *London Review*. Adcock interviewing Colin Keating in *Australia's Radio*.

13. *The Blue Helmets*, pp. 344–345.

14. Ten years after the catastrophe, Michael Hourigan, a former investigator of the International Criminal Tribunal on Rwanda, disclosed that in 1997 he was ordered to close the case as soon it appeared to indicate involvement of Paul Kagame, the former leader of RPF and the current President of Rwanda; Fabrice Rousellot, "La verite n'a pas eté devoilée sur le Rwanda", *Liberation*, March 18, 2004.

15. *The Blue Helmets*, p. 346.

16. "UN Blames Hutu for Rwanda's Genocide," *International Herald Tribune*, July 1, 1994.

17. Dallaire, *After Rwanda*, p. 209.

18. *Report of the Independent Inquiry into the Action of the United Nations during the 1994 Genocide in Rwanda*, New York, December 15, 1999; http:// www.un.org/News/ ossg/rwanda_report.htm.

19. Karen MacGregor, "Survivors sue UN for 'complicity' in Rwandan genocide," *The Independent*, January 11, 2000; Adcock interviewing Louise Mushikawabo in *Australia's Radio*.

20. Case against Georges Anderson Nderubumwe Rutaganda, *The International Criminal Tribunal for Rwanda (ICTR)*, No. ICTR-96-3-I, Transcript of proceedings,

September 30–October 2, 1997, unpublished; Linda Malvern, *Ultimate Crime* (London: Allison & Busby, 1995), p. 13.

21. Case against Jean-Paul Akayesu, ICTR, No. 96–4-I, Transcript of proceedings, February 28, 1998, unpublished.

22. Michael Barnett, *Eyewitness to a Genocide* (London: Cornell University Press, 2003), p. 104.

23. Case against Rutaganda, *ICTR.*

24. Ibid.

25. "Rapport de la Mission," *Le Monde* (Supplement), IX.

26. Philippe Lamaire, "Ligitieuse intervention française au Rwanda," *Le Monde Diplomatique*, July 1994.

27. *Rapport d'information sur la politique d'intervention dans les conflits* (Paris: Assemble Nationale, 1995) No. 1950, pp. 119–124.

28. *The Blue Helmets*, pp. 348–350.

29. UN document A/50/60-S/1995/1, para. 43; Shashi Tharoor," The Future of Peacekeeping," *After Rwanda*, p. 24.

30. *The Blue Helmets*, p. 353.

31. Ibid., p. 365; BBC World News, June 9, 1995.

32. Reuters, International Herald Tribune, April 20–21, 1996.

33. "Rwanda Can Stand Alone," *Newsweek*, April 1, 1996.

34. Case against Akayesu, *ICTR.*

35. *Report of the Independent Inquiry,* supra note 18.

36. Case against Rutaganda, *ITCR.* above.

37. Ibid.; S. Buckley, "General Accuses UN of Failure to Stem Genocide in Rwanda," *International Herald Tribune*, February 27, 1998.

38. Alan J. Kuperman, "A Hard Look at Intervention," *Foreign Affairs*, January/February 2000, pp. 94–118. Kuperman contradicts Dallaire's estimates; even 75,000 of U.S. servicemen would not have been able to bring massacres under a full control—he claims. His is a typical overkill scenario that ignores possible effects of spectacular preventive and punitive actions against the killers undertaken at strategic locations. He also ignores the difference between a full control and reducing the scope of the genocide.

39. Catherine Atlan, "Introduction a la crise rwandaise," *Operations des Nations Unies* (Paris: Fondation pour les Etudes de Defense, 1995), p. 183.

40. Malvern, *The Ultimate Crime*, p. 14.

41. "Un ancient chef militaire de l'Elysee blame l'ONU et defend Paris," *Le Monde*, May 21, 1998.

42. Supra note 18.

43. Marrack Goulding, *Peacemonger* (Baltimore, MD: The Johns Hopkins University Press, 2003), p. 299. Goulding, the UN Undersecretary General in charge of peacekeeping in 1986–1982, admits that poor understanding of the conflicts in Yugoslavia was symptomatic for a weakness, which persisted in the organization. He added that "we did not have time for briefings by experts."

44. Adcock interviewing Michael Hourigan in *Australia's Radio*. Hourigan, who used to be a Crown Prosecutor in Adelaide, and later became a UN criminal investigator in Rwanda, complained that the UN had consistently refused access to its files.

45. *The Blue Helmets*, p. 526.

46. Barnett, *Eyewitness*, pp. 1–20, 154–181.

Chapter 9

1. Markovic was playing games: on June 25, 1991, his government issued in Belgrade a decree of enforcement by the JNA the Yugoslav sovereignty over the state borders and border crossings. Laura Silber and Allan Little, *The Death of Yugoslavia* (London: Penguin Books, 1995), pp. 169–170.

2. Ibid., p. 174.

3. Ibid., p. 184; Statistics of that time seem not very reliable, though, see Mary Kaldor, The Wars in Yugoslavia, *New Left Review*, No. 197, p. 100. According to Kaldor, 64 JNA members were killed to 4 Slovenes, a ratio 1:15 in favor of the victims of an attack.

4. Silber and Little, pp. 180–184.

5. *Unfinished Peace*, Report of the International Commission on the Balkans (Washington, DC: Aspen Institute Berlin and Carnegie Endowment for International Peace, 1996), pp. 31–32.

6. Typical were Milosevic's remarks at the ceremony marking the 50th anniversary of the uprising against the Nazi occupation of Yugoslavia: "The specter of fascism," he said in December 1991, "is knocking on our door. Circumstances have led us into battles with forces that are breaking up Serbia and Yugoslavia. . . . They are dark, conservative forces which we believed had left the historical stage." *International Herald Tribune*, December 11, 1991.

7. Little is known about Serbs' disproportionate presence in public life and especially in police force. According to the 1981 census, Serbs accounted for 11.5 percent of Croatia's population but in 1989 they held 70 percent position in that force. Norman Cigar, "The Serbo-Croatian War, 1991:Political and Military Dimensions," *The Journal of Strategic Studies*, 16(3), September 1993, p. 301.

8. Branka Magas, "The Destruction of Bosnia-Herzegovina," *New Left Review*, No. 196, pp. 203; Silber & Little, pp. 186–208.

9. Javier Perez de Cuellar, *Pilgrimage for Peace* (New York: St. Martin's Press, 1997) pp. 492–494.

10. Hans-Dietrich Genscher, *Errinerungen* (Munich: Goldman, 1997), pp. 955–966.

11. Richard Holbrooke, *To End a War* (New York: The Modern Library, 1999), pp. 31–32.

12. Svebor Dizdarevic, *Le Monde Diplomatique*, March 1993.

13. Magas, *New Left Review*, p. 108.

14. Henry Kissinger, Yugoslavia: Before Sending Troops, Marshal Arguments, *International Herald Tribune*, September 21, 1992.

15. David Rieff, *Slaughterhouse, Bosnia and the Failure of the West* (New York: Simon & Schuster, 1996), p. 17; Paul Garde, Vie *et mort de la Yugoslavie* (Paris: Fayard, 1992), p. 372. These writers differ on the date of the referendum; March 1 is Rieff's, Garde refers to February 29, 1992.

16. Rieff, p. 17.

17. Silber and Little, pp. 247–251.

18. Most of the Bosnians Serbs were living as farmers in the countryside while a high proportion of the Muslim population lived in towns. This fact may partly explain disproportionate relations between the ethnic group and the territory they occupied. This settlement pattern contributed later to the existence of Muslim enclaves on Serb held territories.

19. Mark Danner, "America and the Bosnia Genocide," *New York Review of Books*, December 4, 1997.

20. UN documents E/CN.4/1992/S-1/9, August 28, 1992, para. 6; A/47/666, November 17, 1992, para. 24, 136, 138.

21. Carole Hodge and Mladen Grbin, *A Test For Europe* (Glasgow, Institute of Russian and East European Studies, University of Glasgow, 1996), pp. 51–54.

22. James J. Sadkovich, "War, Genocide and the Need to Lift the Embargo on Bosnia and Croatia," *Journal of Croatian Studies*, Volume XXXII-XXXIII, 1991–1992, pp. 132–163.

23. James J. Sadkovich, *The U.S. Media and Yugoslavia, 1991–1995* (Westport, CT: Praeger, 1997), pp. 205–210.

24. Marrack Goulding, *Peacemonger* (Baltimore, MD: The Johns Hopkins University Press, 2003), p. 309. The name of the "protection force" was due to the complexity of Yugoslavia's political geography. According to Goulding "those to be protected were of course the Serbs in Croatia."

25. *The Blue Helmets* (New York: UN Department of Information, 1996), pp. 513–514.

26. "Mission UN-Moeglich," *Die Zeit*, No. 16/93.

27. Laura Silber, "Balkans: Fighting Casts Doubt on Talks," *Los Angeles Times*, January 24, 1993.

28. Pawel Wronski, *Gazeta Wyborcza*, Warsaw, November 21, 1994.

29. *The Blue Helmets*, pp. 549–553.

30. Sadkovich, *The U.S. Media*, pp. 219–234. Atilla Hoare, "Letters," London Review of Books, February 8, 1996.

31. UN document S/25777, Add. 3 to SC resolution 847, June 30, 1993.

32. Cedric Thornberry, *Statement at the Conference On Preventive Diplomacy*, Stockholm, April 1–2, 1993. UNPROFOR. Unpublished.

33. William J. Durch and James A. Schear, "Faultlines: UN Operations in the Former Yugoslavia," *UN Peacekeeping, American Policy, and the Uncivil Wars of the 1990s* (New York: St. Martin's Press, 1996), p. 253.

34. Lewis MacKenzie, *Peacekeeper* (Vancouver: Douglas & McIntyre, 1993), pp. 135–140.

35. In about one month, and after receiving death threats from both sides of the conflict, the general was recalled on his own request. Ibid., pp. 213–221 and p. 237.

36. Jim Whitman and David Pockock (eds.), *After Rwanda* (London: Macmillan Press Ltd., 1996), p. 237.

37. A negotiating structure composed of representatives of France, Germany, Great Britain, Russia, and the United States.

38. Mark Danner, "Bosnia: The Great Betrayal," *The New York Review of Books*, March 26, 1998.

39. Rieff, p. 149.

40. Whitman and Pockock, p. 231.

41. William Shawcross, "All the Money and Goodwill Won't End Bosnia's Agony," *International Herald Tribune*, December 1, 1993.

42. *The Blue Helmets*, pp. 522–523.

43. Reuters, AP; "UN Intends to Open All Bosnia Roads without a Fight," *International Herald Tribune*, September 23, 1992. Morillon's statement on consequences of

military actions reflected a common in the West view of a superiority of the Serb war machine. But it was largely exaggerated as draft dodging and desertion during the Serbo–Croatian War made evident. Cigar, *The Journal of Strategic Studies*, p. 315.

44. Kuno Kruse and Dietrich Willier, Mission UN-Moeglich, Die Zeit, Hamburg, No. 16, 1993.

45. Larry Hollingworth, the UNHCR representative in Bosnia, reported an agreement by which the UN agreed to surrender an undisclosed share from each supply for the other side. *Oslobodenje*, January 15, 1993.

46. *The Blue Helmets*, pp. 523–524.

47. Ibid., p. 558.

48. UN Troops Fire Biggest Mortar at Serbs, *International Herald Tribune*, July 4, 1995.

49. Thornberry in Stockholm, supra note 32. Tadeusz Mazowiecki reported on those deprived of the aid. In the Cerska enclave in Eastern Bosnia, besieged by the Serbs from the end of May 1992 until the takeover by them in March 1993, children were starving and adults were surviving on animal food, leafs, and tree bark. UN document E/CN.4/1994/3.

50. Rieff, *Slaughterhouse*, p. 242.

51. Silber and Little, p. 294.

52. *The Blue Helmets*, p. 525.

53. General Morillon, *Croir Et Oser, Chronique de Sarajevo* (Paris, Grasset, 1993), pp. 161–181; Silber and Little, pp. 293–303.

54. Morillon, Ibid.

55. Jose Maria Mendiluce, "Bosnia's Bitter Lessons," *Newsweek*, June 7, 1993.

56. *Raporty Tadeusza Mazowieckiego z Bylej Jugoslawii* (Poznan-Warszawa, Fundacja "Promocja Praw Czlowieka—Badanie i Nauczanie" oraz Agencja Scholar, 1993), pp. 243–249.

57. *The Blue Helmets*, pp. 525–526.

58. UN documents S/1994/555, May 9, 1994; S/1994/1389, December 1, 1994.

59. *The Blue Helmets*, p. 559.

60. Ibid., pp. 531–532; *UNPROFOR News*, No. 7, Zagreb, May 1994.

61. Some writers criticize Rose's handling of the Gorazde crisis, see Brendan Simms, *Unfinest Hour, Britain and the Destruction of Bosnia*, (London: Penguin Books, 2002), pp. 189–195; Rose's own account, see General Sir Michael Rose, *Fighting for Peace* (London: Warren Books, 1999), pp. 138–170.

62. UN document A/54/549, para. 175–316. For a day-by-day account see also David Rohde, *Endgame, The Betrayal and Fall of Srebrenica: Euorope's Worst Massacre Since World War II* (Boulder, CO: Westview, 1997).

63. *The Blue Helmets*, p. 557. By May 26, 1995, in retaliation for NATO's air strikes around Sarajevo, the Serbs took about 400 UNPROFOR personnel hostage.

64. UNPF commanded UNCRO in Croatia, UNPROFOR in Bosnia, and UNPREDEP in Macedonia.

65. The weaponry in the Weapon Collection Point was largely useless and also the civilian leadership in Srebrenica objected to its use, fearing that it may encourage UNPROFOR to leave the fighting to the Bosnians. Dick Schoonoord of NIOD in a letter to the author of February 27, 2006.

66. Dutch sources did not find indications that the Bosnian Serbs deliberately fired at Dutchbat. That is not to say that it did not come under fire. Ibid.

67. UN document A/54/549, November 15, 1999, para. 272. The Dutch maintain that Janvier's expectations were at odds with the usual ROE for peacekeeping, still in force. Schoonoord, ibid. The author was not able to get either from the DPKO or from NIOD a confirmation or denial of the validity in 1995 of ROE signed by General Cot in 1993. These authorized the UNPROFOR units to use force against intrusions into safe areas.

68. Ibid., para. 274–275.

69. Ibid., para. 488.

70. Vernon Loeb, Rumsfeld Asks NATO for Bosnia Troop Cuts, *International Herald Tribune*, December 19, 2001.

71. Assemblée Nationale, *Rapport d'Information No 3413*; Report of the Committee of Inquiry into Srebrenica established by the House of Representatives of the Netherlands Parliament on June 5, 2002, introduced in *Press Release vl/mr*, The Hague, January 27, 2003. The Dutch representatives invited by the French and also Yasushi Akashi testified before the French Inquiry. But from the five foreign personalities invited by the Dutch, Maurice Baril, Sahshi Tharoor, Yasushi Akashi, Bernard Janvier, and Rupert Smith only the British General appeared. He was not available for the French Inquiry, though.

72. *Srebrenica: Reconstruction, background, consequences and analyses of the fall of the enclave* (The Hague, NIOD, 2002), www.srebrenica.nl.

73. *Rapport No. 3413*, Volume II, Auditions, testimony of June 21, 201.

74. *Srebrenica: Reconstruction*, Part II, Chapter III, Section 13.

75. Testimony of July 21, 2001 and "La France et Srebrenica," *Le Monde*, Horizons-Documents, November 30, 2001.

76. William Pfaff, "On Bosnia, Futile Policy Can Send Only Futile Messages," *International Herald Tribune*, November 25, 1994.

77. John F. Hillen III, "Killing with Kindness: The UN Mission in Bosnia," *Foreign Policy Briefing*, No. 34, June 30, 1995, Cato Institute, Washington, D.C.

Chapter 10

1. Rosemary Righter, *Utopia Lost* (New York; The Twentieth Century Fund Press, 1995), p. 311.

2. John MacKinlay, "Defining Warlords," *International Peacekeeping*, Frank Cass Journal, 7(1), pp. 48–62.

3. "Darfur and the International Criminal Court I and II," Samantha Power and Stéphanie Giry, *IHT*, February 12–13, 2005; "Don't look away this time," Nicholas D. Kristof, *IHT*, February 24, 2005; by the same author "An American witness to Sudan's systematic killing," *IHT*, March 3, 2005. A former U.S. marine, Captain Brian Steidle, a military adviser to the African monitoring team, witnessed an annihilation of an entire village of Labado of 25,000 inhabitants. He saw small children shot dead or with their faces smashed with rifle butts.

4. SC resolutions 1556, 1564, 1569, 1574, 1590, 1591, 1593, 1627.

5. Jack Straw, "Stop killing, or pay the price," *IHT*, February 17, 2006.

6. UN document S/RES/1590 (2005), para. 1–4, 16 and 17.

7. Contributors of military personnel: Australia, Austria, Bangladesh, Belgium, Benin, Bolivia, Brazil, Burkina Fasso, Cambodia, Canada, China, Croatia, Denmark, Ecuador, Egypt, El Salvador, Fiji, Finland, Gabon, Germany, Greece, Guatemala, Guinea,

India, Indonesia, Italy, Jordan, Kenya, Kyrgystan, Malawi, Malaysia, Mali, Moldova, Mozambique, Namibia, Nepal, New Zealand, Nigeria, Norway, Pakistan, Paraguay, Peru, Philippines, Poland, Republic of Korea, Romania, Russia, Rwanda, Sri Lanka, Sweden, Switzerland, Tanzania, Turkey, Uganda, Ukraine, United Kingdom, Yemen, Zambia, Zimbabwe. Contributors of police personnel only: Argentina, Ghana, Jamaica, Norway, Samoa, United States. http://www.un.org/Depts/dpko/missions/unmis/facts.html.

8. Dan Morrison, "Desperation in Darfur," *US News and World Report*, February 12, 2006.

9. More attacks in Northern Darfur, *UNMIS Newsletter*, February 22, 2006. http://www.un.or/apps/news/ticker/tickerstory.asp?NewsID=17579.

10. Secretary-General Office of the Spokesman, *Off The Cuff*, February 13, 2006, *UN News Centre*, February 24, 2006, http://www.un.org/apps/news/story.asp?NewswID= 17488&Cr=Sudan&Cr1=.

11. Judy Dempsey, "Pressure rises over NATO's Darfur role," *IHT*, February 20, 2006.

12. Ibid.

13. UN document A/54/549, para. 505.

14. Newt Gingrich and George Mitchell, "Rethinking UN Reform," *IHT*, March 14, 2006.

15. Wesley K. Clark, A Month Will Be Not Enough for NATO, *International Herald Tribune*, August 18–19, 2001.

16. Ralf Beste, Olaf Ihlan, Siegesmund von Ilseman, Romain Leick, Georg Masculo, Gabor Steingart, "Das Projekt Mirage," *Der Spiegel*, Hamburg, No. 7, 2003.

17. *The Blue Helmets* (New York: UN Department of Information, 1996), pp. 401– 403. Referring the international legal disputes to ICJ is extremely rare despite the provisions of the UN Charter. In para. 3 of Article 36, Chapter VI, it instructs the Security Council, to consider involvement of the ICJ as a general rule.

18. An Indian peacekeeper died in March 2006 because he could not be flown to the closest hospital in Asmara. http;//www.un.org/apps/news/ticker/tickerstory.asp?NewsID = 17696.

19. Captain Luc Lamaire, *Verbatim of the Testimony*, International Criminal Tribunal for Rwanda, Case No.: TCRT-96–3-I against Rutaganda, September 30, 1997, unpublished.

20. ABC News-sponsored Roundtable on Confederate Flag and Iowa Caucuses, January 23, 2000, and Statement on Defense at Campaign Rally in Kansas City, February 22, 2000, accessed at http://www.foreignpolicy2000.org/library/, accessed on March 18, 2006; Eric P. Schwartz, U.S. Policy Toward Peace Operations, in Thierry Tardy's (eds.), *Peace Operations After 11 September 2001* (London: Frank Cass, 2004), p. 45.

21. Brian Urquhart, For a UN Volunteer Military Force, *The New York Review of Books*, No. 11, 1993; "Give the UN a real force," *International Herald Tribune*, August 8, 2003.

22. Stephen P. Kinloch, "Utopian or Pragmatic? A UN Permanent Military Volunteer Force," Pugh (ed.), *The UN, Peace And Force*, pp. 166–190.

23. Executive Outcomes fought the rebel forces of UNITA in Angola and brought it back to the negotiating table. It was supposedly paid about $40 million yearly; the UN futile UNAVEM III operation deployed over 7,000 men at the estimated cost of $366,523,900 for a period of 14 months. EO had a similar and low-cost success in Sierra Leone. After its contracts were terminated, the civil war returned to both countries. David Shearer, "Private

Armies and Military Intervention," International Institute for Strategic Studies, *Adelphi Papers 316*, Oxford University Press.

24. P.W. Singer, *Corporate Warriors, The Rise of the Privatized Military Industry* (London: Cornell University Press, 2004), pp. 3–18.

25. Brooks, "Messiahs or Mercenaries? The Future of International Private Military Services," p. 138. Peter Viggo Jacobsen, "UN Peace Operation in Africa Today and Tomorrow," *International Peacekeeping*, Kluwer Law International, Volume VII, 2001, pp. 172–174; Eric Pape and Michael Meyer, "Dogs of Peace," *Newsweek*, August 25–September 1, 2003.

26. Singer, *Corporate Warriors*, pp. 185–186, p. 225. Earlier, the Executive Outcomes considered taking out a contract from the government of Rwanda to assist it in its fight against the Tutsi rebels. It was the same government whose elements were responsible for planning and executing of the genocide of Tutsi.

27. UN document A/59/565, para. 300. The Committee, consisting of Joint Chiefs of Staff of the five permanent members of the Security Council, never worked, but it is arguable that the organization should be equipped with an advisory body on military matters.

28. NATO is the only military alliance present in the international military missions. The European Union and African Union are experimenting yet in this field and the only other regional organization substantially involved in such operations under the Security Council mandates was the Economic Community of West African States (ECOWAS) and its military wing, ECOWAS Monitoring Group (ECOMOG) of which Nigeria is the leading member. Its capacity is limited and reputation controversial.

29. Michael Howard, *The Invention of Peace* (London: Yale University Press, 2000), pp. 92–113.

Index

About the Author

ANDRZEJ SITKOWSKI is an independent researcher who has worked with the UN for 32 years as a staff member and advisor to peacekeeping missions.

LIBRARY
ST. LOUIS COMMUNITY COLLEGE
AT FLORISSANT VALLEY